THE KENYATTA ELECTION:
KENYA 1960—1961

THE
KENYATTA ELECTION:

KENYA 1960—1961

GEORGE BENNETT

Senior Lecturer in Commonwealth History,
Oxford University

AND

CARL G. ROSBERG

Assistant Professor of Political Science,
University of California, Berkeley

Published on behalf of
The Institute of Commonwealth Studies, Oxford
by
OXFORD UNIVERSITY PRESS
LONDON NEW YORK NAIROBI
1961

Oxford University Press, Amen House, London E.C.4

GLASGOW NEW YORK TORONTO MELBOURNE WELLINGTON
BOMBAY CALCUTTA MADRAS KARACHI LAHORE DACCA
CAPE TOWN SALISBURY NAIROBI IBADAN ACCRA
KUALA LUMPUR HONG KONG

*Printed in Great Britain
at The Thanet Press*

For
Professor W. J. M. Mackenzie

CONSTITUTIONAL ADVISER*

qu'il puisse dire, avec l'abbé Sieyès,
'J'ai vécu'

* μαιεύεσθαί με ὁ θεὸς ἀναγκάζει
γεννᾶν δὲ ἀπεκώλυσεν

The god compelled me to be a midwife, not a parent
PLATO. *Theaetetus* 150 c [*translated W. J.M.M.*]

PREFACE

The value of an election study must lie in certain measure in the speed with which it appears, that it may still seem closely relevant to all concerned. Accepting this, the writers, one a historian and an Englishman, the other a political scientist and an American, pooled their differing approaches, intending that their report should go to press within six weeks of the election of the National Members on 16th March. Although the end of a lengthy electoral process which had begun with the first nominations on 6th January, this proved not to be the end of the story. The new Government was not formed until late April. The negotiations for this revealed much about Kenya and the elections, which it was clearly essential to include. The book eventually went to press in mid-June. Thus judgments made here must necessarily have even more of a provisional character than was originally intended.

Whilst this was a General Election and whilst there were certain unifying features, the different races and communities of Kenya are sufficiently separate for it to have appeared sometimes as at least five different elections. The writers had thus to pass from one community to another, from one atmosphere to another. In all this, and in the stress of an election, it remains worthy of note that they were received everywhere with remarkable kindliness.

For this generally friendly reception the writers would like to thank all concerned, particularly the politicians of all racial groups who were most generous with their time in the midst of a hectic campaign. The authors would also like to acknowledge with warm thanks the unfailing friendly help of a large number of busy civil servants, both in Nairobi and in the districts, as also the kindness of the Kenya Government which permitted access to the administrative files relating to the election, which was of particular value for Chapter III. The Kenya Government and the officials concerned bear, of course, no responsibility for anything there or elsewhere in this study. The comments are those of the authors alone. They have striven to preserve impartiality in a country in which they were but

Preface

guests and trust that any failings may be forgiven, that no offence may be taken for none was meant.

Generous research grants have contributed to making this study possible: Mr. Bennett acknowledges his debt to the Colonial Social Science Research Council, and Professor Rosberg to the Institute of International Studies, University of California, Berkeley, and to the Carnegie Corporation of New York. Naturally none of these bodies is in any way responsible for the text of this book.

No work of this kind can be carried on without much assistance from many different people. Whilst it may seem invidious to pick out names, the authors could not let pass unmentioned the special help received from certain people, particularly Kenya's Supervisor of Elections, Mr. R. D. F. Ryland, secondly Dr. Gordon Wilson and his Market Research Company of East Africa which allowed the findings of their public opinion polls to be quoted, besides helping in many other ways. The gentlemen of the press gave much assistance, and here particular mention must be made of Mr. and Mrs. Dahya of Kisumu. Our valuable African research assistants were Mr. Douglas A. Jumah in Nairobi and Mr. Robert Odhiambo in Nyanza. At the last stage, the movement of the material towards the publisher could not have been accomplished in time without the considerable help of the secretarial staff of the Institute of Commonwealth Studies, Oxford, and the oversight of its Director, Mrs. Chilver, that most warm-hearted encourager of Africanists. Finally we must acknowledge the tolerance and patience of our wives who accepted long separations at times of family crisis, that we might visit all, except one, of the contested constituencies of Kenya.

May 1961

G.B.
C.G.R.

NOTE

Elections pass into history with such rapidity that we decided to adopt the historian's ungracious practice of dropping all titles in reference to the persons mentioned herein.

In respect of Kalenjin and Masai names we may be somewhat ahead of practice. We noted the growing tendency, in referring to leading members of these peoples, of dropping the 'arap' or 'ole' meaning 'son of' and treating the father's name as a simple surname. We decided to apply this generally.

To any who may feel hurt by either of these somewhat ruthless usages, we would apologize in advance.

CONTENTS

ILLUSTRATIONS

PLATES (*at end*)

1A. Havelock supported by Gichuru and Muliro at a private meeting for African civil servants at the opening of his common roll campaign

1B. Cavendish-Bentinck campaigning in the Rift Valley for the African Vote. See p. 108

2. Mungai Njoroge introduces Peter Marrian to an African audience

3. Kenya Freedom Party makes the KANU sign. (a) *above*, Chanan Singh in Nairobi South. (b) *below*, K. P. Shah's prominent car symbol in Nairobi Central

4. Odinga's Press Conference at KANU's Headquarters in January in which he attacked Mboya, whose portrait is on the wall. *Left to right:* Argwings-Kodhek, Ochwada, Odinga, Njoroge, Kibaki. See p. 132

5. Mboya's eve of poll meeting. Standing in the car Gichuru in striped shirt and Mboya in beaded cap. Note Mboya's aeroplane symbol and the Kenyatta picture with Mboya in the heart of Kenyatta. See p. 179
Inset: Mboya and Gichuru signing a pledge of loyalty to Kenyatta during the campaign. See p. 178

6. Polling station scenes. (a) *above*, Turkana women carrying their registration cards in the traditional cleft sticks. (b) *below*, Kikuyu women queueing in Fort Hall

7. (a) and (b) At Lodwar on 23rd March 1961. *Left*, Mboya, Gichuru, Matano with Kenyatta. *Right*, Odinga with Kenyatta. See page 194
(c) KANU leaders outside Legislative Council building at opening meeting on 11th May. *Left to right*, Chokwe, Mboya, Gichuru, Mwanyimba, Odinga, Mathenge

8. The Governor opening the Legislative Council on 11th May. Government Front Bench, *left to right*, Minister for Works, Jamidar; Minister for Labour and Housing, Towett; Minister of Defence, Swann; Minister for Commerce and Industry, Muliro; Minister for Education and Leader of Government Business, Ronald Ngala; Minister for Legal Affairs, Griffith-Jones; Minister for Finance, K. W. S. Mackenzie; Chief Secretary, Coutts; Minister for Tourism, Marrian; Minister for Local Government, Havelock; and Minister for Agriculture, Blundell

MAPS

Part One

BACKGROUND

CHAPTER I

HISTORICAL PERSPECTIVES

Elections produce uncertainty about the future. When they are also a stage in the process of a British colony moving to independence the tension is heightened. In Ghana and Nigeria this was so in a real sense of struggle between rival groups for the power passing from British into local hands. In Kenya these familiar tensions were intensified by the fact that the elections of January to March 1961 would lead also to a major shift in power between the local communities. For the first time there would be an African majority in the Legislative Council and Africans would also then form the largest unofficial group in the Council of Ministers. Although the minority communities, European and Asian, retained a reservation of seats, all knew that the Lancaster House Conference of early 1960 had opened the way to an African state in Kenya. The Colony would follow the pattern of West Africa. To Kenya Europeans this came with the force of a psychological shock. They had long seen themselves as the northern outpost of European settlement in British Africa. Their feelings were well typified by the settler who cast thirty pieces of silver before Michael Blundell, one of their leaders, on his return to Nairobi from Lancaster House. Many in the community felt that their work over sixty years had been betrayed.

Modern Kenya's story begins only with the twentieth century. Earlier this area of Africa was particularly remote from the outside world. Whilst there were ancient towns on the coast, such as Mombasa and Lamu, with an Arab pattern of life and with other Asian groups settled there, the African peoples of the interior had few external contacts. They continued to live in a self-sufficient economy; some nomadic pastoralists, others shifting agriculturalists. Upon them British power burst and established itself in the last decade of the nineteenth century and the first of the twentieth. In 1901 the developmental backbone of Kenya, the railway from Mombasa to Nairobi and Kisumu, was completed; next year the boundary with Uganda

was shifted from the Rift Valley to the longitude of Mount
Elgon. Although there were some subsequent modifications,
the most important being the transfer of the Turkana country
from Uganda to Kenya in 1926, the shape of modern Kenya
was established.

Much of the country is arid so that the overwhelming majority
of the population is concentrated in the highlands of its south-
western quarter. This may be defined as a rough parallelogram,
formed by the boundaries with Uganda and Tanganyika with
the eastern side an imaginary line north-east from Mount Kili-
manjaro and the northern one running slightly to the north of
Mount Kenya, the snow-clad mountain on the equator which
gave the Colony its name. This area has proved a parallelogram
of force containing the mainspring of Kenya politics. The tension has been racial since successive British Governments
encouraged Europeans and Asians to come into the area to
promote economic development.

At the beginning of the century it did not seem possible to
colonial officials that the required development could be brought
about through the agency of the local African population. They
were regarded as among the most primitive of the continent.
Moreover, there were large areas where the population was
sparse. Human and animal disease had led in the last years of
the nineteenth century to some areas being completely empty,
whilst others again, like the Rift Valley, were occupied but
scantily by Masai nomadic pastoralists. It was found possible
to concentrate that tribe to the south. Their old lands in the
Rift Valley and on the Uasin Gishu and Laikipia plateaus were
taken for European settlement. Small townships sprang up:
Nakuru, sometimes called 'the capital of the (European) Highlands', Eldoret and Thomson's Falls, centres of Afrikaner immigrants, Kitale and Nanyuki in lands beyond. Apart from the
blocks of land around these townships, Europeans settled on
other vacant areas, apparently left by African tribes as no
man's land between them. Nairobi, the capital, grew in such an
area, with settlement stretching east towards the Kamba people
around Machakos and between that tribe and the Kikuyu to
the north of Nairobi. A visiting Under-Secretary of State, the
young Winston Churchill, was not alone in thinking in 1907
that there was plenty of land for all, though he did question the

possibility of the Europeans' aim that this should become 'a white man's country'.[1]

Many of the settlers were from older British colonies, then in the process of becoming self-governing Dominions. It was natural that they in their turn should challenge in this new land the British Government and the Colonial Office, should seek to obtain first a Legislative Council for themselves—which was granted in 1906—and then press for the right of electing members to it. When the first elections took place in 1920 the Europeans considered it right that they alone should have the vote and that their predominant agricultural interest should be represented by eight of the eleven constituencies. Only against European opposition did the Indians obtain the franchise in 1923 and then only on a communal basis: five seats for their population which was more than double that of the Europeans. Although the British Government then acknowledged in a famous declaration that Kenya was 'primarily . . . an African territory', and that the interests of its native inhabitants must be 'paramount', nobody thought at that time that there were any Africans who were capable of expressing these interests in the Legislative Council. Until 1944 this task was left to nominated Europeans. Only then did the Government consider it possible to nominate an African to the Council, the first being E. W. Mathu, a Kikuyu.

The general recognition of Mathu's ability in the Legislative Council marked well the primacy of the Kikuyu tribe in political terms. This, the largest tribe of Kenya, comprises about one-fifth of the African population. Their lands hold a central position in the Colony, stretching north from Nairobi to Mount Kenya. As white settlement took place the Kikuyu found themselves almost completely surrounded by Europeans to whose farms they also went out to work. Under this close European impact the Kikuyu people have changed more than any other East African tribe. Already in 1920 they were stirring politically, forming in that year their first political organization. This, then and later, raised the perennial cry of the lost Kikuyu lands, maintaining that large parts of their tribal area had been taken for European settlement. At the same time the Kikuyu expressed most strongly the African frustration at not being

[1]W. S. Churchill: *My African Journey* (1908)

allowed to grow cash-crops, particularly coffee. Then, too, they were shut out from a place in the political forum. By 1928 they were asking for representation on the Legislative Council by members of their own people. Taking the lead in this demand was the Kikuyu Central Association whose General Secretary was Johnstone (later Jomo) Kenyatta. However his hour was yet to come. He left Kenya from 1931 to 1946 in pursuit of travel and education, studying anthropology at London University and twice visiting Moscow.

During the thirties and early forties the Europeans could continue the economic development of Kenya largely un-troubled by considerations of African politics. The twenties, in comparison, had been a time of political battle with the Indians until 1923 but the British Government's settlement then proved only a brief check to the European struggle to obtain full control of the Government through a European elected majority in the Legislative Council. When this was finally denied in 1931 through the Report of a Joint Select Committee of the two Houses of Parliament, the Europeans sought to obtain financial and ministerial control of the Kenya Government. In this they attained a considerable measure of success, being helped par-ticularly by the conditions of the Second World War. Then the British Government naturally desired full local economic sup-port, and thus granted what was virtually a ministerial position to a leading local European: Major (later Sir) Ferdinand Cavendish-Bentinck. Already Cavendish-Bentinck had played a leading part in seeking the consolidation of the European position in their 'White Highlands'. To guarantee this he had pressed for the promulgation of an Order in Council, which was issued in 1939. At the same time he took the lead in furthering European settlement schemes. In all this activity he naturally clashed with the Indians who were calling for equality of treatment.

Thus the appointment of Cavendish-Bentinck as Member for Agriculture in a re-shaping of the Government in 1945 pro-voked a racial explosion in the Legislative Council. Asians and Africans took this as a sign of European settler control over the future of Kenya. In the next three years the formation of the East Africa High Commission and the new composition of the Kenya Legislative Council raised communal issues concerning racial proportions of membership. Asian and African politicians drew together in opposition to European pretensions. Yet this was an uneasy alliance. Below the leadership level tensions grew as African advancement was beginning to affect the Asian position in the country. Africans could now aspire in increasing numbers to jobs as clerks and artisans, jobs which Asians had filled from the beginning of Kenya's development. Europeans who chuckled over this attack on the position of the other immigrant community were slower to understand the shifting of world power which was soon to affect their position also. The steps to India's independence in 1947 and the repercussions of this process upon African nationalism could still seem distant and unimportant to Kenya settlers remote in highland valleys or on scattered plateau farmlands.

However, it was not long before an African leader, prominent with Dr. Nkrumah at the Manchester Pan-African Conference of 1945, was active in Kenya. This was the former Kikuyu leader, Jomo Kenyatta, who returned from his long absence in 1946. In 1947 he became president of the Kenya African Union (KAU), formed in 1944. Its story showed clearly the initial and fundamental problem of Kenya African politics: tribalism. Although many of the Union's leaders sought to make it, as its name indicated, an organization which would contain Africans from all over the Colony, yet it fell increasingly under Kikuyu domination. It was widely regarded then as no more than a revival of an older Kikuyu political organization. Kenyatta's own personality and previous history contributed to this feeling. His domineering character was resented by some of the leaders from Nyanza. That populous African province of western Kenya, more remote than Kikuyuland from the immediate impact of European settlement, had never shown the same political awareness. Though Kenyatta and other KAU leaders sought to make contact in Nyanza KAU failed to establish successful branches. There the main tribes, the Luo and the Baluhya, remained largely out of politics, despite a few meetings and visits of KAU leaders. KAU was in fact strong only among the Kikuyu— whether in their home reserves or found as labourers across the Colony—and among the Embu and Meru, tribes closely associated with the Kikuyu and situated to the north of them.

Before Kenyatta could succeed in establishing himself as a

true national leader African politics were overtaken by a movement to violence among the Kikuyu: Mau Mau. Whilst this
had a background in secret societies among the Kikuyu and in
strange sects, found across Kenya and often anti-European in
character, this movement was developed as a means of action
by violent and frustrated young Kikuyu. They took advantage
of the possibilities of intimidation always present in an un-
sophisticated people. It has been suggested that Mau Mau
became the Stern Gang, the strong arm movement among the
Kikuyu of KAU. The problem remains of the relationship between the thugs who were the intimidatory power of Mau Mau
and Kenyatta as leader of KAU: who controlled whom? Certainly Kenyatta failed to denounce Mau Mau in terms sufficiently unambiguous to satisfy Europeans and Kikuyu alike
that he was opposed to the movement of violence. In 1952 this
increased in tempo with attacks on missions and government
officials, chiefs and headmen. Finally in October the Government proclaimed an Emergency, arresting Kenyatta and other
KAU leaders and later proscribing the Union.

In the following months the Emergency became a small scale
war. Mau Mau gangs, formed on a military pattern, moved
through the Kikuyu reserves and the forests, attacking Government forces, Europeans on their scattered farms and those
Kikuyu who remained loyal to the Government. In this last
respect the Emergency had something of the character of a civil
war, especially when the Government armed Kikuyu 'loyalists'
and formed them into Home Guard units, centred on chiefs and
fortified posts. To the gangs themselves Mau Mau was a freedom movement. It assailed the whole European position, both
governmental and settler, whilst depending for its strength on
intimidation through bestial oathing which made the movement
all the more repugnant to Europeans. Murder of settlers and
the massacre of Kikuyu at Lari in March 1953 provided the
background to the trial of Jomo Kenyatta who was eventually
found guilty of managing Mau Mau and sentenced to seven
years' imprisonment. Then, in 1954, the Governor, Sir Evelyn
Baring, sought to reassure the loyalists with the promise that at
the end of his sentence Kenyatta would be kept in restriction
and not allowed to return to the Kikuyu country.

The proclamation of the Emergency brought British troops

into Kenya. Their second commander, Major-General Sir
George Erskine, did not rouse settler sympathy with a speech
in Nairobi in which he said that Mau Mau could not be solved
in military terms alone. A political settlement was essential for
the deeper problems involved. In this the British Government,
increasingly committed by troops and money, was likely to have
the deciding voice. With the local Europeans seeking to influence the conduct of the Emergency and with the failure of the
three racial groups to come to any agreement on constitutional
change, the Secretary of State, Oliver Lyttelton, visited the
Colony in March 1954 to put new constitutional proposals. His
idea was the establishment of a multi-racial Government with
full ministerial posts for unofficial members, of whom there
would be three Europeans, two Asians and one African.

The Lyttelton constitution produced the first, and a major,
split on constitutional matters in the European group, being
denounced by many as 'imposed'. Whilst some European
leaders had long realized that progress to self-government would
mean the entry of other races into Government positions the
fact of the new constitution came as a shock. Particularly galling
was the entry of Asians into Government, with one to hold the
long coveted portfolio of Works. However, Blundell, the European leader, and two of his colleagues accepted ministerial
posts. Blundell saw the need for co-operation with the British
Government, and became the one unofficial Minister on the
War Council which Lyttelton also set up to conduct the Emergency.

In July, Blundell and his colleagues were instrumental in
forming the United Country Party with the proclaimed intention of seeking support for the multi-racial principle of the new
constitution. However, it proved necessary to respect the sus-
ceptibilities of the settler community. The new party could only
put forward that members of other races might be allowed to
join it later, whilst, it was announced, the party would continue to maintain the principles of the sanctity of the White
Highlands and of the communal roll method of representation.
In reply there was formed in the same month the Federal Independence Party, soon attacked as being motivated by *apartheid*
notions from South Africa. It suggested 'provincial autonomy'
as the solution for Kenya's problems but found it difficult to

make much headway with this since, owing to the smallness of the European numbers (some 50,000 in a population of six million), no European province could be formed in which the Europeans would not be overwhelmingly outnumbered. It was indeed difficult to see how Kenya could be isolated from the tide of African nationalism, rising on the democratic ideals of the West with the telling cry of 'One man, one vote'. How long, in fact, could Blundell's idea of European leadership in a multi-racial state be maintained?

African leadership was not happy under the Lyttelton constitution. They saw the European position of parity with the other races in the Legislative Council maintained in the new Council of Ministers and, more particularly, were incensed that their overwhelming numbers should be acknowledged by only one ministry, and that one which appeared of little importance. Only after a month of hesitation and a tour of his home province, Nyanza, did B. A. Ohanga agree to accept this post. The weakness of his position then and later was that, like the other African members of the Legislative Council, he was only nominated. Although the Governor had appointed these members after a form of indirect election by the African District Councils the attack could still be made that they were unrepresentative: there had been no proper African elections. Moreover, on account of the Emergency the Kikuyu were debarred from politics. African leadership in this period fell more and more to men from the next largest tribe, the Luo. From them a new figure emerged at this time: Tom Mboya, who was building up his strength as a Trade Union leader.

At the end of July 1954 a new Secretary of State was appointed: Alan Lennox-Boyd, who made it one of his first tasks to visit Kenya. In Nairobi, in October, he publicly reiterated the Government's promise that the Mau Mau irreconcilables would not be allowed to return, that the Europeans had an essential part to play in Kenya and that the British Government would support them, saying that he himself believed in further British immigration. A few days later it was announced that a senior Civil Servant formerly in Kenya, Mr. (later Sir) Walter Coutts, would return to conduct an enquiry into the means of introducing African elections for the Legislative Council.

Meanwhile the prolongation of the Emergency increased

racial bitterness. Europeans opposed the idea of an amnesty which was being urged with African support as a means of ending the operations. Kikuyuland lived under a reign of repression in the attempt to stamp out Mau Mau. There were curfews and tight controls on movement whilst this highly individualistic tribe was forced into villages—all this being done that supplies might be denied to the terrorists. These measures put such pressure on the terrorist leaders that in May 1955 they sought surrender talks. Although these proved abortive, Mau Mau could be spoken of by June as 'only a nuisance'. Soon there was talk that Blundell might leave the War Council and succeed Cavendish-Bentinck as Minister of Agriculture. The idea was not welcomed by Africans who disliked a settler farmer being responsible for a ministry which affected the main economic interest of both races so closely. In the end the change was delayed until the beginning of October, when it was also announced that Cavendish-Bentinck was to become Speaker of the Legislative Council.

In June another sign of the improved security situation was the Government's authorization that Africans might again form political organizations, though at first only on a local basis. In deciding this the Government declared that such associations would be later allowed to join together in 'Conventions'. In this they were using a historic word and following the pattern of European and Asian political organizations. The associations of both the immigrant groups had always been formed on the basis of local associations sending representatives to form central bodies which acted as a mouthpiece for their communities. The Indians' organization was known as the Kenya Indian Congress, and the older European body as the Convention of Associations. Although this had died and been replaced in the Second World War by the Electors' Union, the name continued to hold the European political imagination. In December, a Luo lawyer, C. M. G. Argwings-Kodhek, formed in Nairobi the Kenya African National Congress. The Government replied that the name was not acceptable, and that the organization would be refused registration; it would thus be illegal. The Government was not yet prepared to allow African political organizations above the District level.

In January 1956 the Coutts report on African elections was

published. Although Coutts acknowledged that some half of the
Africans who had given evidence were in favour of universal
adult franchise he preferred a more conservative approach. He
recommended that the vote should be given only on certain
qualifications such as age, education, and experience in posts
of responsibility—with additional votes for people possessing
more than one of these. It was estimated that on the basis of
this report some 40% of adult males would be entitled to vote,
but the Government in a Sessional Paper issued with the Coutts
report announced a further widening of qualifications so that
60% of adult males were likely to be enfranchised. However, it
did not seem possible to carry out the necessary preparations
for the African elections on this franchise to be held at the
same time as those for the European and Asian communities
already announced for September. Africans were by now looking beyond, to a demand for an alteration in the racial composition of Legislative Council: a change from European
parity with the other unofficial members to one, as in Uganda,
of African parity.

As the European and Asian elections in September drew
near, two important incidents occurred. First the able and
influential Asian Minister without portfolio, A. B. Patel,
announced that he would retire from politics, preparatory to
withdrawing to a religious centre in India. His departure left
the Asian non-Muslim community without an outstanding
leader to hold them together, a loss the greater since Patel had
gained considerable respect among all communities as a media-
ting influence in the multi-racial government established in
1954. Then, as the election campaign developed, the split
among the Europeans, present since 1954, deepened. The
election for the European communal seats was fought mainly
between two groups: one led by Blundell who accepted the
Lyttelton constitution, and the other, under the leadership of
Group-Captain Briggs, which denounced it as 'foisted' upon
Kenya. Some other candidates, standing as independents,
were known supporters of the multi-racial ideals of the Capricorn Africa Society but they were overwhelmingly defeated.
Yet other candidates stood in the name of the Federal Independence Party. Significantly the Blundellites and the Briggsites
stood as 'Independents', seeking to avoid the name of Party, a

word long anathema to the Europeans who realized the dangers
of divisions in their ranks before the pressures of African numbers around them. In the outcome, the Federal Independence
Party was overwhelmingly defeated. Its member who came
nearest to success stood as an independent against Blundell's
party and ministerial colleague, W. B. Havelock. The election
result was a marked set-back for Blundell's policy of co-
operation since the Briggs group obtained eight of the fourteen
seats, leaving the other six to Blundell and his supporters.
Despite denials in the election campaign, Briggs shortly agreed
to accept a ministry whilst the two groups announced their
unity in the European Elected Members Association in the
Legislative Council, and, in January 1957, the United Country
Party was formally dissolved.

Meanwhile, registration of electors for the African elections
was proceeding but slowly during the last quarter of 1956.
Although the Government conducted a propaganda campaign
to persuade voters to register, a fundamental difficulty arose
from African suspicions aroused by the necessity to disclose
taxation particulars to obtain the vote. As there were still only
eight African Elected Members the constituencies were enormous. There was, for example, only one for the heavily populated Central Province. There registration could only be low
since among the Kikuyu, Embu and Meru the vote was allowed
only to loyalists in the Emergency. In the result the Meru tribe,
whose registration was highest, obtained a member and the
politically conscious Kikuyu did not. Only two of the new
African Elected Members had previously been in the Legislative
Council. African leadership there passed to Tom Mboya, the
Luo trade unionist elected for Nairobi where he defeated
Argwings-Kodhek.

Under Mboya's leadership the African members were soon
demanding fifteen more seats. At the same time they denounced
the Lyttelton constitution as imposed during the Emergency,
saying that in the elections they were pledged against it. Mboya
went on to demand that Kenya should follow in Ghana's path
towards self-government. In July the European Elected Members issued a statement that they would accept an increase of
African representation without asking, as they had in the past,
for any European increase to maintain parity. On the other

hand they looked for a form of self-government in which all races could co-operate and for a constitutional agreement sufficiently binding to give a future period of stability, adding that it was essential to this that Africans should join the Government as Ministers. Mboya and his colleagues rejected any idea of conditions and argued for 'undiluted democracy', meaning thereby equal rights for all individuals though with safeguards for minorities.

Then, in October 1957, Lennox-Boyd arrived in Nairobi to begin lengthy negotiations with the leaders of the racial groups. Since there had been an agreement that the Lyttelton constitution should continue until 1960, he first obtained the resignations of European and Asian ministers. The Lyttelton constitution was thus considered to have broken down, leaving the Secretary of State with a free hand for the discussions. In November he announced his award: the Africans were to receive an extra ministry and six more elected seats. This last brought them to an equality of numbers in the Legislative Council with the communally elected Europeans. At the same time it was announced that no more communal seats would be created and that the racial proportions for communal seats would be fixed for ten years. As an approach to common roll elections in the future Lennox-Boyd accepted the idea that the Council should sit as an electoral college to choose twelve Specially Elected Members, four each for Africans, Asians and Europeans —the idea behind this being that such members could claim to have support from other races beside their own. Besides this, the Government would have power to nominate sufficient members to maintain a Government majority. The new constitution received support from Europeans and Asians, one leader of the latter calling the institution of Specially Elected Members 'the first step to a common roll', an Asian objective from the beginning of Kenya's electoral history.

However, the Lennox-Boyd constitution was rejected by the African leaders, who announced, in particular, that they would boycott the Specially Elected seats. When the elections for these were held, it was found that eight Africans were willing to stand, despite denunciations as 'stooges, quislings, and black Europeans', traitors to the African cause. These attacks turned particularly against Musa Amalemba, a Muluhya from North

Nyanza, for he not only obtained one of these seats, but, after his election, accepted also the post of Minister of Housing, despite the African call for a boycott. A dramatic incident occurred during the choosing of the Specially Elected Members. As a result of the African boycott the most liberal European candidate, Ernest Vasey the able Minister of Finance, was defeated. He obtained an equality of votes with Humphrey Slade but lost when lots were drawn. The African members subsequently moved a motion of confidence in Vasey, but the story is one indication of a tragedy of Kenya's history: the impossibility of gaining fully the confidence of a community other than one's own without losing the support of one's own.

In the months that followed the introduction of the Lennox-Boyd constitution the gulf between the races widened with a new temper rising in African politics. While the Emergency continued a nominal existence, scandals arose about some of the prison camps. In a Legislative Council debate calling for an enquiry in June 1958 Oginga Odinga, the Luo member from Central Nyanza, referred to the imprisoned men as leaders respected by the African people, and mentioned specifically the name of Kenyatta. In September Mboya's Nairobi People's Convention Party called for the observance of the anniversary in October of Kenyatta's arrest as a day of fasting. In November the Governor thought it necessary to speak in the Legislative Council of the danger of the development of a cult of Kenyatta. However, Dr. Kiano, a Kikuyu member of the Council, spoke of Kenyatta as a freedom fighter equal to Nkrumah whilst attending in December the Pan-African Conference at Accra, and in the same month Arthur Ochwada, Assistant General Secretary of Mboya's Kenya Federation of Labour, referred to the Mau Mau as 'gallant freedom fighters'. This interpretation of the past made more difficult than ever a reconciliation between the races in Kenya.

At the same time the African leaders, having rejected the Lennox-Boyd constitution, were pressing for a new constitutional conference. Their demand was for an African majority but Lennox-Boyd insisted that there would be no increase of communal representation and said also that he wanted to give the Council of Ministers a longer chance to prove itself. In January 1959 the African members announced a boycott of the Legislative Council until a decision was taken that constitutional talks would be held.

In March Blundell expressed the view in the Council that rejection of a conference was unwise. He then began to seek to build a multi-racial party with a multi-racial policy. His policy statement in April was a revolutionary document for a European, for it argued for the ending of all racial barriers, even for the opening of the European Highlands to land-holding by other races. Blundell followed this by resigning from his post as Minister of Agriculture to lead a multi-racial New Kenya Group inside the Legislative Council. Whilst he could claim that a majority of the Council, forty-four members of all races, had signed his policy statement, there was no African or Asian constituency elected member among them. However, the fact that he had amassed such support for a review of the constitution re-opened the issue. Lennox-Boyd replied in the House of Commons by outlining the conditions he considered necessary for the transfer of power and agreed there should be a conference well before the Kenya General Election scheduled to take place in 1960. In these circumstances the African members returned to the Legislative Council, Odinga expressing his satisfaction with the Secretary of State. Blundell's action had not increased his popularity among the settlers and soon Briggs was expressing their hostility to the idea of a conference. He began to mobilize European opinion in opposition to Blundell's New Kenya Party as the Group became outside the Council. In August Briggs formed the United Party, based on an amalgamation of his old 'independent group' supporters with those who had been in the Federal Independence Party. The new organization's policy was proclaimed as being the ending of the Legislative Council and the developing of independent local government bodies.

During these months new groupings were being formed among the other races. In July an Asian, Arvind Jamidar, announced in the Legislative Council that a multi-racial Kenya National Party had been formed, backed in the first instance by ten African, one European and six Asian members of the Council. The European was the very independent-minded S. V. Cooke whose action commanded little support in his own community but on the African side the grouping was to prove embryonic for the future. Masinde Muliro from Elgon Nyanza became the party president and it received moderate African support. However, the prominent Luo and Kikuyu leaders stood aloof. Late in August a new party, the Kenya Independence Movement, was formed among them with Odinga as president and Mboya as secretary. Since the party seemed interested only in an African membership the question soon arose whether the Government would permit a colony-wide African party for the first time since 1953. Registration had not been conceded by the end of the year and in November the Kenya National Party also announced that its membership would consist henceforth only of Africans. It had become clear that multi-racialism was an idea with no political future among Africans.

In October two most important and dramatic changes took place. The Kenya Government issued a Sessional Paper declaring the objective of the removal of all racial barriers, including those in education and on entry into land in the Highlands. For the latter a new, and multi-racial, Board was to be established, the sole criterion for ownership in the Highlands to be that of good husbandry. Angry settler meetings denounced the paper, Briggs declaring it to be the breaking of all the pledges of previous British Governments. The Sessional Paper appeared at the very moment of a change in Britain. Iain Macleod succeeded Lennox-Boyd as Colonial Secretary after the British General Election. A month later the new Secretary of State announced in the House of Commons that the Emergency would shortly end and in December he visited Kenya in preparation for a constitutional conference over which he was to preside. The Sessional Paper announced the destruction of the fundamental European position in respect of land. It remained for the British Government to complete the work with regard to settler political power.

THE LANCASTER HOUSE CONFERENCE

The Constitutional Conference on Kenya's future met in London, at Lancaster House, whilst Macmillan, the British Prime Minister, was travelling around Africa, noting in speeches from Accra to Cape Town 'the wind of change' blowing across the Continent. It was known that many new independent African states would emerge during 1960. Against this background of victorious African nationalism Kenya was to be the first British Colony where would be tested the relationship between that nationalism and the older but declining political dominance of white settlerdom. The challenge was the greater since the nationalists of Kenya had raised the question of the release of Kenyatta, the African leader most feared and detested by Europeans. In the last weeks before Lancaster House the nationalist demand had gone further: that Kenyatta should be released to attend the Conference as one of the delegates. Five days before the Conference convened the Kenya Governor, Sir Patrick Renison, replied that even if Kenyatta were free he could not attend since the Conference was one for members of the Legislative Council only.

Thus to London there came in mid-January 1960 all but one of the Constituency Elected Members of the Council, with ten of the twelve Specially Elected Members and two Nominated Members, one to represent the Northern Province, and the other the senior Arab official, the Liwali of the Coast, whilst official representatives were the Governor of Kenya and his Attorney-General, E. N. Griffith-Jones. Among the non-officials there were four main groups: on the one side the four-teen African Elected Members and on the other the four United Party members, Europeans under Briggs, the Asian and Arab group led by Dr. S. G. Hassan and a multi-racial delegation of the New Kenya Group led by Blundell. The first and last of these groups were by no means homogeneous. Whilst during the Conference divisions emerged in Blundell's group, the African members had previously been divided into two groups in the Legislative Council.

The African agreement to work together at Lancaster House was acknowledged by making Ronald Ngala, a member from the Coast and of Muliro's group, leader, with Mboya as secretary. Mboya, through his American contacts, was responsible for the choice of the American Negro lawyer, Dr. Thurgood Marshall, as adviser to the delegation. This set up repercussions in which the lead was taken by Odinga who wanted a second adviser, more knowledgeable of Kenya politics, in fact a representative of Kenyatta. A telegram was sent to Accra to Peter Mbiyu Koinange, formerly one of Kenyatta's closest associates. He was then a member of the Bureau of African Affairs in Ghana whence he arrived in London five days before the Conference began. The Secretary of State then refused to accept him for he was regarded by the British and Kenya Governments as one of the two Africans outside Kenya more particularly responsible for the events leading to Mau Mau. In view of this refusal the African Elected Members boycotted the opening of the Conference. The Government's action brought them together at least temporarily, for they had been by no means unanimous in the request for Koinange.

Five days of negotiations ensued before a compromise formula was devised whereby a blank pass was issued on which the Africans could write Koinange's name for entry to Lancaster House, though not to the Conference chamber. Whilst the Government thus curiously salved its conscience in not officially recognizing Koinange's presence, there was wide feeling that the Conference was proceeding on African terms, that African nationalism had scored a first and significant triumph. Acceptance of Koinange was difficult, not only for the Kenya Europeans present but also for moderate Africans who were supported by a telegram of protest from Kikuyu loyalists in Kenya. Blundell's multi-racial group was divided over this so that only after several hours heated debate did they agree to continue in the Conference. The United Party representatives took yet longer to accept. Briggs was initially for withdrawal but after a week-end's thought agreed to take part. European weakness was well demonstrated in that they dared do no more than make a token abstinence of one afternoon from the discussions.

The central subject of the Conference was clearly the form of elections in the process of building 'a nation based on parliamentary institutions on the Westminster model and enjoying responsible self-government', the objective set in his initial speech by Macleod. The Africans wished to break completely with the communal elections of the past and proceed immediately to universal adult suffrage on a common roll basis of 'one man, one vote'. In the opening of the Conference debate Ngala and Mboya put these views. Blundell, speaking between them, said that his group agreed that Kenya must move away from racial seats, and that they would accept a reduction in their number but, he pointed out, a 'common' roll effectively meant an African roll. They sought a system whereby all members of all races would be answerable to responsible electors of all races, that the number of persons elected on a non-racial basis should, if possible, outnumber those who were elected racially. However, next day an Asian member of his group, I. E. Nathoo, the Muslim Minister of Works, came out clearly for the common roll, saying that if the Africans wished to abolish communal seats the Conference should agree. This speech came as a surprise to the Conference, to the New Kenya Group, and not least to Nathoo's fellow Asians. Traditionally the Asians in Kenya had always advocated a common roll. In the twenties it had been a weapon of the East African Indian National Congress against the Europeans but now many Asians feared that with its introduction they, like the Europeans, would be submerged in the African mass, and so they hesitated to support Nathoo.

After the lengthy debate in which all but one of the forty-seven non-official delegates spoke, Macleod replied with the British Government's proposals. He was for a marked reduction in the size of the Legislative Council by ending the system of Government nominees—a change which had the Kenya Governor's expressed approval—and by limiting the number of members to forty-eight. He saw the danger of too abrupt a change to a common roll and wished to bridge the transition by a system of rolls with progressively higher qualifications for voting. Half of the forty-eight seats would, however, be open to voters with 'very low' qualifications, similar to those already operating in Tanganyika, so that these seats would thereby become African dominated. Macleod further suggested that these twenty-four seats should come from twelve two-member constituencies in which voters would each have but one vote and thus some protection might be given to minority opinion. Although the proposals were supposed to be confidential they immediately leaked to the Nairobi press. Word went round the African areas that the Colonial Secretary had announced that the Africans were to receive independence and some African rioting occurred. In London the United Party leaders expressed their sense of 'shock' and talked of doing no more in the Conference than maintain a 'watching brief'.

Macleod had suggested that the Conference should break up

into committees but Blundell insisted that committees on the executive and on the proposed Bill of Rights could not function until the all-important question of the franchise and the shape of the legislature were settled. In this he was strongly supported by the African Elected Members. In the end it was found that progress could only be made through informal discussions between the various groups. In these the Africans stood firm on the common roll, whilst Nathoo's speech had opened the possibility of negotiations through the divisions in Blundell's group. Both these groups proceeded to produce suggestions for constituency planning and involved negotiations ensued. As these proceeded Slade, from Blundell's group, and Briggs flew back to Nairobi to inform their supporters of the progress of the discussions. The growing European anxiety was immediately reflected in a slump in the Nairobi stock market and a standstill in all property dealings. Even before the Conference was completed, a loss of confidence thus started through uncertainty about Kenya's future.

Meanwhile in the negotiations in London the African members came to accept that some form of safeguard for the minorities by communal seats might be retained, though they insisted that this should be brought about without compromising the principle of the common roll. The continuation of Specially Elected Members, the group which provided the majority of Blundell's support, proved a more difficult hurdle and had to be handed back to Macleod for decision. Ngala told the press that having agreed to a reservation of seats—which, however, would only be a temporary provision—he could not see the need for the Specially Elected Members. In the end, a month after the Conference first met, Macleod produced a final plan. Although it was insisted that this was not a cut and dried solution incapable of further amendment, the various groups knew only too well the complexities of reopening the discussions. The three largest groups agreed to accept, though none did so with any relish, and each expressed reservations. Only the United Party were entirely opposed to the proposals.

Thus was laid down the new constitution: a Legislative Council of sixty-five members, with an effective African majority. Thirty-three would be elected from open seats, the first in Kenya's history, and the franchise would be so wide as to ensure that the electorate would be overwhelmingly African. Twenty seats were to be reserved for candidates from the minority communities: ten for Europeans, eight for Asians, and two for Arabs. This meant both a decrease of four seats for Europeans and an increase of two for Asians, parity being thus established between European and non-European reserved seats. To ensure that candidates commanded a following in their own communities before they went to the same common roll electorate as in the open seats, a form of primary election would be held in the community concerned. The Kenya Europeans had seen with horror Europeans and Asians elected in open seats in Tanganyika with the support of the Tanganyika African National Union. They were determined that their reserved seats should not go immediately to people whom they regarded as 'stooges' of African nationalism. However, the Secretary of State made no decision on what percentage would constitute 'effective and genuine support' from a community in the primary election—this was left for subsequent determination in Kenya. There would be twelve National Members, four each for Africans, Asians and Europeans. Two changes from the Specially Elected Members made these more palatable to the Africans: officials would not vote in the new Legislative Council electoral college, and, through the proportions of open to reserved seats, African electors would have the major voice in the choice of the new National Members. Whilst the Governor would retain the right of nomination, it was hoped its use might prove unnecessary. Responsible government was not proposed. The Governor would still choose his Ministers and no provision was made for a Chief Minister. However, the proportions in the new Council of Ministers would change radically: the officials would be cut from seven to four, the Europeans from four to three, the Asians from two to one— whilst the Africans would increase from one to four.

Briggs's reactions were outspoken. He called the new constitution 'a victory for Mau Mau', whilst his party in Nairobi described it as 'a cynical abandonment of the Europeans in Kenya'. They considered that the franchise proposals would result in the community's disenfranchisement and lead to 'taxation without representation'. The coming months would decide whether Blundell could reassure his supporters, both

Europeans and moderate Africans. On the other hand, the African Elected Members had achieved neither full adult suffrage on a common roll nor an African Chief Minister. They also would find it difficult to convince the African electorate of the advantages of the new Constitution. As for the Asians, their organizations, the Kenya Indian Congress and the Kenya Muslim League, came together to send a cable to Macleod alleging unjust treatment, saying, in a traditional way, that they regarded equality with the Europeans as the minimum compatible with their rights and honour. Although they had increased their number of seats in the Legislative Council it was bitter that they should lose one of their ministries.

There remained one further matter of dispute. The African elected members had wished to give no more safeguard to the immigrants than through a Bill of Rights. For this their legal adviser, Dr. Marshall, was asked to prepare a first draft. When this was discussed the Europeans insisted on safeguards for land and education, in a form which, said the Africans, went beyond the scope of the Bill. Moreoever, the Africans regarded many of the European titles as being in dispute. In the end the members of the Conference simply agreed to note the suggestions on expropriation made by Macleod.

Thus European land was clearly one fundamental issue for the future. Another, raised in the Conference, was that of the Kenya Protectorate, the ten mile coastal strip leased from the Sultan of Zanzibar under an Agreement of 1895. The Arab representatives suggested in characteristically gentle terms that they would regard it as a breach of faith if the British Government devolved its administrative powers on to another Government, namely the successor African Government in Kenya. On the other hand the African members of the Conference made it plain that they did not recognize the Agreement of 1895, regarding it as null and void.

As the Conference broke up there was in these and other ways a foreshadowing of coming political developments. Throughout there had been strong feeling among the African members at the way Mboya was ever in the limelight, being treated by the British press and television as the effective leader of the African delegation. In a final press conference both Ngala and Muliro commented adversely on this. At the same time Muliro paid tribute to the honesty and sincerity of Briggs, acknowledging that the fears which dominated men like him could not 'be brushed aside lightly'. Briggs himself made it plain that the British Government's offer to underwrite £5,000,000 for land settlement was insufficient; he thought a figure of £30,000,000 was necessary to help stabilize land values in the transitional period.

The Lancaster House Conference had set out a new consti-tution. Yet it would require some time before the elections under it could take place. The period of preparation would necessarily be one of uncertainty. Already reactions in Nairobi to the reports of the Conference indicated the danger for Kenya's economy if this were a lengthy process. Could confi-dence be maintained or would political activity make the situation worse?

When the various leaders returned to Nairobi from Lancaster House Ngala commented that they had broken 'European domination' and Blundell was denounced at the airport by Europeans as a traitor, though this led Africans present to raise a counter-cry, 'Mr. Blundell, we'll vote for you if necessary'. Muliro's comment to reporters was that the Africans were now ready to take three ministries. Certainly it had been under-stood at Lancaster House that this would now happen. How-ever, Mboya, arriving in Nairobi a few days later, raised the question of the future in an acute way. He commented that they were not committed to the duration of the new constitu-tion, adding later that it would not last four years, the normal life of a Legislative Council, that it was already out of date. When discussions began on possible ministries Mboya an-nounced that he would not accept one for himself, for, he said, 'our struggle is still to be won'.

Not until the very end of March was the appointment of three new African ministers announced. In fact a fortnight before, Ngala said on behalf of all the Africans that they were agreed that none should enter the Government whilst the Lennox-Boyd constitution was still in force. This decision was made after a lengthy meeting which in itself showed the develop-ing differences between moderate and extreme opinion among the African leaders. Admittedly one of their problems was that the Government wished to retain one of the four ministries allotted to Africans in the hands of Musa Amalemba, and nationalist feeling was strong against him. In the end the Government managed to persuade the African leaders to accept the three other ministries, not just as part of the Lennox-Boyd constitution but as sharing in 'a caretaker Government' until the election could be held. On this basis Ngala accepted the portfolio of Labour and Social Security, J. N. Muimi, of the Kamba tribe, Health and Welfare, and Kiano that of Commerce and Industry, a ministry which, it was widely believed, the Government had hoped Mboya would accept. African nationalist leaders had now joined the Government, producing at long last the effective multi-racial ministry which had been hoped for when the Lennox-Boyd constitution was established in 1957.

However, the month's delay in the entry of the Africans into the Government and the speeches made by African leaders during that month heightened the atmosphere of uncertainty about the future. Already in the third week of March, Major Roberts of the United Party was claiming that £900,000 a week was leaving the Colony and there was talk of the possibility of currency restrictions.

European difficulty in entering the new world was well brought out by the resignation, on 4th March, of Cavendish-Bentinck from his post as Speaker. He gave as his reason that he was 'out of sympathy with the trend of current events'; he felt he 'might be unable conscientiously to discharge the functions of the office of Speaker with that complete detachment and impartiality which are essential'. In a fuller statement a few days later he attacked what he called the '*volte face*' of the British Government, saying that it was failing to honour the many pledges made to the settlers by British Governments in the past. He explained that he felt he must support the interests particularly of those whom he had encouraged over the years to settle in Kenya in reliance upon these pledges. The European settlers began then to rally around their old leader of the thirties and forties so that he was able to announce, on 20th March, that he was forming a 'Kenya Coalition'. He announced his primary aim as that of greater co-operation among Europeans and thereafter among all whose interests were in jeopardy. The Coalition claimed later that it sought to represent 'the minorities'. In this it was hamstrung since its leader was the known elder champion of the Europeans. It therefore made no appeal whatever to the Asians, nor did its approaches to the smaller African tribes have any greater success. The Coalition became the last-ditch rearguard action of the Europeans.

Whilst Europeans sought to defend the past, African leaders were discussing their new position in relation to the Government and forming new political groupings for the future.

CHAPTER II

THE GROWTH OF AFRICAN POLITICS

The return of the African Elected Members from Lancaster House did not lead to the formation of a single territorial-wide political organization as in many other African countries, though the attempt was made, but to two national African parties: the Kenya African National Union (KANU) and the Kenya African Democratic Union (KADU). They differed not only in the basis of their support, but also in their approach to politics and organization. KANU was the first to emerge and, throughout the election, remained dominant. It regarded itself as the principal instrument for achieving freedom and independence. Its motto was, 'Duty to one's country is duty to God', and it attracted to its banner the more militant and determined nationalists. KANU's objective was the unity of all Africans and the organization of a mass movement in which power and authority would be concentrated in the party's central executive institution. The objective of an all-embracing party was shattered almost immediately by the formation of KADU, which bitterly opposed the idea of an absolute unitary mass party. Throughout the election KADU retained the character of an opposition party. It lacked the dynamic force and thrust of KANU. While KADU sought 'freedom', an equal emphasis was placed on its watchword, 'peace and justice'. Formed from an alliance of tribal and regional associations, it accepted a concept of collective national leadership in which divergent interests were accommodated.

These developments can only be understood as part of a larger historical process. Both KANU and KADU have their roots not in the immediate events after Lancaster House, but in a nationalism whose growth and organization have been both uneven and fragmented. Fundamental to this disunity has been tribal parochialism in the absence of a united organized mass movement. Kenya has numerous tribal groups varying greatly in size and development, and among all the consciousness of separation remains prominent. Not only has the tribe continued to command the loyalty and identity of most individuals, but social and political changes have encouraged this.

Africans form 97 % of Kenya's population, being estimated in 1959 to number 6,171,000. With twenty-seven main tribes, the African people may be divided into four major groups: Bantu, Nilotic, Nilo-Hamitic and Hamitic, these being both linguistic and cultural classifications. Though over 70 % of the population are Bantu, the greatest land area is occupied by Hamitic and Nilo-Hamitic peoples. The Luo, a Nilotic agricultural people, are settled in Nyanza Province around Lake Victoria. Nilo-Hamitics—the Masai, the Turkana and a group known as the Kalenjin, comprising Kipsigis, Nandi, Elgeyo, Marakwet, Tugen and Suk, together with several smaller tribes—occupy a broad stretch of western Kenya running from the northern to the southern boundary, while Hamitic peoples —Somali and Galla—inhabit the north-eastern part of the country. The Bantu—Kikuyu, Embu, Meru, Kamba, Taita, Giriama, Kisii, Baluhya and others—form large clusters of population in southern Kenya.

A significant feature among most Kenya Africans has been an absence of chieftaincy or any centralized traditional system of authority. Before the arrival of the British, the majority of these tribes lacked any effective political unity. In Nyanza Province, for example, nineteen tribal entities, each loyal to its own land area, made up the Luo people, while numerous tribelets with different political structures comprised what are now called the Baluhya.

British administration stabilized tribal boundaries, recognizing each tribe as a separate entity through a system of tribal reserves. These units became the focal point of administration. Government policies in, for example, law, primary and intermediate education and local government had the effect of strengthening tribal loyalties. Trans-tribal awareness and mobility have been further hindered by the slowness in building a modern market economy embracing African farmers. When cash crops were encouraged, controls on production and marketing have often served to perpetuate local loyalties through the way they have been operated. The impact of urbanization, so often a process producing wider loyalties, has been limited by the lack of opportunity for an independent, permanently settled urbanized community to develop. The necessity for the majority of African wage earners, through low wages and the difficulties of accumulating capital, to have to look to the reserves for security in old age, unemployment or sickness, prevent the growth of a stable urban society; people need to retain association with land ownership. A recent survey in Nairobi found that few Africans had been there for as long as three years residence. Under all these conditions, the individual interests and loyalties of the vast majority of Africans have thus remained with the tribe.

African political development has taken place in an environment of non-African dominance, in a social order whose standards and values were European. The ability of African leaders to force major political changes has been lacking until the last four years. Contributing to their weakness has been the general disunity, disorganization and backwardness of the African population. This is reflected in the poverty of the rural areas, the low African wage scale and the limited educational opportunities. Besides this, racial considerations long obstructed African entry into the European dominated social order. Thus until recently there have been only a small number of educated Africans; few of these sought to function as a national élite, or were able to do so.

Before World War II, political action by Africans seldom reached the national level, although many local social and political associations arose in response to land and other grievances resulting from European settlement and government policies.[1] The granting of the franchise to Europeans in 1920 was a factor in the early growth of such associations. These sprang up predominantly in Kikuyuland, through a collection of grievances and the more profound initial impact of western civilization. Associations did develop among other tribes and some efforts were made by the most important of the Kikuyu organizations, the Kikuyu Central Association, for limited trans-tribal action. This, and other bodies, agitated for direct representation in the Legislative Council, but more particularly for consideration of African land claims and greater educational and economic opportunities. None of these associations had any

[1]For details see G. Bennett: 'The Development of Political Organizations in Kenya', *Political Studies*, vol. V, no. 2, June 1957.

effective influence upon Government policy. The majority were
considered unrepresentative of African opinion, while some
such as the Kikuyu Central Association, were thought sub-
versive and disloyal in agitating against constituted authority.
Nonetheless, the activities of these associations and their leaders
had an impact on post-war political action: a significant sector
of the African population, especially the Kikuyu, had become
highly socialized for political action. Both KAU in the immediate post-war years and the more recent leaders have been
able to build on this early political involvement and recruitment. Amongst the Kikuyu, and a few other tribal groups,
politics is thus a second generation phenomenon.

The history of KAU, from its founding in 1944 to its proscription in 1953, vividly illustrates the defects of mass political
movements in Kenya in terms of trans-tribal nationalism. The
paucity of educated English-speaking Africans and the inade-
quacies of a network of social communication embracing the
larger and more important agricultural tribes prevented the
building up of a mass following on a national scale. Although
branches were established in various parts of the country, they
were, outside the Kikuyu areas, largely ineffective. Kenyatta,
who returned to Kenya in 1946 and became president of KAU
in June 1947, was compelled to found his activity on the greater
possibilities for mass mobilization among the Kikuyu. In KAU,
while a few from other tribes continued as senior officers, the
leaders and the mass following were overwhelmingly Kikuyu.

From the beginning, no tribe in Kenya had been more influenced by the advent of western civilization or had closer
contact with Europeans. The Kikuyu were increasingly
drawn to nearby Nairobi but closer communication bred
greater dissatisfaction. With the boundaries of the Kikuyu reserves fixed by government, the growing population had no
room for expansion; opportunities for work in the European
economy were not enough to absorb all the landless who
began to appear. By reason of their closer proximity to European
settlement, by which they were almost surrounded, the Kikuyu
were subjected to discriminatory treatment to a greater extent
than members of other tribes. For these and other reasons,
particularly the bitterly felt grievances over the loss of land,
the Kikuyu were more restive and dissatisfied than any other

people of Kenya. They were therefore more responsive to organization in a mass political movement, wanting only effective leadership.

A number of circumstances favoured the emergence of political leadership among the Kikuyu. After 1945 communications developed which allowed easy movement between the rural areas and Nairobi. Meetings were held attracting thousands of people. Vernacular news sheets and papers appeared in great numbers, a few achieving large circulations. The growth of voluntary associations quickened the process of mass organization and helped to define public opinion. These associations, as well as the independent schools and separatist African churches dating from the twenties, all helped to foster concepts of Kikuyu and African unity.

By 1952 the inconsistent policies of British rule—encouraging white settlement and acquiescing in its demands for a major influence in government, while at the same time accepting the principle of African political development—reached deadlock. With Jomo Kenyatta as the charismatic leader of a militant nationalism which repudiated the social, economic and political privileges enjoyed by Europeans, the majority of the Kikuyu no longer accepted the legitimacy of the political and social order imposed on them. Debarred from meaningful participation in a European-dominated political order and thus believing there was no way to achieve immediate reforms, some Kikuyu began to plan violent opposition, an idea which thrived in the atmosphere of frustration and social bitterness. Their secret and conspiratorial organization exploded into the Mau Mau rebellion.

After the declaration of the Emergency on 20th October, 1952, and the arrest of Jomo Kenyatta, Achieng Oneko, Paul Ngei, Bildad Kaggia and other leaders, violence rapidly gained the ascendancy. KAU, however, was not immediately banned. With Kenyatta in prison, Walter Odede, a nominated member of the Legislative Council, became acting president until he, too, was detained in March, 1953, suspected of association with Mau Mau and of spreading its methods among the Luo. Then W. W. W. Awori, also a nominated member of the Legislative Council, was acting president until KAU itself was proscribed on 8th June, 1953. KAU's aims at this time were not immediate African self-government, but the abolition of the colour bar, a new land policy, educational and legal reforms, the restriction of European and Asian immigration into Kenya, African parity of unofficial representation in the Legislative Council and a common electoral roll based on a limited franchise.

Until 1955 all African political organizations were prohibited. The publication of independent African newspapers ceased with the outbreak of the Emergency for several years. *Baraza*, published by the *East African Standard*, continued, however, to reflect some African opinion and to present news about African affairs. Whilst the African nominated members of the Legislative Council had considerable latitude in criticism of government policy, yet there was an almost complete cessation of normal political life for Africans. In this vacuum, the African labour movement, with its headquarters in Nairobi, achieved an increasingly important role in voicing African political aspiration. Its influence and power was strengthened by the emergence of a young, intelligent and vigorous leader: Tom Mboya. In October 1953, Mboya became general secretary of the Kenya Federation of Registered Trade Unions, which became, in 1955, the Kenya Federation of Labour. With the successful settlement of the Mombasa Dock Strike in March 1955, his leadership was clearly established. As general secretary of the Federation, Mboya criticized various aspects of government policy concerning the prosecution of the Emergency, inadequate representation of Africans on all government bodies, the encouragement of tribal associations, and the continued restrictions on the formation of a new African political organization on a colony-wide basis.

In February 1956, the Government decided to act against the increasingly political role the Federation had assumed. Their decision was provoked in part by Mboya's press statement in London on 9th January censuring a wide range of government action and calling for constitutional reforms similar to those advocated by the proscribed KAU. In Nairobi, the Federation had also issued a long criticism of the Coutts Report on African elections to the Legislative Council. Rejecting the recommendations for a restricted franchise, the Federation maintained that there should be universal adult franchise, that the granting of only six seats to elected African members was 'ridiculously' inadequate, and that a general constitutional conference should be held to make the national institutions more representative of the people of Kenya. The Federation held that these were the views of the majority of the population. To avoid having its registration cancelled, an act tantamount to proscription, the Federation had to give immediately an undertaking to restrict its activities to matters directly concerning the members of its constituent trade unions in their capacity as employees. Apart from prohibiting the Federation from expressing political views, the Government was determined to prevent the existence of a colony-wide political body under any guise.

The Government's framework for African political development had been set forth in June 1955. Then the Emergency ban on all African political organizations was relaxed, but the formation of political associations was confined to a district basis. To encourage a 'simple and orderly development of African political life' and the growth of responsible opinion, Government envisaged these district associations eventually forming a connection with the member of Legislative Council representing the area. At a later stage, a colony-wide convention of associations would be permitted, but only after constituency conventions had matured and learned to solve some of their own local problems. The prohibition on political organization in the Central Province was retained, though a nominated Advisory Council for the Province was eventually established for the discussion of government policy by loyalists. With the authority of Emergency powers, the Government hoped to shape the development of African politics after a pattern of their own making. In place of the militancy of KAU, they pictured 'sensible and stable' men working up from the local level and gradually assuming greater responsibility in the affairs of the country at a pace controlled by government.

By the first direct African elections for members of the Legislative Council, in March 1957, a limited number of district associations had been brought into existence, mainly under the leadership of a new generation of leaders. An early one was a body led by Argwings-Kodhek, one of the first African lawyers. In a partially defiant mood, this originally sought registration, in December 1955, as the Kenya African National Congress. Like the Kenya Federation of Labour, it maintained that tribalism would be encouraged if political activities were limited to the district level. Government reacted by refusing registration because of the Congress's declared aim of becoming a colony-wide party; they said that experience had shown that such organizations had been employed to further the aims of terrorists. After modifying its name and focus, the Congress was registered in April 1956 as the Nairobi District African Congress. Shortly before the 1957 elections a split took place which eventually led to the formation of the Nairobi People's Convention Party. Though the Congress continued as a separate organization under Argwings-Kodhek until KANU was formed in 1960, its influence steadily declined as the Nairobi People's Convention Party came to dominate Nairobi African politics.

Among other district associations that emerged were the Mombasa African Democratic Union, the African District Association (Central Nyanza), the Kisii Highlands Abagusii Association of South Nyanza District, the South Nyanza District African Political Association, the Taita African Democratic Union and the Nakuru African Progressive Party. The organization and membership of these associations was rudimentary, and their role in obtaining support for candidates in 1957 was nearly everywhere negligible. Nonetheless, these associations represented the new beginnings of politics, embracing an ever larger number of major tribal groups. The danger remained that the pace of political development between districts would continue to be uneven and that parochialism rooted in tribal loyalties would be encouraged at the expense of African unity.

The African elections of March 1957 formed a watershed in African politics and, indeed, in Kenya's political history. African members of the Legislative Council could now assert that their views were sanctioned by a substantial electorate. With the African population linked to newly elected leaders, a strong parliamentary position and a constitutional focus for reform had been achieved. But the system of communal electoral rolls marked even more sharply the nature of racial politics.

The elections also reflected the growing group of educated

leaders. Though limited in number, these men represented a greater proportion of tribal groups than hitherto. They formed the vanguard of a new generation of politically aware Africans benefiting from the expanding educational and economic opportunities. However, there was still a marked disparity not only between urban and rural areas, but also between districts. These differences affected the emerging pattern of political organization across the country. The African Elected Members came to the Legislative Council as individual leaders committed to political reform, but not under the discipline of a national party. There was neither an agreement on corporate leadership, nor a willingness to accept fully any one of the Elected Members as the established national leader. This leadership problem increasingly faced African politics after 1957, despite the struggle for self-determination.

At first, the overwhelming need for concerted action was sufficient to hold the African Elected Members together. Even before these first eight joined the Legislative Council, they asserted, in March 1957, that Britain should recognize Kenya as primarily an African country which would be developed towards an 'undiluted democracy' based on a universal adult franchise. Condemning the Lyttelton plan, they demanded either an immediate increase of fifteen additional members (thus giving Africans parity with all other racial groups combined) or a general discussion of the whole Lyttelton constitution. To bring into jeopardy the multi-racial character of government and precipitate a constitutional crisis, they refused to accept ministerial posts. At each and every parliamentary opportunity, they attacked restrictions on African political organizations and meetings, lack of adequate representation in municipal bodies, social discrimination and various aspects of government policy.

Although the Lennox-Boyd constitution of November 1957 did not result in the abandonment of the Lyttelton principle of multi-racial government, African members achieved a major success in gaining in it equality of representation with Europeans in the Legislative Council. While they were adamant in their rejection of the new constitution, they did not believe that a boycott of the Legislative Council at this time would promote their demands. In the last week of March 1958 elections were held in six new constituencies, and African voters again installed members pledged to oppose the new constitution and not to accept ministerial posts. Then the decision by eight moderate Africans to stand as Specially Elected Members was regarded as a betrayal of the African struggle. The African Elected Members boycotted the election in the Legislative Council for these seats and vigorously attacked the candidates, more particularly Musa Amalemba, regarded as the leader and because he subsequently accepted the post of Minister of Housing. Thereby, the Government could claim that the constitution was effectively 'multi-racial'.

By the middle of 1958, the problem of an organizational focus for African nationalism in Kenya was becoming increasingly apparent. To achieve some degree of co-ordinated action on the part of the various district associations and greater support for the African Elected Members, a number of leader conferences representing the associations had been held periodically since October 1957. In May 1958, a Convention of African Associations was formed to foster unity amongst these disparate district associations and develop a common policy with the African Elected Members. The Convention, however, was refused registration since Government policy continued to prohibit any kind of African colony-wide organization. Political unity was, therefore, still dependent on the maintenance of cohesion and agreement amongst the African Elected Members. Although they were able to display an appearance of concerted action until the formation of the Kenya National Party in July 1959, their need for political unity at this time was overlaid by factors of personality and leadership conflicts, divergent views and interests and the pressures of tribal parochialism.

Perhaps more fundamental to the eventual open split amongst the African Elected Members in July 1959, and the formation of two national African parties after the Lancaster House Conference, was the disharmony between the patterns of urban- and rural-orientated nationalisms. Each of the African Elected Members tended to be identified with one or other of these forces. Each sought political change, but the urban-orientated nationalism of the Luo and Kikuyu was the more militant and uncompromising. Amongst the Kikuyu and Luo particularly— and to some extent the Kamba and Baluhya—in Nairobi, this nationalism was most significantly expressed in the Nairobi People's Convention Party, although it had some voice in organizations in other urban centres and rural areas. Denied organizational opportunities on a colony-wide basis by Government regulations, and with disunity and conflict present in its leadership, this militant nationalism substituted the symbol of Kenyatta's charismatic leadership for a mass country-wide movement. The substitution was not only inadequate in binding people of diverse areas into a common movement, but it also had the effect of intensifying the differences between the tribes associated with the two kinds of nationalism. By the middle of 1959 the leaders of rural nationalism resented the influence and power of urban nationalism, fearing at the same time its eventual ability to dominate their areas and usurp their established positions.

The disagreements arising from these divergent manifestations of nationalism and concepts of leadership, reinforced by personal rivalry, became polarized in the formation of the Kenya National Party and the Kenya Independence Movement in July and August 1959. These two groups proved to be precursors of the two national African parties formed after Lancaster House. African leadership in the Kenya National Party, which was multi-racial until November, came from eight of the fourteen Elected Members, the prominent roles being played by Muliro, Ngala, Towett and Moi. The party's core support was derived from rural constituencies, and it found difficulty in gaining an adequate hearing in the towns. On the other hand, the Kenya Independence Movement, led by Odinga, Mboya and Kiano, commanded widespread urban popularity and could also depend upon the rural support of at least the Kikuyu and Luo. The dynamic potential of the Kenya Independence Movement continued, however, to be thwarted by Government's ban on country-wide African parties. Then the need for a united front at Lancaster House made it mandatory that the African Elected Members should submerge their differences to present an effective case which would give them a maximum advance towards independence.

THE FORMATION OF NATIONAL AFRICAN PARTIES

A new chapter in African politics opened after Lancaster

House with the lifting of the ban on colony-wide African parties. The unity achieved for the Conference began immediately to disintegrate and there ensued a shifting pattern of alliances which eventually crystallized into two national African parties.

A leaders' conference was called for 27th March at Kiambu. Two days previously a policy statement appeared, signed by ten of the African Elected Members, proposing the formation of the Uhuru[2] Party of Kenya. Significantly absent from the signatories was Mboya; at least some of the party's founders intended to exclude him from a position of national leadership. Behind this masked effort to isolate Mboya politically was a complex of allegations and rivalries. Many of the African Elected Members had become incensed over what they regarded as Mboya's arrogant behaviour in posing as the African leader to the press and television during the Lancaster House Conference. It was said that he was working for his own ends and that he had used funds from American labour organizations to further his own political career. Old opponents, like Odinga and Argwings-Kodhek, were particularly anxious to remove Mboya from leadership and they found support in men such as Arthur Ochwada, a former deputy general secretary of the Kenya Federation of Labour. Perhaps the most important challenge emanated from some Kikuyu leaders who were reasserting Kikuyu political power in this post-Emergency period. With the Kikuyu forming the majority of the African population in Nairobi, it was vital to Mboya's future political position to retain the support of this community.

These allegations and manoeuvres did not command universal support. Some of the African Elected Members had second thoughts about the proposed exclusion of Mboya. The leaders' conference was attended by a majority of the African Elected Members, including Mboya, as well as by delegates from thirty African political organizations. Rejecting the Uhuru Party, the conference decided to form a mass organization: the Kenya African National Union (KANU). This name had the advantage not only of incorporating the title of the old KAU, but also, in looking forward to a greater East Africa, of resembling the name of the dominant party in Tanganyika: the Tanganyika

[2]Swahili for 'freedom'

African National Union. Significantly, the colours and symbols of the new party were to be those of KAU.

Despite organized opposition at the conference to Mboya, he was appointed, together with Ngala, Kiano, Odinga, Argwings-Kodhek and two others, to the committee to draft KANU's constitution. James Gichuru, a former president of KAU, was appointed chairman and Dr. Mungai Njoroge secretary of the committee. By the time KANU held its elections for its national officers, at a second Kiambu meeting on 14th May, Mboya had mobilized his forces. His strength resided not only in his own ability but in the organizational network he and his supporters had been building across the country for several months. Branches of the People's Convention Party were established in strategic districts, forming nuclei for a colony-wide party. With this potential power, he secured election as KANU's general secretary. Gichuru was confirmed in his position as acting president, Mboya's opponent Odinga was elected vice-president, and Ochwada was made deputy secretary. Ngala, the Labour Minister in the Caretaker Government, was *in absentia* elected treasurer, and Daniel arap Moi, the senior Kalenjin member of Legislative Council and also absent, deputy treasurer.

However, the Kiambu conferences and the formation of KANU did not command the full support of all African leaders. There were immediate attacks alleging that the new party was dominated by Kikuyu and Luo leaders. Apart from Muliro, who had refused to co-operate in organizing a single mass African party, the Kalenjin and Masai leaders regarded with great suspicion both the objectives and leadership of KANU. Their distrust was aggravated when Towett, Kalenjin leader and the newly appointed Assistant Minister for Agriculture, was shouted down at the second conference. A network of alliances between organizations which felt their interests to be threatened and subordinated began to take shape in opposition to KANU.

A focal point in this was Muliro's Kenya African People's Party, a skeleton of the former Kenya National Party. Of greater significance was the formation of the Kalenjin Political Alliance in March and April. This evolved from the four district Independent Parties (Baringo, Kericho, Nandi and Elgeyo-Marakwet) which Moi had led the way in forming in 1958-9.

4

The Alliance claimed to represent about 900,000 Kalenjin-speaking people and aimed to provide determined and effective representation for their rural interests. Moreover, the Alliance was resolved to make clear its prior claim to control over land in western Kenya, though it had no wish to interfere with European agriculture in the Highlands. This was based on the assertion that much of the land in the western highlands of Kenya belonged to the Kalenjin before the Europeans arrived. Meeting in Eldoret on 21st May, the governing council of the Kalenjin Political Alliance elected not to join KANU, and invited other 'gentle and well-behaved' Africans to join with them and develop a nation-wide organization. Already links were established, for Muliro and Tipis (an Elected Member of the Legislative Council for a vast area including Masai) had joined the Kalenjin elected members, Moi and Towett, in addressing a mass meeting on the formation of the Kalenjin Political Alliance at Kapkatet in Kericho district on 21st April.

Paralleling the emergence of the Kalenjin Political Alliance was the formation of the Masai United Front, equally concerned about the future of the Masai land areas and fearful of domination by the Kikuyu and Luo. Meeting at Ngong at the edge of Masailand on 22nd May, the Masai elders gave their approval to the younger leaders who had formed the United Front and were opposing KANU.

By early June links were established between the Kenya African People's Party, the Kalenjin Political Alliance and the Masai United Front. At Mombasa another organization was formed, the Coast African People's Union, headed by Ngala who had declined, on his return from the United States, to become treasurer of KANU. Finally, on 25th June, a conference was held at Ngong of the leaders of these four newly formed parties, and of the Somali National Association. United in opposition to KANU and fearing the dangers of one-party government, they merged to form the Kenya African Democratic Union (KADU), Ngala and Muliro shortly becoming Leader and Deputy-Leader. Thus urban and rural nationalism had become aligned in two opposed parties to contest the forthcoming elections.

PARTY ORGANIZATION

From the moment of its establishment KANU was unable to achieve its aspirations and intentions of building an all-embracing, centralized and unitary type of mass party. Two closely related factors help to explain why KANU never advanced beyond a confederal type of political organization.

Undoubtedly the prime consideration was the problem of leadership. This was crucial, for, in the type of organization envisaged by KANU's founders, power must reside at the top and probably in a single leader who monopolizes legitimacy. KANU was never able to solve this, though it believed an answer had been found by recognizing Jomo Kenyatta as the leader *in absentia*. Kenyatta was the logical choice; no one else was identified so fundamentally with the struggle for freedom. To the majority of Kenya Africans, Kenyatta was not the leader into 'darkness and death', the phrase the Governor used in May, but rather the father and symbol of their nationalism, being referred to, with African respect for age, as '*Mzee*' ('the old man' or 'elder'). For over seven years he had been suffering for his people, first in prison and later in restriction at Lodwar, a remote government centre in the Northern Province. His release had been demanded by the militant Nairobi People's Convention Party for over two years; his very name was now invested with a mystique and was invariably linked with the cry for freedom at political meetings.

When KANU was first formed Kenyatta was elected and proclaimed president. But the Government refused to register the party so long as Kenyatta was even the titular head. In his place the Governing Council elected James Gichuru, who had stepped down from the presidency of KAU for Kenyatta in 1947. The link with the past seemed established, Gichuru being once again apparently cast in his historic role. But this attempt to solve KANU's leadership problem failed: the party required something more than an image and symbol of leadership. It needed a leader with authority able to sort out its structural and policy difficulties and give the party overall guidance and focus. The dilemma was that only Kenyatta possessed this authority, but he was far removed from the contemporary political arena. Moreover, none of KANU's leaders, such as Mboya, Odinga or Gichuru, could claim to share this authority; if they sought to assume a dominant role, they would be accused of usurping Kenyatta's position and might well destroy their own political careers. In such a situation any national leader could be, and was, easily challenged by other contestants for power. Even KADU's leaders could employ this political weapon against the leaders of KANU in their effort to weaken that party. The result of this *immobilisme* and vacuum in the leadership was that the national executive institutions of the party remained weak and practically every decision of any national leader was challenged.

A second consideration arising directly from this situation was that leaders were encouraged to maintain or develop their own source of power, even if it might jeopardize the electoral opportunities of the party. Factions were fostered in a competition for influence and control of the party; they then became an end in themselves, their success being more important to certain leaders than the success of the party as a whole. As KANU branches evolved from previous local district associations, many took on the characteristics of local autonomous parties, sending delegates rather than 'representatives' to the national Governing Council. Moreover, conflicts over the leadership of branches could not be adequately resolved by the national headquarters and this in many cases critically inhibited the effectiveness of the party in the area concerned. While the election had the effect of stimulating party organization, it also encouraged the growth of parochialism in the absence of a united national leadership. With a leadership divided into competing factions, the immense task of building a unitary mass party before the election was beyond the realm of possibility. What emerged was a loosely knit organization, vigorously resisting any suggestion that any one man could impose his leadership. In a real sense the party was haunted by the authority of Kenyatta: his judgment was continually appealed to, but his court could never sit. Power and authority would have to meet if the party was to be a dominant factor in the future.

KADU was seeking to establish a fundamentally different type of party. Authority was dispersed and shared between the leaders and a sense of corporate leadership clearly prevailed. In seeking unity the party placed a high value on compromise, to attract and accommodate divergent interests and peoples. It stood in opposition to the militant and urban-orientated nationalism of KANU, representing the interests of the less politically conscious areas. It believed that the first essential in political organization was unity and strength at the local level, that individuals would in time learn to graft their loyalties on to the national growth. Organization could not be imposed, but must develop from the people's own efforts and institutions. To give meaning and coherence to the party, major emphasis was placed on the ideology and achievement of democracy in a free Kenya.

Neither KANU nor KADU was able to organize itself adequately to conduct an effective, 'national', election campaign. At the centre, party secretariats were slow in developing an efficient administration; far too many tasks had to be performed by a limited number of the parties' senior officials. Neither party's executive officer took up his duties until the campaign was well under way. Though the party constitutions outlined the duties and responsibilities of the various organs from the local to the national level, it was usually individual leadership rather than party organization that became decisive.

At the constituency level both parties sought to create a network of branches, but this immense task was hardly begun before the critical phase of the campaign started. In only a few areas did party organization play a prominent part in the election. Far more important was the commitment of the main tribal groups to one or other of the parties. KANU made a ready appeal to the Kikuyu as the heir to KAU, but for the Kamba the 'commitment' was made quite specifically. Influential leaders from the two Kamba districts of Machakos and Kitui met on the Yatta plateau, and, after discussing which of the two parties it was better for the tribe to support, opted for KANU. This incident provided perhaps the most dramatic illustration of the pattern of Kenya's African politics: one-party tribes. KANU's advantage was that it had the effective support of the Kikuyu, Embu and Meru, the Kamba, Luo and Kisii. This represented 60% of the African population and control of fifteen of the open seats. Moreover, KANU appeared to have a major advantage in Nairobi and Nakuru where members of these 'KANU tribes' made up the majority of the population.

KADU derived its strength from the Kalenjin tribes of western Kenya, the Masai of the Southern Province, from some of the coastal tribes and from a sector of the Baluhya of Nyanza. The Kalenjin and Masai were the backbone of KADU, although the Leader and Deputy Leader of the party had a substantial following among their respective peoples, the Giriama and Baluhya. Only in Mombasa did KADU have sufficient ethnic support to be a major force in an urban constituency. Elsewhere the ethnic following of both parties was in doubt and other considerations played the major part in the election.

After the establishment of KANU and KADU, the vast majority of the earlier district parties and associations were either dissolved, or merged into the formation of branches of one of the two new national parties. This process was a gradual one, and indeed in KADU the original tribal alliances continued to exist as affiliated units. There was also a significant difference in local structures: KANU built its basic unit on the administrative district but KADU on the location or ward, the sub-divisions of the district. This difference had no appreciable effect on the outcome of the election, but did demonstrate KANU's concern for centralization of party activities and KADU's ideal of achieving a truly democratic system by having people at the smallest administrative unit initiate political action. In the case of both parties theory and practice seldom met; organizations evolved around dominant personalities rather than structures. This was inevitable, for political organization in many areas was new, rudimentary and fragile. Politics were rooted in personalities; although the election fostered party development, it also gave rise to struggles for local leadership. In such situations support for individual candidates was more important than party discipline and organization.

Neither of the parties succeeded in establishing effective branches or gaining substantial followings in the committed tribal areas of the other party. KANU tried to build a following in the Kericho district (an overwhelmingly Kipsigis area) and in Elgon Nyanza, and KADU similarly among the Kamba of Machakos, but these efforts had no real success. Only in two rural open constituencies did party prospects appear evenly balanced: in North Nyanza where both parties were poorly organized and were opposed by a more effective tribal party, the Baluhya Political Union; and in Taita where KANU probably had an advantage as a result of inheriting the leadership and structure of the local district party, the Taita Citizens Union. Aside from the three open urban constituencies, the party branches in other towns played no significant part in the election, except in some of the reserved seats.

With KANU and KADU dominating the national scene, the few local parties that continued a separate existence or evolved in the pre-election period were of negligible importance in the election with the exception of the Baluhya Political Union. The B.P.U. had its headquarters in Nairobi with branches in Mombasa and Nakuru as well as in North Nyanza. It sought to unite all Baluhya into a single organization which might in the future affiliate to one of the two national parties. In essence it became the political vehicle for the election of Musa Amalemba, the Minister of Housing. In the sparsely settled but vast territory of the Northern Province there were five separate parties, all based on regional interests. Only one, however, was of any significance—the Northern Province People's Progressive Party, which claimed to represent the interests of the Somali. It boycotted registration and sought secession of the province from Kenya and its unification with Somalia. The Shungwaya Freedom Party contested the Tana-Lamu constituency and sought (as did the Arab-motivated Coast People's Party) a form of autonomy for the coast. One party which claimed some 15,000 supporters and announced during the pre-election period that it would contest half the open seats, was the 'go slow' African Liberal Party. It supported the Coalition, saying that Kenya should not attain independence for at least fifteen years. In the surge for self-government and independence, it was a voice crying in the wilderness.

CHAPTER III

ESTABLISHING THE ELECTORAL MACHINERY

Introduction

The Lancaster House conference was concerned with a power-struggle between the racial groups, not with the details of the machinery for the elections which would follow. This appears to have been the reason why surprisingly large and important questions were left for a Working Party which was to be appointed by the Governor of Kenya to consider the election arrangements. Constituency boundaries and the numbers of voters in different constituencies may well settle the fate of an election. For this reason such questions have been referred elsewhere to an outside Commission, as before the Nigerian Federal Elections in 1959. Yet the Lancaster House conference was content to leave this and other matters of no less importance for the result of the election to a Working Party to consist of 'probably the Chief Secretary and the Attorney-General' in the Kenya Government. Thus Coutts and Griffith-Jones, the officials concerned, were appointed to recommend 'the rules which would govern the registration of voters, the qualification and nomination of candidates and the election of Members to the Legislative Council, including the delimitation of constituencies'.

In elections elsewhere it has been normal for the Committee or Commission establishing constituencies to examine these on the ground. The Working Party explained that they did not do this for two reasons: 'the necessity for submitting our report quickly and partly because of our other commitments'. This comment is indicative of much about the administration of the Kenya election. There was, indeed, a need for speed to bring about the elections as quickly as possible to terminate the deep uncertainty about the future produced by the Lancaster House conference. At the same time all this hard extra work of organizing an election had to be undertaken, as the Working Party sentence suggested, whilst normal administrative duties

were being carried out. There remained a certain feeling of
speed and improvisation throughout the election. This feeling
found expression in the final debate on the arrangements, on
the Legislative Council Bill in December, which took place
only three weeks before candidature day for the reserved seats.[1]

As the Working Party did not propose to visit the various
parts of the country a notice was inserted in the Official Gazette
saying that members of the public might submit memoranda.
Particular interests, from Nyanza to the Coast, and members
of all races did in fact do so. The Working Party announced
that they would not receive oral evidence though they would
have meetings with the various groups who had been represented at Lancaster House. Among the submissions the Working
Party received were some recommending a return to communal voting, this they naturally regarded as a 'major
variation of the Lancaster House Agreement' and outside their
terms of reference.

The Constituencies

At first glance the constituencies would appear, especially
when looked at after the registration of voters, to be full of
anomalies. Whilst this was to be expected for the 20 reserved
seats, it was no less so for the 33 open ones. Among them figures
of registered voters ranged from 1,622 to 88,738 in single-
member seats and from 14,000 to 142,458 in two-member
constituencies. These extremes were produced in part by
considerable differences in enthusiasm at registration. More
fundamentally, the proportionate principle of 'one man, one
vote' so much demanded by Africans was not extended by
them, either at Lancaster House or subsequently, into a demand
for a proportionate representation of numbers by constituencies.

The Lancaster House Report suggested 'it might be appropriate that representation should be based on districts' and this
was taken as the main term of reference by the Working Party
in setting up the constituencies. During the conference itself
some of the African leaders urged that there should be one seat
per district as the basis of representation. Already Coutts had

[1]Throughout this chapter references to debates in the Kenya Legislative Council
concern those on the Working Party's report, from 14 to 21 June, and on the
Legislative Council Bill, from 14 to 16 December.

found this desire, in the representations made to him in 1955 when he was touring to prepare his report for the first African elections of 1957. The period of British administration has given the districts a reality in African minds. Whilst some may be natural, like Nandi or Meru representing tribal areas or, like Machakos and Kitui, ancient divisions within a tribe, yet others, especially those of Nyanza, represent only artificial administrative units. Nevertheless, interests such as those of local government have been built around them so that it seemed as if the African request paralleled at this new stage that of the Europeans who, in 1917, first patterned their constituencies in Kenya on 'interests', not on population.

Whilst districts provided the foundation of the electoral pattern, the Working Party considered also factors of 'population, area and communications'. Their interconnection was well illustrated by Moi in discussing the Working Party report in the Legislative Council. He recalled the physical impossibility of covering the vast area for which he was initially elected in 1957, an area he put at 40,000 square miles. Although his area had been subsequently reduced he still had 16,000 square miles to represent in contrast to some members with only 100 to 600 square miles. In welcoming the Report he spoke particularly for the pastoral tribes. In terms of population they certainly did well from the district system of constituency: the Nandi and the Kipsigis received a seat apiece. The Working Party report put the Samburu district with Moi's own Baringo district, which contains a number of small tribes, the largest being his own Tugen people, but Samburu was subsequently transferred to Northern Province West. On the other hand the Elgeyo and the Marakwet, already administered in one district, had added to them West Suk in what proved to be one of the only two combinations of districts outside the Northern Province. The Elgeyo, Marakwet, Suk amalgamation was, indeed, awkward to administer electorally and raised the question why, if that combination could take place, the Masai were, despite their small population, granted two seats, one each for their separate administrative districts of Kajiado and Narok.[2]

[2]The populations in the 1948 census were: Elgeyo-Marakwet 64,497, West Suk 42,831, Kajiado 29,482, Narok 37,648.

The sparsely populated districts of the pastoral tribes contrast markedly with the concentrated populations of the agricultural tribes. Among them the Working Party developed from Lancaster House a solution which enabled them again to keep to the district basis: the institution of two-member constituencies. These, Coutts explained, were allotted to districts having a population of more than 350,000.[3] Another device was to anticipate the coming division of South Nyanza into two districts, and to recognize it by dividing it already into the two constituencies of Kisii and South Nyanza.

Nevertheless, there has been some marked under-representation, in proportion to numbers, of the Central and Nyanza Provinces. Perhaps the most extreme case has occurred among the Kikuyu. By population the largest tribe, they might have been entitled to six or seven seats; in fact they received only four. The discrepancy was so great that Wanyutu Waweru, the Kikuyu Assistant Minister for Education, took this up in the Legislative Council. He explained that he was in a very difficult position since Coutts, in introducing the Working Party report, had asked that members putting a claim for increased representation should suggest where the seats might come from, reminding them that there were only thirty-three seats for distribution. Waweru still thought that seven seats for Central Province against twelve for Nyanza was 'very unfair', and he went so far as to suggest, as an alternative, that one of the four seats allotted to the Kamba (Machakos and Kitui) might be taken—a suggestion which would not have been popular with a tribe which had put in a claim to the Working Party for seven. The difficulty was that, as F. J. Khamisi, member for Mombasa Area, acknowledged later in the debate, the African members had been unable to agree among themselves on the distribution of seats. They had been asked to put suggestions either as groups or as individuals. At Lancaster House they had most detailed ideas but their subsequent divisions prevented them putting anything effective to the Working Party. Thus the officials had very largely a blank sheet on which to work.

[3]Coutts was commenting on the fact that Kiambu, for which a second seat was claimed, had, he thought, only about 300,000 population. The difficulty was that the most recent census was that of 1948, when Kiambu was recorded as having 258,607. The officials could only work on estimates, but their figures have neither been published nor challenged by the politicians.

The Working Party did draw two constituency boundaries which raised questions of a wider political significance. Having decided to allot two seats to the sparsely inhabited Northern Province, they took as their division between the two constituencies not district boundaries but 'the Somali line', the line up to which Somali nomads moving from the east are allowed to graze their cattle. This caused questions in the Northern Province: whether this further recognition of an administrative line had a meaning for the future as a definition of the area which might be allowed to join Somalia. The second politically charged unit was the formation of the Protectorate constituency, one of the two Arab reserved seats. Its southern half took away the populous area of Kwale district, leaving a very thinly populated area to return one member for the rest of that district. The strict definition of the Protectorate constituency in terms of the 1921 Kenya Protectorate Order in Council drew public attention to the fact that the Sultan of Zanzibar's ten-mile Coastal Strip runs from Tanganyika north only to the Tana River, including otherwise only Lamu island; the Sultan's flag and an Arab administration has been, incorrectly it would seem, employed in the area of the old and annexed Sultanate of Witu in the Lamu district. The mainland parts of that district were joined with the sparsely populated Tana River district as one constituency, despite the different interests of the Arabized coastal people, the Bajuns, and the tribal Africans on the Tana River.

In respect of the reserved seats the Working Party was determined to end the old Kenya pattern of overlapping racial constituencies. They recommended instead clearly separated geographical areas for these seats. Another revolutionary change was to accept for the first time the fact that about half of Kenya's European population live in the two towns of Nairobi and Mombasa. They thus ended the heavy weightage in favour of the European rural areas and granted five seats to the towns, one to Mombasa and four to Nairobi if we include in the latter the residential area of Nairobi Suburban. Already some African hostility had been voiced because of the likelihood of the European rural seats being in one great contiguous block, the old White Highlands. To assuage this feeling the Africans were given in that area Nakuru Town as an open seat. Otherwise, the

rest of Nakuru district was, on the district pattern, to be one
constituency, but, when the Working Party report was debated
in the Legislative Council, a European suggestion was accepted
that Naivasha district should be added, and not put in Central
Rural. Thus was reconstituted the old Rift Valley constituency,
the traditional seat of the European leader. Elsewhere the
diminution of European, and particularly rural, seats compelled
amalgamation of former district constituencies: Trans-Nzoia
and Uasin Gishu to form West Kenya, Nanyuki and Laikipia
to be North Kenya, whilst the old Ukamba and Kiambu constituencies formed the basis of the new Central Rural. There,
and in Kericho, definition was by 'settled (i.e. European) areas'
of the districts concerned so that odd shapes appear on the
constituency map. Central Rural was made up of four separated
areas and Kericho of three. One other European constituency
was defined as the 'settled area' of the Nairobi Extra-Provincial
District, except for Nairobi City, and named 'Nairobi Suburban'.

Inside Nairobi city and Mombasa municipality the Working
Party left the detail of the geographical divisions to local agreement, doing no more than specify the number of seats by races.
In Nairobi the District Commissioner arranged meetings of the
sitting members of the Legislative Council. Through the residential racial segregation there the problem was comparatively
easily solved. The African area to the East became an open seat.
The European residential area in the West was to provide three
seats but there was one complication. Since it had been agreed
that there should be two-member constituencies among the
Africans the Government insisted that the same principle should
be extended to the other races. Thus Nairobi West was to have
two members, despite some European protests, and Nairobi
South-West the third.

Slightly more complicated were the Asian seats for, whilst no
provision had been made at Lancaster House for separate
Muslim and non-Muslim seats, it had come to be accepted—
and the Muslims had insisted that this should be so—that the
existing division should be maintained. Thus in Nairobi the
non-Muslims received two seats in separate areas: one which
included the Government buildings and commercial centre
becoming Nairobi Central and the other, a residential area,

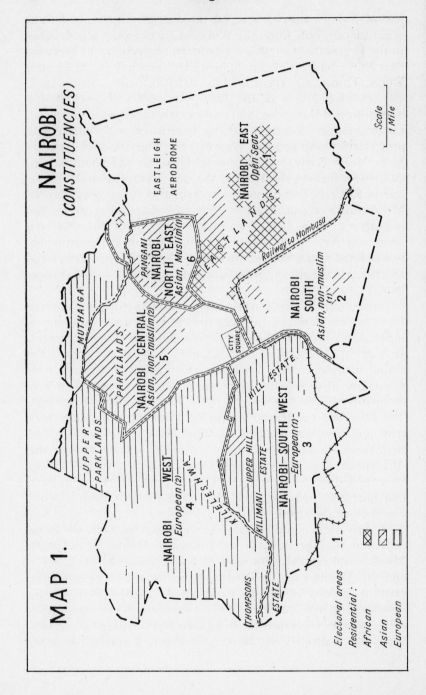

MAP 1.

NAIROBI
(CONSTITUENCIES)

Scale
1 Mile

EASTLEIGH
AERODROME

NAIROBI EAST
Open Seat
1

E A S T L A N D S

Railway to Mombasa

PANGANI
NAIROBI
NORTH EAST
Asian, Muslim(1)
6

NAIROBI
CENTRAL
Asian, non-muslim(2)
5

NAIROBI
SOUTH
Asian, non-muslim
(1)
2

MUTHAIGA

PARKLANDS.

CITY
SQUARE

HILL ESTATE

UPPER
PARKLANDS.

NAIROBI
WEST
European(2)
4

UPPER HILL
ESTATE

NAIROBI-SOUTH WEST
-European(1)-
3

K I L E L E S H W A

KILIMANI ESTATE

THOMPSONS
ESTATE

Electoral areas ..1..
Residential:
African
Asian
European

Nairobi South. The effect of the creation of this latter seat was to give a good chance to a member of the Sikh community which had never been granted separate communal representation in the Legislative Council. For the Muslim Asians a seat was created, known as Nairobi North-East. In this last seat there was some sense of artificiality of boundaries in dividing it from the non-Muslim constituency. (Map p. 52.)

This feeling of artificiality was greater at Mombasa where the various Asian groups live together in intermingled harmony. Thus the Mombasa sitting members of the Legislative Council, meeting under the chairmanship of the Provincial Commissioner, had a most complicated task to draw up separate constituencies. There was even a proposal that Mombasa might be designated a single multi-member constituency with reservation of seats for the various communities. In this constituency each voter would have, as elsewhere, but one vote. Since this was likely to produce simple communal voting, and as the members became less in favour of the idea the more each thought of representing the whole area, this was soon dropped. It was first easy to cut off the European areas along the sea-front and at Port Tudor, and also to designate the predominantly African areas on the mainland and on the west of the island as an open seat; far more complicated was the designation of the Arab and Asian seats. At one stage there was even a suggestion of dividing the area in half to create a western seat for the Asian Muslims and a two-member seat in the east for Arabs and Asian non-Muslims. In the end the complicated design shown on the plan (p. 54) emerged, the Arab seat being based on the old town with a westward extension. More complaints about the boundaries of constituencies arose in respect of Mombasa than anywhere else. When the results of the negotiations became known, S. G. Hassan, the sitting Muslim member, was attacked since the Ismaili community, his strong supporters in the past, had been split between two constituencies so that their voting strength, traditionally an important factor in Mombasa Muslim politics, was broken. Equally A. J. Pandya, the sitting non-Muslim, was attacked by the Mombasa Indian Association under the presidency of a young lawyer, I. T. Inamdar, for failure to consult the Association during the negotiations. The claim was made in the press that two predominantly non-

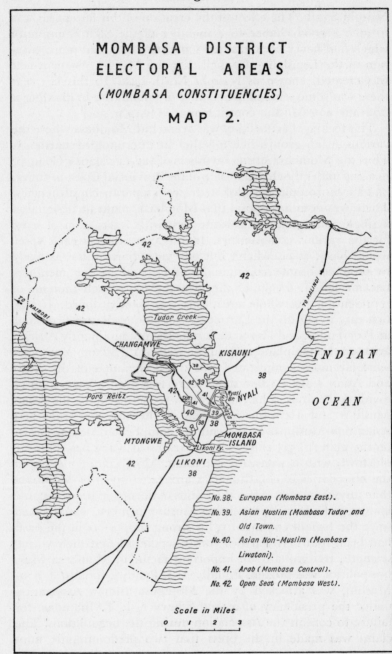

MOMBASA DISTRICT
ELECTORAL AREAS
(MOMBASA CONSTITUENCIES)
MAP 2.

No. 38. European (Mombasa East).

No. 39. Asian Muslim (Mombasa Tudor and
Old Town.

No. 40. Asian Non-Muslim (Mombasa
Liwatoni).

No. 41. Arab (Mombasa Central).

No. 42. Open Seat (Mombasa West).

Scale in Miles
0   1   2   3

Muslim Asian areas had been unjustifiably cut off from the new constituency and the suggestion was current that this was convenient to Pandya since these were inhabited by certain Hindu groups unlikely to support him. The protests of the Mombasa Indian Association were made in August after the constituencies had been gazetted, but by then it was considered too late to take any action.

Of the other three Asian seats two were given to Kisumu Town. There again the two groups, Muslim and non-Muslim, were very intermingled. It was decided to create a single two-member constituency with reservation of seats for each group, despite the possibility of communal voting. One final Asian non-Muslim seat remained for allotment. On this the Working Party consulted the Asian members of Legislative Council who wanted somehow to have represented the Asian interests of the smaller townships. Nakuru was closed to them by the decision to make it an open seat. The Asian members first suggested that two or three of the townships might be combined to provide their final seat, an idea the Working Party would not accept, insisting rather on the choice of one. In the end one Asian, Travadi, put up his home town of Nyeri, although in fact it is twelfth in township population. This idea found its way as a suggested constituency into the Working Party report where it caused much consternation and amusement. After further discussion with the Asian members, it was finally agreed that Nairobi might have this extra seat, so it was thrown into the already constructed Nairobi Central to make another two-member seat.

The lengthy Legislative Council debate on the Working Party report expressed mainly congratulations to the two Civil Servants on a very difficult task carried out in a remarkable way in drawing up these constituencies. Little was said by way of criticism, though Mboya expressed some doubt at their keeping so close to the administrative districts, raising particularly the cases of the heavily populated Kiambu and South Nyanza districts, the latter being his home area.

Later the Africans began to be more seriously perturbed by the idea of two-member constituencies where a voter would have but one vote. Although European and Asian politicians were to share in the difficulties of explanation that these

constituencies occasioned it seems surprising that the idea had
been accepted by the African leaders at Lancaster House in the
first place. There it was put forward as a means of protecting
minorities, a crude form of proportional representation. Whilst
a similar device had operated in Britain in the nineteenth
century, African nationalists today desire to follow the modern
British practice. The truth is that at Lancaster House they
were not interested in the minutiae of constituencies and elections. Indeed no questioning of this form of seat was raised in
the June debate on the Working Party report. Only later did
African and European politicians request the Government to
split these constituencies into single-member ones. Coutts,
replying in the Legislative Council in December, was able to
say that, as these representations were received only after registration, it was impossible to take action since the Government
would be liable, in any division of constituencies, to be accused
of rigging the partition in favour of one party or candidate.
Specifically in the case of the European reserved seat of Nairobi
West, division was impossible since registration of voters had
been carried out on a single list for the constituency as a whole,
as in all urban seats; as Nairobi addresses are by postal box
number, not by geographical location, the electoral roll gave
no basis for a division.

Absentee Voting

In a recent survey, *Elections in Developing Countries*, it has
been commented: 'Kenya has gone further than any other
British Commonwealth territory—and perhaps too far—to be
kind and helpful to African voters.'[4] The writer was referring to
the elaborate arrangements made in the African elections of
1957 for absentee voters to record their vote when outside their
own constituency. Also, by long tradition in Kenya's European
and Asian elections, arrangements had always been made in the
past for postal balloting for their absentee voters. This latter
practice had led to many accusations of abuses, these being
well summed up by Coutts and Griffith-Jones in their report:
'There has been in the past so much difficulty about the
arranging of postal ballots, and in many cases so much exception
has been taken to them with the result that a degree of

[4] T. E. Smith: *Elections in Developing Countries* (1960), p. 236.

instability has been introduced into the conduct of elections, that we consider that the time has now come when postal ballots should be abolished altogether.' Likewise, the Government accepted the above quoted comment in respect of African absentee voting and did not intend to repeat the complicated system of boxes for each constituency, stationed at every polling station across the country, as had been done in 1957. However, the Government found itself unable to stand firm under pressures for a reconsideration of these decisions.

In this respect perhaps the most important was the request from Musa Amalemba, the African Minister for Housing, for a retention of some form of absentee African voting. In the months that followed Lancaster House he was engaged in building up the political awareness of his own Baluhya people and this found expression in July in the formation of the Baluhya Political Union. The Baluhya form an important element in the migratory labour pattern of Kenya; many are employed as domestic servants and in other ways in Nairobi. Amalemba was concerned that their vote might be 'lost', submerged among other voters. In his position in the Council of Ministers he was able to bring about a reconsideration of the original refusal to make no provision for absentee African voting.

The decision was taken that in the three towns of Nairobi, Mombasa and Nakuru there would be absentee voting for certain constituencies, those supplying the major elements of the labour force. Since, unlike 1957, this was not to permit of all absentees voting for their home constituencies, there were bound to be anomalies. Some of these were curious and illustrated something of Kenya's migratory labour patterns. The home-provinces mainly concerned were Nyanza for the Luo and the Baluhya, and Central for the Kikuyu, Embu and Meru. It was agreed that all the constituencies from these two provinces might have some extraneous voting. On the other hand, it was felt that the Kikuyu district of Kiambu was so close to Nairobi and Nakuru as not to need polling stations in those two towns whilst, likewise, no provision need be made at Nairobi for voters from Fort Hall. Subsequently representations were made on behalf of the Kamba of Machakos and Kitui in the Southern Province, though it was then decided that they were found in significant numbers only in Nairobi and Mombasa and would not need to poll at Nakuru. Polling was arranged there for members of the Kipsigis tribe, pastoralists employed as cattlemen on the European farms of the Rift Valley.

The announcement of these arrangements came at the very beginning of registration in August. How would they affect registration during the following weeks ? Two political leaders in particular saw the importance of this absentee voting. In Nairobi Argwings-Kodhek, defeated there by his fellow Luo Mboya in 1957, took the opportunity of organizing a personal vote in his home area of Central Nyanza. He formed a committee to persuade potential voters from this district to go before the Registration Officers to have their forms attested for transmission home. Requests were particularly noted when registration was carried out in the railway workshops, many of the workers there being Luo. Argwings-Kodhek's committee collected the attested forms and posted them in batches to Kisumu for entry on the register. Wild estimates circulated of the number of votes thus taken back but a final post-registration report of the District Commissioner in Central Nyanza showed that the total number for the district from the whole Colony was only 1,274. Whilst this was done for one candidate, Amalemba carried out a similar exercise for voters from North Nyanza, but with a less specific objective. His Baluhya Political Union simply urged the Baluhya to register in North Nyanza to build up an impressive registration there and not lose the tribe's votes in the towns where they worked. The Baluhya Political Union again collected attested application forms to forward in bulk to the registration centre at Kakamega, the district headquarters. There no exact figures could be obtained, but Amalemba estimated personally that the number was something between two and three thousand.

After registration the electoral authorities, desiring to make arrangements for the extraneous voting at the three centres in February, asked the home districts to provide figures of postal applications. Unfortunately, many districts had not kept records. Moreover, it was possible under the law for people to register personally in their home districts, but at election time take the opportunity of voting in one of the three towns if they happened to be away then in employment. This might well have been important in respect of the Kikuyu, Embu and

Meru voters with their increasing outflow to employment during 1960 after the ending of the Emergency restrictions on their movement. Thus the authorities were largely in the dark in making arrangements for the actual polling; they could only estimate the number of polling-booths and ballot papers required for each district at each of the three centres. As it happened, one district, Embu, only provided three hundred ballot papers for its extraneous voters in Nairobi; by the end of the morning's polling these had been exhausted and a patient queue of some fifty voters developed whilst further papers were rushed down by car from Embu town, ninety miles away.

In Nairobi voters approached the extraneous polling station through a crowd of supporters of candidates from, it seemed, all over the Colony. Their good humoured competitive cries and display of slogans provided the background to the polling. At the same time this voting and the crowd at the polling station attracted voters registered in other constituencies. Many from Fort Hall were turned away. They might have to travel seventy or more miles to vote but there were no facilities for them, yet on the other hand there were boxes for people from Kisii and South Nyanza, constituencies which in reality provided only fourteen and twenty-eight voters respectively in Nairobi. The importance of the vote clearly concerned only North and Central Nyanza. Of the 5,330 extraneous voters in Nairobi, 2,223 were from Central Nyanza, indicating a marked increase of labour coming in from that area, whilst 2,007 were from North Nyanza. In Nakuru's 573, those from North Nyanza predominated, there being 230 from that district, against 152 from Fort Hall and 99 from Central Nyanza. In Mombasa, where less than 100 voters had had their forms attested and sent away, there were 382 extraneous voters.

The question arises whether the complicated system can be justified. It had one serious drawback in providing the possibility of multiple voting with little chance of detection. An unscrupulous voter could have voted on one day in Nairobi, travelled to Nakuru where the extraneous voting was two days later, and then finally gone to his home district. More important, it was an added factor in causing Africans to maintain their identity with their home districts rather than with their place of work, a question of social importance and now, through the operation of this system, with political implications also. Some wondered whether the effects of the removal of Luo voters would have an adverse affect on Mboya's strength in Nairobi. In the outcome this did not prove to be of any consequence there but, on the other hand, the system did have a certain effect in ensuring that in the European residential areas of Nairobi the African numbers would not swamp the European voters in the reserved seats.

As this system had infringed among Africans the original principle of no absentee voting, the decision that there should be no postal voting was likewise eroded. Inside the Government pressures were put to allow the security forces to continue this old privilege. Early in August it was announced that this would be allowed to members of the police and of the King's African Rifles. This soon raised demands from other Government employees: first from prison officials, often in remote places but nearly all away from their home districts, and also from administrative officers likely to be employed on election duties at polling stations distant from those where they had the vote. Outside the Government certain groups of people, whose employment would be likely to keep them from the polling stations, called for a return to the old Kenya system of postal votes for all who applied: White Hunters who might be conducting game shooting parties round the remote Northern Province or out of the Colony in Tanganyika, railway workers and air crews. The case of these last was taken up particularly by the independently minded European member of the Legislative Council for Nairobi, Air-Commodore Howard-Williams, who, in the debate on the Legislative Council Bill in December, called them 'some of the best people in this Colony'. Earlier, in June in Legislative Council, Usher from Mombasa had urged consideration for the sick and bedridden. Coutts referred back to this in replying in committee to a final plea for the reinstitution of the postal vote from Sir Charles Markham, who made an impassioned appeal on behalf of White Hunters. The Chief Secretary said that, with the exception of the King's African Rifles and the police, the Government remained as 'adamant on this point' as the members of the Working Party had been. He made the obvious point: 'if you start making exceptions it is difficult to know where to draw the line'. Nevertheless,

Markham, Howard-Williams and a third European, Bompas, continued to press the matter. Markham asked, with the support of an African member, Nyagah, why there should be special provision for absentee voting for Africans but not for others.

The matter did not end with this debate. With Howard-Williams's support, the Air Lines Pilots Association continued to press their particular case. They had not been successful in obtaining any action by the time of the European primaries but, in a Legal Notice published in the Official Gazette on 7th February, twelve days before the final election, a special concession was granted to air crews. By all canons, administrative and political, this was a most extraordinary decision, made under the Governor's Rule-making powers. Hard cases, when yielded to, make very bad law. Other people, particularly railway workers and Government officials engaged in administrative duties on polling day, had a justifiable complaint that their representations had not borne fruit. More seriously, the decision was taken in the last stage of an election campaign; it was a yielding to the representations of one particular candidate. Were the voters concerned predominantly in his constituency? Would he not get their postal votes? The outcome of this curious little Kenya farce was that of the 148 air crew concerned only two voted postally.

Registration
'Ay! register, register, register!' said the Duke, 'those were immortal words.'

'I can tell your Grace three far better ones,' said Tadpole, with a self-complacent air, 'Object, object, object!' (Disraeli: *Coningsby*).

In modern Britain, though not in the United States, all potential voters are registered automatically. In British colonial Africa registration is an exercise of fundamental importance, in much the same way that it was to Disraeli's election agents in England 130 years ago. In some West African elections, as in Kenya in 1957, Governments have considered it part of their function to encourage registration through the persuasive devices of the administration and of the Government Information Services. In Kenya in 1960 the Information Service was prevented by a lack of funds, in the worsening economic position of the Kenya Government, from mounting any such large exercise. It did, however, issue booklets in six local languages (Swahili, Kikuyu, Luo, Luhya, Kalenjin, and Kamba) explaining what registration was about, and put out information through the Kenya Broadcasting Service and the vernacular newspapers it publishes at the various provincial centres.

As for the administration, it received instructions that registration was to take precedence over all other work, except the vital minimum. Beyond this, administrative officers received no general direction from the centre on the part they were to play in encouraging registration. There was a feeling that, with the development of African politics, the persuading of Africans to register was now a function of the political parties—as, indeed, it should have been, had they been sufficiently organized. It might, therefore, seem that the final registration figures would indicate where the political parties were well organized and where they were weak at this registration period which lasted from 8th August to 7th October. However, examination of the various constituencies soon indicated that the registration pattern was more complex. Both politicians and administrators played significant parts, varying in proportion in various areas.

Nobody could say whether or not a good registration had been achieved for two reasons: it was not possible accurately to assess the potential number of voters, the absence of any census since 1948 and the impossibility of calculating what percentage of the population over twenty-one possessed one of the many qualifications for the franchise.[5] The vote was given to all over forty years of age, and to those above twenty-one with one of certain qualifications: literacy, an income of £75 per annum, property worth £200, membership of a Local Authority Council (including Locational Councils) or employment as a sub-chief or tribal policeman, the property or income qualifications of a man making his wife or wives eligible also.

The first difficulty in any African election is to assess age. Here a further complexity arose since knowledge was required at two ages; twenty-one and forty. Since Africans do not

[5] *The East African Standard* stated (19 February, 1960) that the qualified franchise was expected to produce an electorate of ¾ million, compared with 3¼ million by universal adult franchise.

normally have documentary evidence of age the Working Party suggested that District Commissioners should specify the age-grades which would qualify. Thus for the labour-migratory Kikuyu an age-grade list was prepared by a District Officer at Nyeri and circulated across the Colony, similar lists for other tribes with age-grades being prepared and used locally. The Europeans' wars provided some help. One rough guide suggested to some Registration Officers was that they might assess age twenty-one by asking if the applicant was born before the *Vita ya Italiani* (the Italian war, i.e. the Second World War) and age forty by whether he had been born during or just after the *Vita ya Germani*, as the first World War is locally known. The Working Party considered that Registration Officers should 'muster a Committee of local Elders' to advise on the age of applicants—an idea which was opposed in the Legislative Council as likely to lead to intimidation.

On property and income values Registration Officers received guidance from locally prepared lists. Thus in Meru, land was assessed according to different zones at a value of between £5 and £20 per acre, whilst animal values ranged there from an adult grade cow at £40 to sheep and goats at £1 per head; the value of a typical African hut was put at £10, and an 'improved house' with a corrugated iron roof at £150. In the same district, which produces large quantities of cash-crops, the annual income from coffee-trees was assessed at 10/- per tree, from potatoes, beans and maize at, respectively, £30, £16 and £10 per acre. In the poorer and more arid district of Kitui, sheep and goats were given the same value as in Meru and cattle were averaged at £7 10s. per head; land was assessed at no more than 10/- per acre in most areas, with £2 in the better places, whilst a mud and wattle shop or house was priced at £20 and a stone one at £100 or above. The difficulty with all such lists was, naturally, that people resented their in-quisitorial character.

Similar resentment was felt among tribes where there is no age-grade system when Registration Officers attempted to determine age by asking for tax-receipts. Africans tend to hoard these documents over the years so that a person with three or more could be assessed to be over twenty-one: he had been paying tax for at least three years, for tax in Kenya is collected

from all above the apparent age of eighteen. Registration
Officers were soon attacked for asking for tax-receipts; it seemed
they were exceeding their function to become tax-inquisitors.
James Nyamweya, a lawyer and later a KANU candidate, and
others in Nyanza Province made representations, as a result
of which instructions were issued that the practice should cease.
Elsewhere the harm may have been undone but it is possible
that among the Luo of South Nyanza this was the fundamental
reason for the low registration there: potential voters were
scared initially from registering.

Nyamweya's other point of protest concerned the marital
status of women appearing for registration: it would be, he
said, ridiculous to turn the registration offices into 'petty matri-
monial tribunals to establish the legality of any *de facto* or *de jure*
existing union between a man and any wife or wives'. Certainly the status of marriages under African customary law is
a subject which has caused much ink to flow from the pens of
lawyers, anthropologists, administrators and religious leaders
alike.

All desiring registration had to make a personal appearance before a Registration Officer. At first these officers
attempted to assess possible voters for the various qualifications,
employing the help of teams of local people, much in the way
that the Working Party suggested. As registration went on this
proved increasingly impracticable. First, Registration Officers
were compelled to travel and could neither take teams nor
assemble them in remote areas. Moreover, many administrators
believed that the qualifications were so wide that it was virtually adult suffrage. Thus, with the administrative discretion
they necessarily exercised in examining potential voters, and
with the pressure under which they worked as the numbers of
people coming forward to register increased, there were some
areas where the strict application of the qualifications broke
down; it just was not possible to examine people closely on
their voting qualifications. In these districts Kenya virtually
passed in this election to adult suffrage.

Although no official directive was issued that the administration was to encourage a high registration, in two particular
provinces, Nyanza and Central, a competitive spirit emerged
among District Officers and others. Lists soon circulated showing

week by week, the estimated percentage of potential voters which had been achieved. Central Province produced the most consistently high proportion of registration. Although these can only be guesses related to population estimates it would seem that figures of the following order were produced: Fort Hall 94%, Embu 88%, Nyeri 86%, Meru 79% and Kiambu 70%. In view of the background of the Emergency one of the most striking features was the good relationship in large parts of Central Province between the administration and the politicians. This proved to be the basic reason for the high registration. It was achieved by a genuine co-operation, acknowledged in the Legislative Council in December for one district, Embu, by the sitting member, Nyagah, who wished to thank the Government for the methods they had used making for a 'very easy and intensified registration'.

Meru district immediately to the north registered the second highest number of voters in the country. It was widely known that in 1957 the high registration there had been largely achieved by the activity of the administration. On this occasion the District Commissioner summoned the co-operation of the school-teachers. At first there was some difficulty because they felt they were being conscripted. A local missionary Supervisor of Schools issued a letter to his teachers, telling them that it was essential that registration should take place, that without the teachers registration would be impossible among the illiterates; finally, he adjured his teachers: 'the work which you are asked to do is to enable your own people to vote.' The result of the teachers' activity was such that by the end of August over 100,000 of the Meru had registered during the school holidays. A fortnight later the District Commissioner sent a letter of thanks to the school-managers, saying that without the teachers' help registration would have been impossible for they had 'filled up most of the forms'. These application forms for registration were printed in two languages, English and Swahili. Meru was by no means the only district where the vast majority of applicants for registration, being totally illiterate, could do no more for themselves than make a thumb-print.

One striking feature in the Kikuyu country was the high proportion of women among the registered voters. This was said to be as high as 80% in one part of Kiambu district. Such a figure is to be explained in part by the high Kikuyu labour migration, particularly from the southern area to Nairobi, and in part also by the high male death roll of the Emergency. Moreover, the Emergency has made the women a highly conscious political group, among both the Kikuyu and their associated tribes, particularly the Embu. The high registration of women in the Central Province and in some districts elsewhere provided a marked contrast to the African election of 1957 in Kenya when, through the then existing qualitative franchise, less than 1% of the registered electorate were women.

The density of the Kikuyu population, and their concentration in villages as the result of an Emergency measure, made registration in that tribe comparatively easy. In other areas Registration Officers soon saw the need to tour—to go out into the highways and byways, to be present at markets and in other places where people congregated. Wherever there were active political agents, demands were soon voiced that this should take place. In the sparsely populated Kitui district, equal in size to the whole of Central Province, KANU agents called for greater activity from administrative officers, just as they did in Central Nyanza, the home of Odinga, one of the KANU leaders.

It was among the Luo that there was the greatest suspicion during the registration period. More complaints than anywhere else were made in the politically charged atmosphere of Central Nyanza. There KANU was early and quickly organized around the flamboyant personality of Odinga. He himself was outside Kenya during most of registration, travelling widely and even visiting Peking, his speeches there making him even less popular in Government circles. When he returned late in September, he inserted a curiously misleading advertisement in *Ramogi*, the Luo weekly newspaper: 'Register your vote . . . Each and everyone—children, women and old men should appear in the registration office and register their votes. The registration date is Friday, 30th September, 1960 [sic. the original closing date]. We shall tell you the name of the other fellow to be voted for later.' In Odinga's absence KANU agents were nevertheless active early in the registration period, badgering the administration into visiting the more remote areas to conduct registration and asking that, as people had been slow to realize the meaning of registration, the officers should revisit certain other areas. After registration had been in progress for a month the District Commissioner met some twenty KANU representatives from the whole district and discussed with them their complaints. Although they were then appreciative of the arrangements in one particular division, a guerilla warfare of complaints continued until finally the KANU branch organizing secretary went so far as to cable the Secretary of State for the Colonies, saying that registration arrangements were unsatisfactory and completely unsuitable, and maintaining that the administration had some 'ulterior motive' for hampering registration. This was organized nationalism on the attack, by nature suspicious of all action of the colonial rulers.

In South Nyanza, in marked contrast to Central, the organization of KANU, the predominant party, was weak. This arose partly because there was no separate branch for the constituency. KANU's constitution only allowed of one branch per district. As the separation of districts into Kisii and South Nyanza was not to take place until 1st July, 1961, KANU's branch headquarters remained at Kisii town for the whole area. During registration KANU sought to build up numbers by touting for membership in South Nyanza in the vicinity of registration officials. The latter believed that such KANU action scared many away from registering, since people had no wish to be dunned at the time into paying 5/- for a party membership fee.

North Nyanza was the district with the highest registration: 142,458. According to a statement published by the Information Department this represented 95% of the estimated potential. Various factors contributed to this high figure, of which undoubtedly the most important was the growing political interest of the Baluhya people. In the two districts of North and Elgon Nyanza they were determined to show their strength. There was evidence, too, of Government chiefs being active in encouraging registration. Government officers were supposed to do no more, in addressing the people in *barazas*, than give information about registration and the facilities for it. However, the old fine line, impossible of definition, between information and advice on the one side and active encouragement on the other which had applied to Government officials forty years before in respect of labour recruitment was now effective in regard to the registration of voters.[6]

Among the Kalenjin there was an outstandingly high registration in Kericho district. The Kipsigis had sprung into political awareness in the months following Lancaster House. The large meetings that their leader, Towett, then held and the organization he developed in first the Kalenjin Political Alliance and then in KADU, and the part that he played in the latter, provided the background for the tribe's high registration. In contrast, the neighbouring Kalenjin tribe to the north, the Nandi, displayed such a marked lack of interest in registration that the administration closed it down for a month, from mid-August to mid-September, preferring in that period to do more publicity through *barazas*. Efforts were made to persuade the Nandi to register so as to justify the allocation of a constituency to them. By the re-opening of registration it had become apparent that there would probably be a contested election so that registration then became meaningful, something which had previously been doubted.

It was, of course, among the scattered pastoralist tribes that registration was naturally expected to be low. A surprisingly high figure was achieved among the Turkana. As a result they dominated the constituency of Northern Province West, since some 10,600 Turkana registered against 2,400 Samburu and 1,500 others. In that constituency those Boran who were of the Muslim faith boycotted registration, as did the vast majority of Somalis in Northern Province East, who adopted this tactic to demonstrate their desire not to share in Kenya's *Uhuru*.

In the other constituency whose boundaries had like political repercussions, the Arab reserved seat of the Protectorate, it was the Africans who considered boycotting registration. Among them there was much resentment that they were to be represented by an Arab. In the southern part of the constituency the

[6]A survey designed to study voting behaviour (see pp. 160-3) was carried out by the authors in the two constituencies of Central and North Nyanza. Voters were asked how they came to register. 34% in North Nyanza and 14% in Central claimed they had acted without any persuasion. In both constituencies a high proportion said they had been persuaded to register by Government officials, from District Officers to chiefs and headmen: Central 69%, North 60%. The figure for persuasion by a political leader was only 4% in Central and 2% in North Nyanza.

Digo tribe had apparently come to believe that the constituency
would be drawn so as to exclude their African land unit. When
they found that they had to register in an Arab reserved seat
their political organization, the Kwale African Democratic
Union, made a series of representations to the authorities, saying that Africans did not accept the Agreement of 1895 with
the Sultan of Zanzibar, and in these representations they later
received the support of KANU officials in Mombasa. Similar
anger was felt by Giriama in the coastal strip to the north of
Mombasa. At first both groups boycotted registration but then
their political leaders, KANU to the south of Mombasa and
KADU to the north, saw that there was a possibility of a more
effective and dramatic demonstration by registering their numbers and then boycotting the election if they received no satisfaction from the Arab candidates. Thus the last weeks of registration brought in the bulk of the African voters in the constituency.

Yet this was not untypical of African reaction to the reserved
seats. They did not like the idea of having to be represented by
a person of another race. At first African registration was slower
in the reserved seats than in the open ones, until the political
leaders, seeing the importance of registration there, persuaded
Africans to come in. In this they were most successful in the
rural constituencies, the outstanding example being the Rift
Valley. There in the end the figure of 23,242 non-European
voters was achieved, which could clearly overwhelm the
European 2,286. In Nanyuki, in the North Kenya constituency,
the newly formed KANU branch urged Africans to register
but this went on to cries of 'disenfranchisement'. There it was
noted that the more politically conscious Kikuyu were readier
to register in the European seat than were the Kalenjin who
chose their home constituencies, for the law allowed the option
of registration in the constituency of employment, residence,
or property ownership. One explanation for the low registration in Kiambu was that one Kikuyu leader was there persuading people to take the option of registering in places, like
Thika, where they worked, to influence the outcome of the
Central Rural election. A striking case of an African rush to
register only at the last minute, to influence a reserved seat,
occurred in Kisumu Town: 2,177 voters registered in the last

week from a total of 5,672. In contrast, in the reserved seats in
Nairobi and Mombasa the African political parties failed most
conspicuously to persuade people to register in sufficient numbers to obtain the influence they might have exerted on the
results. Apart from Kisumu, where the highly organized KANU
branch was active in registration, the only town reserved seat
where the community for which it was reserved was not in the
majority was the Asian Muslim one of Mombasa Tudor and
Old Town.

Among Europeans there was a widespread apathy to
registration during August. Whilst it was true that this was
the holiday month, Kenya has long been known as 'the land of
bado kidogo' (a little later); it has an atmosphere of 'do it
tomorrow' which affects the Europeans no less than the other
races. This apparent apathy was mingled, however, with a
considerable feeling of dislike for the new constitution, the fear
that it meant European 'disenfranchisement'. Certainly few
Europeans registered in the open seats; a check in the Central
Province open constituencies showed that far less than one half
of the potential European voters had registered there. The only
open seat where Europeans registered in any numbers was
Nakuru Town, where, already at registration, there was talk
of the possibility of a European candidate. That candidate later
estimated that 740 from a possible 850 Europeans had registered, largely through his persuasion. In the end a high
European registration was achieved in many of their reserved
seats, the District Commissioner of Nakuru putting it at 100%
for his district!

One of the difficulties of registration was, it was sometimes
reported in the African seats, that people were unwilling to
register because they did not know for whom they would be
asked to vote—something seen in the above-mentioned advertisement of Odinga in *Ramogi*. All this indicated the weakness
of party and the interest in personality, in which all the races of
Kenya have shared. Certainly it was widely believed in Mombasa that the reason for the comparatively high initial registration for its Asian Muslim constituency, where 2,973 Muslims
registered in the three weeks of August from the final total of
4,266, was that one of the candidates was already known.
Equally it was expected that the sitting member, A. J. Pandya,

would contest the adjacent non-Muslim constituency and there by the end of August 1,509 non-Muslims had registered, just under half of the final figure. Behind both these candidates—as throughout the Asian constituencies—fundamental in registration, as later in voting, was the activity of the organizations of the various Asian groups: religious, caste or regional.

As September went on there was a wide feeling that voters had not been registering in sufficient numbers, particularly among the Europeans. When, therefore, demands came from Africans also that the registration period should be extended this was quickly agreed, on the unanimous representations of all the political parties. It was then announced that registration would finally close on 7th October, a week later than intended. Also, to help registration in the towns and in the two constituencies of Central Rural and West Kenya, representations for Sunday registration, which had come particularly from the Asians of Nakuru, were yielded to: offices would be open in those constituencies on the two final Sundays of the registration period. After two months of great activity by Government officials, political agents and many others, a registration figure of 1,325,878 was published for the whole country,[7] for the first election in Kenya in which all races were treated equally from the point of view of qualifications.

There was some particular grumbling from the oldest established voting section, the Europeans. Like everybody else, they had had to appear in person before a Registration Officer, and obtain in exchange for their completed application form a card to be retained for presentation at the polling booth at the election. European complaints concerned the residential qualifications required: residence in Kenya for one year preceding registration and a connection through residence, occupation or property with the constituency concerned of not less than three months. This last bore hardly on Government officials and businessmen who had recently been transferred. Many complaints were sent in and the matter was taken up in the debate in December on the Legislative Council Bill, where, on Bompas's representations it was agreed to reduce the latter period in the future to two months. It might seem that this qualification could be removed altogether. Its point was to establish identity

[7] *East African Standard*, 21 October 1960.

with the constituency: yet surely this would be achieved automatically, as in Britain where no such provision is made, by the period between registration and the election.

The Legislative Council (Constituency Members) Regulations 1960, issued in August, laid down clear provisions for the publication of the registers and a period for claims and objections. These have been few in the past in Kenya and were even fewer on this occasion. The organization of Kenya's political parties had not yet reached the second stage of Disraeli's election agents: an understanding, not unknown among some parties in Nigeria, of the importance of objecting to the names of opponents on the register. The difficulty was that the registers were only exposed to view at the central point of the constituency, the Returning Officer's headquarters. In the large rural constituencies of Kenya this made consultation of the registers a formidable undertaking. As Mrs. Shaw put it in Legislative Council in December, it was not likely that in her constituency voters would go forty miles to Kericho to ensure that their names were on the register—and her constituency was one of the smaller rural ones. Only after the period for claims and objections was over and the voters' rolls had been certified did one Asian candidate's agent protest, in December in the press, that he had had no opportunity of examining the rolls. As he was in Nairobi he was not under the same difficulty as those in the rural areas. It would seem a feeble complaint that he had missed the announcements in the Official Gazette concerning the availability of registers for consultation—an alert agent should have noted this from the Regulations. An apt comment on this matter, applicable to all races, was made in the Legislative Council by Nyagah in December. After confessing that he had discovered 'only the other day' that the voters' roll in his constituency had been closed he added, as he appealed for more time: 'we are learning some of these things.'

The Method of Voting

Perhaps the most surprising feature of the election was the decision that voting should be by the voter placing a cross against the name of the candidate in the British fashion. This was the first common roll election in Kenya and the first in which elections for members of all races would occur simultaneously.

Clearly, it was decided, there could be no racial differentiation in the method of balloting. Indeed there was talk in Government circles that 'if they (the Africans) wanted an election they must do it properly'. Thus the decision was taken, at an early stage, that the system employed in the African elections of 1957 and 1958 would not be used: namely, boxes for each candidate marked with his symbol, the voter placing a ballot paper into the box of his choice. This system, adopted from India for use in British African territories, was certainly open to many abuses. With secret balloting behind a screen a voter could refrain from putting his ballot paper in a box and then sell it outside the polling-station for a candidate's agent to insert later in the day in the box of his choice. The question was whether, with the large number of illiterates in Kenya, an overwhelming majority in many constituencies, the 'X' system could work at all.

The original intention was even more remarkable: that no specific help should be given to illiterates, that the ballot papers should have, in the full British manner, nothing but the names of the candidates with spaces against them in which the voter would mark his cross. This was apparently agreed to by the Council of Ministers, a decision in which some, if not all, of the African Ministers appear to have concurred. Then some people began to have second thoughts. It was realized that there was a danger that presiding officers might be overwhelmed in many polling stations by a flood of illiterate voters who would have to be helped in marking their papers. Administrators in the field were asked their opinion and many recoiled in horror. Some advocated the employment again of the candidates' box system as in 1957/8. But there was a possible half-way house and this was finally adopted: as in previous Asian elections in Kenya a symbol would appear on the ballot paper against the candidates' names. Asian illiterates had thus been helped to perform their civic duty; surely, it might be possible for African illiterates similarly to mark their own ballot papers with an 'X'—after all the 'X' sign originated in Britain from the traditional way for an illiterate to 'make his mark'!

The next problem concerned the symbols to be used. Past experience had led to the belief that certain symbols conveyed an advantage. In 1957 it was said that the cock had greatly helped Mboya in Nairobi (in Swahili and Kikuyu the same word means both 'cock' and 'hero'). The cow symbol was naturally desirable for there is a 'cattle-complex' among many East African tribes, a complex comparable only to the cow-worship of the Hindu—and there would be Hindu voters in this election also. Clearly such symbols with particular significance to particular communities had to be eliminated. A powerful multi-racial committee was set up by the Government to examine the whole question. They had to be knowledgeable of the prejudices and predilections of the various religious and racial communities and had to choose symbols meaningful to widely varying peoples in a country where habitat-regions range from tropical sea coast through desert and bush to the fertile hill valleys of the highlands. The committee had a basis in the symbols used in the past. After much discussion, eliminating some and adding others, a sheet of sixteen symbols was issued. One curious instruction was issued: the hoe was to be held in reserve—there was some feeling apparently that this typical African agricultural instrument might be considered derogatory—yet in Nigeria it had been the symbol of a party. In Kenya, in contrast to West African elections, there were to be no symbols for parties. These were for individual candidates only and were to be allotted at nomination by ballot by the Returning Officer. Some first discussed the symbols with the candidates and agreed that, if there were any which were generally disliked, they might be eliminated from the ballot. Thus in Meru seven were cut out: the thorn tree, the giraffe, the ostrich, the bunch of bananas, the aeroplane, the railway engine and the hippopotamus. Certainly this last symbol was widely regarded with aversion among Africans—its name in Swahili is 'kiboko', the word meaning also a hide-whip—whilst a railway engine was, of course, an unknown and therefore unrecognizable object in many of the districts of Kenya.

When the Legislative Council met to discuss the Legislative Council Bill in December the decision that balloting would be by a cross on a ballot paper with symbols against the candidates' names had not been published. Mboya regretted that Coutts in opening the debate had made no statement on the matter; he went on to refer to the representations the African members had made on the subject. In the Bill itself there was no mention of the voting system; this was to be left to the Governor to prescribe by his Rule-making powers under the Bill. Many of the African members put a request for the use of symbols. Whilst it was apparent that by this they meant the 1957/8 system of separate boxes for each candidate marked with symbols they were—with one exception—not explicit in saying this. Had it not been for Odinga, who clearly explained that system and the popular African demand for its reintroduction, the Government might have been able to believe that by putting symbols on the ballot papers it had done as much as was desired. In replying to the debate, Coutts chose to pass over the matter of separate ballot boxes in silence—and he was not taken up on this by the African members. Nyagah put his finger on a major reason why the 'X' system was chosen when he said that symbols should be used for candidates of all races—'let us not make a "fingerprint" issue out of this', he added, referring to a campaign of the forties when the Europeans had refused to accept that they should carry, like Africans, fingerprinted identity cards.

The Asians, too, knew the need for symbols, Jamidar again being worried that no mention of them was made in the Bill. Whilst the Asians were likely to be content with their traditional method, the one that was in fact to be used, Pandya did ask that, as in the past, the names of candidates might appear on the ballot paper in other characters as well as the Roman. However, in the interests of uniformity in this election, the various Indian scripts (Gujerati, Urdu, Gurmukhi, etc.) were dropped.

Mboya pointed out clearly the defects of the system that was to be employed. The Africans, he said, did not believe that the secrecy of the ballot could be maintained when the illiterate elector had to pass on his vote to someone else for, he added, 'however trustworthy and honest that man may be, it immediately creates doubts and suspicion as to the results of the election'. The Government's method of maintaining secrecy was by administering an oath of secrecy to all admitted to polling stations. There was nevertheless a danger of intimidation through the secrecy being violated and at least one District Commissioner made representations on this point because, he said, interpreters would be needed to assist presiding officers to communicate with voters from the more remote areas of his district.

There was a yet more serious possibility of suspicion: that the Government, or certain administrators, might be suspected of favouring one party or one candidate rather than another. The danger, in its extreme form, was that a nationalist might make the burden of his election campaign an attack on the colonial Government and then lose the election. However, the Government, secure in the knowledge of its own integrity, had decided to accept the risks of what became in many constituencies—as many administrators knew would happen—an overwhelmingly large whispering vote. In one constituency suspicions of the administration were voiced. Odinga, a nationalist with seemingly apparent Communist connections, announced in the middle of his campaign that the Government was hostile to him, that he would not be able to trust the presiding officers taking down the whispered votes of the illiterates. Perhaps fortunately for all concerned—at least in respect of this issue—Odinga topped the poll, outdistancing his rivals by a long way. He was thus able to tell the crowd in Kisumu at the announcement of the poll 'that originally he had thought the polling station officers were "imperialists", but he had changed his mind and wished to thank them for the fair way in which they had handled the election.'

Fears of the violation of the secrecy of the ballot arose in another way at the time of the primary elections. When the ballot papers were handed out some Europeans noted that their voting numbers were being entered on the ballot paper counterfoil and that there was a number at the top of the ballot paper. Agitated letters appeared on the subject in the local press, something which has happened in previous Kenya elections with regard to this. Again the authorities had to reply that this was normal British practice, that after the election the ballot papers and the counterfoils would be sealed up and could not be examined before being destroyed six months later unless there was an election petition and a High Court judge, conducting the enquiry, ordered an examination to discover if there were any irregularities. In these elections the presence of the number on the ballot paper was more apparent than is normally the case since it was printed on the face of the paper, instead of the reverse, the practice in Britain.

The complexities of this election meant that voters of all

races had to be given clear instructions on what to do in the
polling station. It had to be explained to Europeans, Asians
and Arabs alike that in the primaries they were to delete the
names they did not want, but in the common roll election to
mark an 'X' against the name of their choice, a task about
which European and Asian politicians protested. As in previous
Asian and Arab elections tents were set up on polling day in
the vicinity of the polling stations; there last minute instructions were given to voters by means of blackboards and sheets
of paper. This same process of education had then to be
extended in the second stage of the election to African voters.
They recalled the previous system. As late as three weeks before
the polls one schoolmaster candidate in Central Nyanza still
did not know that this had been given up. He translated from
the Luo his short poster to the writers of this study as follows:
'Vote your card carefully for Mr. ——. He has taken a key
symbol which will have to open up everything in Kenya.
Vote your card carefully in the box of the key.' In this he displayed both his unawareness of the new election procedure and
the play that candidates were soon making of the symbols
allotted to them. More wide-awake candidates carried large
sheets of paper or blackboards around with them, demonstrating to voters the method of marking an 'X', or else they
handed out handbills of specimen ballot papers, showing the
cross in the appropriate place against the candidate's name
and symbol.

At polling the result of this propaganda was in some constituencies surprisingly effective. Naturally enough the higher degree
of literacy in the towns, fortified by agents' final instructions,
allowed the system to work there reasonably well. Unfortunately
the way voters had marked their papers was, in many cases,
then disclosed to all in the polling stations since candidates'
agents had not also given instructions on how to fold the voting
paper before placing it in the ballot box. Perhaps more voters
had to be helped to do this than to mark their papers in these
town polling-stations.

In the country districts the whole system collapsed into a
whispering vote. Civil servants knew that masses of people
were not only illiterate but had never even held a pencil in
their lives—it just was not possible to teach them to make their

mark in time. Among the Giriama—a coastal tribe which has for over a hundred years resisted Westernization and education despite encouragement by missionaries—vast numbers of illiterates were seen whispering their votes to officials in the polling stations. One presiding officer working here said that only five from the five hundred he had dealt with in one day were capable of marking the ballot paper themselves. Large numbers of illiterate women, whose voting qualification was that either they were married or aged over forty, were timidly entering screened booths to whisper their votes—at least one fled before the tension of the moment, the proximity to a strange white man. Such scenes of assistance could not be avoided: the overwhelming mass of Kenya's population is illiterate.[8]

One final problem emerged: there were illiterates or semi-literates, too proud to accept help, who thought they could mark their papers as instructed. Hence the large numbers of spoilt papers which reached over a thousand in three constituencies: North Nyanza 1,955, Central Nyanza 1,625 and Fort Hall 1,351. Fortunately in all these cases the majorities were so large that the spoilt papers could not affect the result. Meru, where no spoilt papers were reported, was one of the constituencies where voters had to be helped in large numbers. Moreover, Returning Officers were allowed to use their own judgment as to the nature of the mark they would accept and its place on the ballot paper. It is understood that the number of spoilt papers in many constituencies might well have been higher if many Returning Officers had not decided to exercise a liberal discretion.

.   .   .   .

It is sometimes said that academics should not make un-constructive criticisms. Accepting this challenge, we would point out that other methods of voting do exist. The Federal Commissioner for Elections in Nigeria suggested in 1959 that the system used in the former French colonies might well be adopted. There the voter enters a screened booth and tears off a sheet, coloured or marked with a symbol, for the candidate of his choice. Then, after placing the sheet of paper in an

[8]For two descriptions of polling scenes among illiterate voters see the *Kenya Weekly News*, 10 March 1961. The second article concerns Arab women in the Protectorate seat.

envelope to conceal his choice, the voter places the whole in the ballot box in the open. This system is clearly to be preferred to the whispering vote which most voters in Kenya used in 1961, and it avoids the abuses of the multiple box system whereby, as commented above, votes may easily be sold. The snag appears to be that, as was found in Nigeria in 1959 when this suggestion was put, Africans are no less conservative than other people and prefer what they know. However, Kenya Africans have now tried two different methods —why not a third and a safer one in the future?

The Primary Percentage

One other major matter, and one of vital importance, was left for the Working Party: the percentage which candidates in the reserved seats had to obtain from their own community before proceeding to the common roll electorate. This proved to be the most controversial point of the report, though it was not taken up fully until the debate in December on the Legislative Council Bill. Then the Europeans raised the question as their major topic. In the six months since the June debate on the Working Party report it had become a matter of major concern in the beginnings of the election campaign, since all involved had come to see clearly that the percentage was likely to have a vital effect upon the election result in certain of the European reserved constituencies.

The necessity for a form of primary election for the reserved seats arose from the European insistence at Lancaster House that they would not follow the Tanganyika election pattern. When the principle of the primary elections was conceded, that candidates should have 'effective and genuine support within their own community',[9] the other horn of the dilemma appeared. Could this support be defined in such a way that the Africans' insistence that the principle of the common roll would be maintained, by ensuring that there would be at least a

[9] A curious argument developed in Kenya that the Working Party had changed the words of the Lancaster House report, which in this respect appears to have been carelessly drawn up. On page 6 of the report it did say 'the effective and genuine support of their own communities' which clearly means far more than 'within their own communities', the phrase on page 7. However, all present at Lancaster House knew full well that the latter represented the intention of the Conference. It was unfortunate—to say the least—that this verbal ambiguity should have been left for European politicians in Kenya to seize upon.

choice of candidates who would go forward to the common roll election? This question had both political and sociological implications. Clearly a community solid within itself would be able to prevent more than one candidate going forward unless 'effective and genuine support' was defined by a ridiculously low figure.

From previous history it was likely that the divisions within the Asian communities would prevent them from being able to achieve any such solidarity. Hence, the debate about the percentage was almost entirely confined to the Europeans. Whilst fighting elections as personalities among themselves in the past, they have at least understood the need to draw together in the face of a common danger. When it became known that at Lancaster House 20% was the suggested figure there were many observers of the Kenya scene who thought that even this might be too high to allow more than one candidate emerging in many European rural constituencies. One other method was discussed during the conference: that nomination papers should be signed by members of the community concerned in a sufficient number to denote 'effective and genuine support'. After numbers from as low as twenty to as high as two hundred had been discussed the idea was dropped. It was agreed that a percentage should be fixed but the actual figure was left to the two Civil Servants in Kenya.

On this point the Working Party received many suggestions. One went so far as to suggest that the figure should be set at 40% of the registered voters, leaving aside the actual numbers who could be persuaded to go to the poll—perhaps they recalled some low European polls of the past. The effect of this and of some other suggestions would clearly have been to produce a return to a communal election by excluding all but one candidate. On this the Working Party stood firm. They knew that 'effective and genuine support' did not constitute a majority; they accepted that their task was to define what minimum constituted that support. They tried to put over the view that what was in question was support, not opposition. They said that the true purpose of the primaries would be fulfilled if each voter were asked not to select only one candidate—'which would be tantamount to a pre-election'—but to express acceptance or rejection only at the subsequent common roll election. They wanted voters to be required to indicate by writing 'yes' or 'no' against each name, showing thus whether they were suitable candidates, not that they were the final choice. At the count the 'yes's' against each name would be expressed as a percent of the total number of valid ballot papers. The endorsing of a candidate by 25 % or more would count as a nomination for the common roll election. It proved impossible in practice to put this idea over to the majority of the voters of the races concerned, European, Asian and Arab alike. As the subsequent debates in the Legislative Council showed, few of the European leaders accepted the spirit of the arguments of the Working Party.

When the debate on their report opened, Briggs, the United Party leader, condemned it as unrealistic. The fact was that, by their rejection of the Lancaster House report, his Party was mentally debarred from effective speech. Markham, who through illness had not been present at Lancaster House, took up the argument on the primaries and became by December the leader of the attack on the 25 % figure. In June, however, the interest of the debate lay more with the attitude of Blundell's supporters in the New Kenya Party. They then supported the figure not of 25 % but of 33⅓ %, which had been put to the Working Party as the united view of all the European Elected Members. The first of the New Kenya Party men to speak, Bompas, uttered words he was later to regret when they were quoted against him in the election campaign. After saying 'the figure should be no less than 50 %' he went on to declare: 'if in a preselection I secured 27 % or 30 % of votes, I would certainly not be prepared to continue to the next stage.' He considered that 25 % opened the way to 'some plausible crackpot succeeding in a preselection'. Slade advocated 33⅓ %, saying there was 'a big difference' between that and 25 % for he was prepared to accept that a man might have support if he had two to one against him, rather than three to one—he had, in what became a typical European fashion, shifted the ground from examining support to regarding opposition. Blundell, the leader of the group, likewise came out for 33⅓ %, though he added that he did not agree with those who thought that 'a 25 % proportion must of necessity mean collusion with extreme nationalists or extreme political wings of other racial thought'. Alexander had the most novel and interesting argument: he recalled that Ernest Bevin had admitted that for a Trade Union '17% in certain circumstances could mean that the Union was the effective and genuine voice of the workers'.

The Asians evinced little interest in the question during the debate. Their most extreme speaker, Nazareth, confessed that, whilst he would have preferred a figure between 30 and 35%, he was prepared to accept 25%. At the same time he drew attention to the announcement in a newspaper that morning that a new group among the Asians, the Kenya Freedom Party, had said that 25% was too high. Travadi, after revealing that at Lancaster House 20% had been the figure discussed, fairly summed up the Asian view when he accepted 25% as 'a good compromise'. In Kenya the Asians are perhaps better at compromise than are the Europeans. To them Pandya tried again to put the view that it was not whether 75% were against but whether 25% would indicate that the candidate had effective support.

Such arguments made little impression on such a blunt, outspoken independent member as Howard-Williams. In June he called the Working Party report 'bogus and ill-digested'. The first, a favourite word, he applied in December to the whole election, a view in which large numbers of the European community concurred. By then Cavendish-Bentinck, the leader of the Kenya Coalition, had come out with a clear call to voters to leave only one name on the sheet at the primary stage. His policy was thus to deny the intention of Lancaster House and of the Working Party; he was seeking to make the reserved seats communal again. Moreover, his tactic contrasted with the view that Markham, his chief lieutenant in the Coalition, had put in the Legislative Council in June. He had then recounted that the sub-committee of the European Elected Members had considered it undesirable that Europeans in the constituencies should adopt what he called 'Tammany Hall tactics' to ensure that only one candidate went forward; he did not want, he then said, American methods of rigging elections to be imported into Kenya.

In December it was Markham who led the European attack on the figure of 25%, opening with a long speech and the threat of a filibuster. He maintained that the question was not a party

issue, and appealed to the New Kenya Party members to
follow their leader's previous speech and accept the amendment
he, Markham, would propose of 33⅓%. He further announced
that he would fight on this to the bitter end, moving first an
amendment for 40%, and moving down by stages, until in
time he reached 33%. Mboya, in a series of interjections, re-
torted that it was not purely a European issue. Speaking later
in the debate, he recalled that the purpose of Lancaster House
was to move away from communal representation, that in this
spirit they had agreed to leave a large number of Africans to
be represented by Europeans, Asians and Arabs. He did not
like Lancaster House but he had agreed to try it and he asked
the Europeans to do the same. Finally he said that if Markham
moved his amendment, the Africans would move to reduce
the figure below 25%, and he tabled the figure of 10%; in
support, Khamisi declared that even this was too high—
he wanted the Tanganyika system. This line from the African
members pricked Markham's bubble, as he later conceded in
a newspaper letter—and all amendments for changing the
figure were dropped after Coutts had announced that the
Government would stand firm on 25%.

The newspapers, though, seized on Blundell's speech as, for
the Europeans and their election campaign, the most important of the debate. In a fighting speech, tense and moved, he
recalled the spirit of Lancaster House and warned Europeans
that if Cavendish-Bentinck's advice were accepted so that only
one candidate went forward in the European constituencies,
it would be 'the end of a European contribution to the political
development of this country'. In an undiplomatic fashion which
may have cost him votes in his own community, he went on
to say that the difference between 33 and 25 was 'a very small
matter indeed for it was far more important for the candidate
who gets in at the Rift Valley to earn the confidence of 1000
African voters, than it is to capture 50, 60 or 100 more European voters because in the ultimate analysis the contribution
of our community in this country will entirely depend on
the confidence and friendship we can establish with the African
people.' Members, he said, who sought to sabotage the form
of election failed to see this: if the Lancaster House constitution,
based on the common roll, were then sabotaged it would 'be

remembered for future constitutional discussions'. Unfortunately for Blundell the sincerity of this speech was damaged by
people who recalled his earlier position in June. One member
used Shakespeare's description of Cleopatra to say: 'Age cannot
wither him, nor custom stale his infinite variety.' The European
election campaign was being fought in this debate.

Before it was over the real feelings of the Europeans were
voiced by Roberts, the former leader of the Federal Independence Party. He found his justification for $33\frac{1}{3}\%$ in the European and Asian contribution to the country in the past: 'their
initiative, skill and finance' which had built the country and
their worries that all this 'could be so easily wrecked'. For this
reason, said Roberts, the Europeans wanted 'true representation' in the next Government and, to obtain this, wanted the
percentage raised from 25 to $33\frac{1}{3}\%$, although, if the Asians
were content with 25%, let them retain that figure for themselves.

In replying to the debate, Coutts naturally rejected this last
idea of racial differentiation. He explained again the point that
so many Europeans and Asians found difficult to follow—as
late as the primary election itself—that in the primary elections
everyone had virtually as many votes as there were candidates.
Percentages would be calculated for each candidate against
the total number of valid ballot papers, and thus no candidate's
percentage could affect that of another. He also announced
that it had been accepted that the return or forfeiture of deposits
on the reserved seats would be decided on the result of the
primary election alone: those who failed to receive 25% of
permissive votes would forfeit their deposit. Later, in the committee stage, Nyagah asked that the common roll principle of
the election should apply here too so that the common roll
election should adjudicate on this—a point, indeed, of importance to candidates for reserved seats.

Thus passed into law the novelty of the system of the primary
election on the basis of 25% support within the community
concerned. As it had turned out this was the main issue in the
last stage of establishing the machinery of the election: the
passage in December of the Legislative Council Ordinance,
1960.

Part Two

CAMPAIGNS

CHAPTER IV

THE RESERVED SEATS

In Britain, whilst some preliminary sparring is necessarily expected in the last weeks or months of the old Parliament, the election campaign itself is generally reckoned as being short: from nomination, or dissolution, to the actual election day. In Kenya, on this occasion the period of infighting was doubled: candidates for the reserved seats had two stages before them. First, from candidature day, 6th January, to the primary elections held on different dates between 18th January and 23rd January. Next day was nomination day for the open seats, the opening of the general campaign for all the seats together, with the actual elections in the period between 19th February and 27th February. Candidates in the reserved seats had thus a lengthy period of some six weeks of electioneering. In the first stage they had to convince their own community; in the second, whilst seeking to hold that support, they had to appeal to the general body of the common roll electorate. Yet these weeks were only the culmination of a much longer period. The first candidate, an Asian Muslim in Mombasa, had declared himself as early as the previous August, but there was a real sense in which the whole time since the Lancaster House Conference ended in March 1960 had been one long election campaign for the reserved seats—particularly was this so among the Europeans.

The year following Lancaster House was a difficult one which did nothing to strengthen European confidence in the future. During the conference itself, as we have noted, there was already a fall in stock and land prices. There soon followed in March the quick rejection by Mboya of the new constitution as having no real permanence, and then the delay in forming a Government with new African ministers. However, some comfort came from Kiano, who sought, in the responsibility of holding the portfolio for Commerce and Industry, to rebuild confidence by moderate and responsible utterances both in Kenya and elsewhere. The difficulty was that other African leaders, outside the Government, were, as they formed their own groups in preparation for the coming elections, raising issues which could only intensify European fears. They were demanding again the release of Kenyatta, talking of the expropriation of the European highlands after *Uhuru*, and making other promises for that freedom and independence which, it was said, the elections would bring. In the background, there were reports of a recrudescence of oathing and Mau Mau songs among the Kikuyu, and the Governor considered it necessary to re-affirm in May that Kenyatta would not be released. Sir Patrick Renison spoke then of Kenyatta as a 'leader to darkness and death', saying that his release would glorify Mau Mau, 'identify it with African national advance', and encourage violence, holding back constitutional advance for many years; 'the administration would be demoralized'. On this Odinga commented in Legislative Council: 'let Africans choose if they want savagery or not.'

June was a bad month, intensifying European fears. It opened with the publication of the Corfield Report on Mau Mau, which recalled in detail old horrors. Then, in the middle of the month, the first Europeans fleeing from a Congo chaos they regarded as inevitable with that country's independence arrived in Nairobi. The subsequent happenings in the Congo, which provided a continuous background to events in Kenya, more than proved their fears. Kenya settlers, and others in the Colony, could not but ask what Kenya's fate would be in independence.

After Lancaster House the call for European unity was soon raised and much pressure was put on Blundell to join Cavendish-Bentinck. Before the end of May, the recently revived Europeans' organization, the Convention of Associations, asked the latter to visit London on behalf of the settlers. At the end of the first week of June, the *Financial Times* noted two things: a 10% decline in the value of local ordinary shares since Lancaster House but at the same time a continuance of Kenya's economic expansion at the rate of $3\frac{1}{2}\%$ per annum, and it mentioned particularly Shell's interest in a £14 million refinery at Mombasa. Already the *Kenya Weekly News* had pointed to the contrast of attitudes: a continuing confidence among firms with headquarters in Britain and the rising fears of the local European

farming community. London had had experience in dealing
with nationalism in newly-emergent independent countries in
Asia and Africa; the Kenya settlers had not. Remote and
isolated in their Highlands, they could only listen to the roar
of the voices of the rising tide of African nationalism lapping
around them. Fear begets fear. There can be no doubt that,
through the fears of the settlers, transmitted also to London by
Cavendish-Bentinck's spending six weeks there, from late June
to mid-August, the position was made worse. Only the formation of a new Government after the elections could answer the
question whether these fears were justified. Unfortunately the
setting up and operation of the election machine took a whole
year from the ending of the Lancaster House conference to the
declaration of the results. During this time Kenya's economic
situation continued to worsen, as confidence drained away. In
August it was reported first that many Asians were applying
for passports—taking the first step if they should need later to
leave in a hurry—and then that an East African Pioneering
Society meeting at Kitale was discussing the possibility of a
mass exodus of European farmers to South America.

European fears over land-titles and the search for a guarantee
of land values was the main European interest after Lancaster
House. This interest naturally formed the major subject of
European concern in the election. Much discussion then went
back to Cavendish-Bentinck's visit to London, where he asked
for the establishment by the British Government of a revolving
fund of £35 million to guarantee land-values in Kenya, a
request in which he was joined by Peter Marrian, the president
of the Kenya National Farmers' Union, then making his second
visit of the year to London to represent European farmers'
worries. At the same time Blundell was in London. Whilst also
seeking security for land he believed, as he told the press, that
Sir Ferdinand's figure was too high: the total value of land
concerned was only £20 million. Blundell's actions in London
led to the accusation in Kenya that he had sabotaged Cavendish-
Bentinck, that he had broken a promise at the Convention of
Associations that he would not in any way work against him
during his London visit. The European leaders met with a
refusal from the Secretary of State to provide any guarantee
fund which they considered sufficient, or to accept liabilities in

the post independence period. Cavendish-Bentinck's conclusion was they must battle on to secure this from the Government and he later made this a main point in the Coalition election manifesto. Blundell, on the other hand, warned, in November in the New Kenya Party's manifesto, that he did not believe that the British Government could be persuaded to change its view, that confidence could only be restored by meeting African land pressures by African settlement schemes, and the development of agriculture in the African land units. Here, on land, was revealed the major difference between the European parties in the election: the Coalition seeking terms from the British Government and the N.K.P. believing that confidence could only be restored by coming to terms with the new Africa.

Here was the central problem of all the non-African communities as they faced the election. Could they come to terms, or would they seek to defend themselves from the positions of the past? In the case of the Arabs, this meant insistence upon the sanctity of the Coastal Strip in the Agreement of 1895 between Britain and Zanzibar; for Asians maintenance of the reserved seats under the new constitution. All these interests were under attack from African politicians: European land titles, the Coastal Strip, the reservation of seats. Moreover, what confidence could the immigrant groups have when Gichuru, the president of KANU, who had sought in October as a moderate to reassure British investors in London, was reported in November as saying to an African audience in Kenya that after *Uhuru* 'Europeans and Asians will kneel to us'? A few days later, Mboya, who had gone to London with Gichuru, proclaimed that after the elections Kenyatta would be named as Chief Minister. Here was the figure and the problem which loomed over all else. African meetings proceeded to antiphonic shouts from platform and crowd of 'Uhuru na Kenyatta' (freedom and Kenyatta), but how could Europeans accept any dealings with the man they regarded as the originator of Mau Mau? His name became the shibboleth of the campaign. Nothing else tied the meetings of all races together except the mention of his name, the pressure upon the candidate seeking votes to declare himself if he had not previously done so, to define his attitude towards the man in restriction at Lodwar in the Northern Province.

European Seats

Early in September it was announced that Cavendish-Bentinck's Kenya Coalition, described by its leader as a 'movement' rather than a 'political party', was to contest the elections. At the same time Briggs proclaimed his support and that of his United Party. Cavendish-Bentinck had been requested to take this action by the executive of the Convention of Associations. The Convention itself met formally in Nairobi a month later to consider this, with a motion before it supporting the Executive Committee's action. Members of Blundell's N.K.P. sought to block this on the grounds that the Convention was traditionally a forum, not a political party, and therefore could not line up with one. To this the executive's reply was that the Convention had repeatedly urged the political parties to sink their differences, and, as they had not done so, the Convention had now to take a stand with the political party which represented their views.

Cavendish-Bentinck then spoke, outlining the Coalition's policy in what proved to be the first salvo of the election campaign. He attacked Blundell as progressing through multi-racialism to a mono-racialism under which, it seemed, the minorities would be allowed to remain in Kenya only under sufferance. He believed that Europeans and Africans would get on better on a basis of mutual respect and a recognition that they were different; he did not believe that Africans would vote for Europeans. He attacked the N.K.P. as men created and brought together by the former Governor, saying they were 'very closely allied to the British Government'—always a powerful line of attack in a colonial territory. The new franchise system he called 'disgraceful'; it was 'designed to keep certain people in power', men who would not be genuine representatives. Blundell rose to say that he did not know that Sir Ferdinand would be making these attacks but made no reply. He was, said the press, 'a rather lonely-looking figure . . . obviously aware that the feeling of the Convention was strongly against him.' The voting on the motion for support for the Executive's action soon showed this, for it was passed by 38 votes to 4.

As the campaign developed, Cavendish-Bentinck's main insistence was that they should concentrate on economic rather than on political questions: Macleod's great mistake at Lancaster House had been his failure to see the economic implications of his actions. Blundell replied that trying to halt political change in the present circumstances of Africa was 'like trying to hold up the Zambezi'; they must seek to guide and harness change, not to retire into sterile opposition; he would be prepared to co-operate with the African members in the new Legislative Council. This led to the inevitable question: his views on Kenyatta. Speaking to students at Makerere, the University College in Uganda, late in November, Blundell was reported as saying that Kenyatta should be released 'at a suitable time after independence'. This caused such a furore among Europeans that Blundell issued a statement in amplification, saying it was as well to give Kenyatta an opportunity to prove that his motives were no longer a menace to security whilst Britain was still responsible for law and order. The implication of this appeared to be that Blundell meant 'before', not 'after' independence—and this was what the Makerere students reported, in a letter to the press, he had in fact said. The Coalition seized on these remarks and quoted against Blundell words uttered in September in which he had opposed Kenyatta's release.

Here was one of the prime issues over which they built up an attack on Blundell as the 'man of many voices . . . a politician'. In contrast, the image of Cavendish-Bentinck projected was that of the honest man with no axe to grind who had left his honourable position as Speaker to defend the interest of those whom he had encouraged to come as settlers to Kenya— his resignation was not the action of a time-serving politician. He himself maintained, speaking in the Rift Valley at the end of November, that he had no intention of standing in the election. These contrasting images of the two European leaders were most successfully put over, and proved a vital point in the campaign. It is more than arguable that the failure of the N.K.P. to capture the European vote turned very largely on the personality of their leader.

The two parties published their manifestoes at the end of November and the beginning of December. Cavendish-Bentinck, writing an introduction to the Coalition's, the second to appear, admitted that the manifestoes might appear somewhat similar in content, and insisted that the difference lay in 'the reasoning, the intent and the consistency' which underlay the statements. There was much truth in this. The Coalition's document, *Now and the Future*, gave an impression of determination, forthrightness and a spirit of do-or-die which appealed to European electors who felt that they had their backs to the wall. Cavendish-Bentinck declared that his party would not 'as others have done, sail vaguely hopeful, but blindly, before the winds of change'; the Europeans had largely created the country; they could not stand aside 'in a craven attitude of abnegation' but must 'help shape the future'. The N.K.P.'s document, *Plan for Success*, was longer by half. It began with a justification for being a 'Party', admitted the attraction of 'Independent' candidates to Kenya voters in the past, but claimed that the new constitution made a party system a necessity; their objective was 'to play a real part in the government', and this could not be done effectively by 'a group of Independents with varying policies'. There followed a map of Africa to show the overwhelming mass of independent seats; against this background they sought to develop their policy, explaining that at Lancaster House they had accepted constitutional proposals which went beyond the limits they considered desirable because they believed that an agreement with the African leaders was the only basis for Kenya's future political and economic development. They supported this by the claim that African leaders had demonstrated responsibility in office in the Caretaker Government since Lancaster House.

The policy statement looked to the larger electorate from whom the party had to seek votes by its reference to the franchise. It was unrealistic to suppose that 'one man, one vote' would not be the franchise of the future, though they still wanted reservation of seats 'until such time as racial prejudice disappears'. On this, the Coalition was again on the attack, but again only in a way which appealed to European voters. They recorded that the European Elected Members had been 'unanimously agreed' on $33\frac{1}{3}\%$ as the figure for the primaries. The Coalition leader's policy was that voters should delete all but one name at the primary stage. If Blundell was to be attacked for changing his position over the percentage figure, it could no less be said that Cavendish-Bentinck, by making deletion of all but one name the tactic of the Coalition, had refused to accept the spirit of the Lancaster House conference: that the common roll should decide.

Both manifestoes spoke of the need for an independent judiciary and for the maintenance of law and order. The N.K.P. insisted that an opposition should be free to criticize without fear of reprisal, whilst the Coalition underlined the need for 'security from violence and intimidation', saying that the latter was 'always liable to rear its ugly head'. Both made much of the security of land title and both sought reassurance for the Civil Service, a vote important in particular in the Nairobi constituencies. On education, the Coalition recognized the 'feelings and prejudices' of European parents about racial integration in the schools, towards which, it had been recently announced, the first steps were to be taken. The wording of the two statements on this, a highly emotionally charged issue, was curiously similar, both leaving the matter to consultation between boards of governors and parents' representatives. Both supported the idea of East African Federation and both mentioned the possibility of a second chamber, though in each case the N.K.P. did so in greater detail. Some thick black words on the Coalition's last page provided one of the catch-phrases of the election: 'We thus regard our role as that of watchdogs, and not lapdogs'; in reply to which N.K.P. speakers described themselves as 'guidedogs into the future'.

The similarity of much of the wording of these manifestoes showed again the belief of politicians that it is necessary to court the middle of the road uncommitted voters. Did any such exist among the Europeans? The Coalition was determined to destroy the view that it was a reactionary party, and must have been pleased with the comment of the critical *Daily Nation*[1] that 'despite its ebullient style, however, this is by no means a reactionary document'. The Coalition reacted strongly to any suggestion that it was dominated by the old United Party so that, when it came to choosing candidates, it carefully avoided any who were known to have had a close connection with that body. Indeed, two of the Coalition's first candidates to be announced, Markham for Central Rural and David Cole for North Kenya, had had a previous connection with the

[1]For comments on the press in the election see Appendix II.

N.K.P.; then for Kericho, Oates, chairman of the Convention of Associations, and Harry Macallan, a Nakuru lawyer and contributor to the *Kenya Weekly News*, for the important Rift Valley constituency, which Blundell had by then declared he would contest.

On the N.K.P.'s side the first candidates announced were, in mid-November, Mrs. Hughes and Bompas for the two-member seat of Nairobi West. Both took the opportunity to say that they were moving from their old areas because of the amalgamation of constituencies but it was known that both had had tiffs with their former constituents, in the Uasin Gishu and Kiambu respectively. Another early candidate was Commander Goord for West Kenya, the N.K.P.'s adviser at Lancaster House and one of the original signatories of the N.K.P.'s policy statement. One of Blundell's closest supporters was Havelock who, after being a Specially Elected Member, chose now to stand in Nairobi South-West. In North Kenya the party seemed to be having some difficulty in finding a candidate for it accepted, in December, Laurie Campbell, a missionary educational adviser—*prima facie* a weak choice in a place where it was more than necessary for the candidate to appeal to settler farmers. One candidate, who had been expected but did not appear, was Rhoderick Macleod, the brother of the Secretary of State. He knew the unpopularity of the name of Macleod among the Kenya Europeans and thought it wiser to remain a back-room boy, the efficient organizer of the party's campaign. The strongest of the N.K.P. candidates, as it turned out, was Mrs. Shaw in Kericho. Although her constituency was reduced in size she was known there as a popular member who had over the years paid close attention to her constituents' needs; indeed she was heard to say in speeches, 'You can trust me', and some people took as an implication 'even if you don't trust Mr. Blundell.'

Whilst these were some of the more interesting party candidates to emerge during November and December, no Kenya European election would be complete without independents and without some indication that politics at the Coast were different. In Mombasa East neither party put forward any nomination—the only European reserved seat the Coalition did not contest; thus we may conveniently leave consideration of this for the section on the Coast seats. In Central Rural, Marrian, the former president of the Kenya National Farmers' Union, appeared against Markham. Rumour had it that Marrian had preferred this to his home constituency of North Kenya, for there, in the former Mount Kenya constituency, he had lost his deposit in the 1956 election when standing as a known supporter of Capricorn. The N.K.P. decided not to oppose Marrian since his political ideas were not dissimilar from theirs, even if in economic matters and application for farm-guarantees to the British Government he had been with the Coalition. In the oldest Kenya traditions of independents, there stood for Nairobi West Howard-Williams, the editor earlier of a weekly journal *New Comment*, notorious for outspoken remarks about Africans until the Government suppressed it under the Emergency Regulations. In his election manifesto the candidate aligned himself with Cavendish-Bentinck's 'sane and praiseworthy approach', and insisted that, as in the old Council and at Lancaster House where he positioned a Union Jack on the table before him, he would remain an independent and '*not* join any political party'. Howard-Williams had stood for Parliament for Cambridge University in 1945—perhaps for this reason his staccato manifesto recalled a famous manifesto of Sir Alan Herbert as candidate for the senior University some years before. Half a page will suffice to indicate the flavour:

'Private Enterprise
     Yes, please!
Employment
     Please see Agriculture.
Forestry
     I have no knowledge of forestry as such.
Communism
     We have no place for this sort of nonsense.
The Truth
     The Truth must prevail.
Freedom of the Press
     If you have goodwill you have something priceless—
     like charm of manner.'

—the last two sections being clearly a veiled reference to his suppressed journal *New Comment* and a column 'Truth' he used to write.

These were some who submitted candidature papers on 6th January. Three days previously the Coalition leader announced that he would stand for the Rift Valley, superseding Macallan and saying that he had yielded to the pressures that he should stand since things were so bad in the country that he must be at the country's disposal if wanted. The decision produced a gladiatorial atmosphere in the great arena of the Rift Valley, in the clash between the European leaders. Blundell expressed regret that an ex-Speaker whom he respected should be in the hustings against him but added 'In one way, however, it is good because it makes the Kenya Coalition less of a "headless wonder".' From the African side Mwai Kibaki, executive officer of KANU, declared that the contest would decide the future of the Europeans in Kenya: the Africans would decide between a man who wanted the Europeans to leave 'after being paid a colossal sum of money' and a man 'who encourages them to make the country their own provided they adjust themselves to the conditions.'

The Africans were thus in the wings of the Rift Valley election, watching this contest with perhaps more interest than that for any other reserved seat. Blundell, unlike his opponent, acknowledged the common roll nature of the election by having one African, Herman Oduor, the general secretary of the General Agricultural Workers' Union, and two Asians sign his nomination paper. The Coalition tactic, on the other hand, was to fight the primary and the common roll elections as two different campaigns. When, at the end of 1960, Blundell paid a forty-five minute visit to the KANU branch in Naivasha and obtained their support, the Coalition seized with glee on a newspaper photograph of Blundell leaving the building. They circulated it prominently in an election pamphlet to indicate their opponent as pandering to Africans.

Cavendish-Bentinck's entry made one significant change in the nature of the Rift Valley campaign. By long tradition Kenya European election opponents are wont to travel round the constituency together, addressing joint meetings. Blundell and Macallan were already doing this. Cavendish-Bentinck, after one joint meeting, ended the arrangement. He was soon independently addressing larger meetings than Blundell. More serious for the latter was the social intimidation which became

an important feature of the campaign. There was talk first
among Coalition supporters of boycotting Blundell's meetings.
When this failed there were threats of violence against Blundell:
debagging, rotten eggs and tomatoes and even shooting were
talked of. As a result the Naivasha District Commissioner cancelled the licence necessary under the law for one meeting, so
that in one part of the constituency Blundell could only meet
people privately. In the end the detestation and contempt
which so many settlers felt for Blundell could not be denied
violent expression. In a meeting at Londiani, six days before the
poll, a member of the audience called him a 'traitor' for his
part at Lancaster House and this was the signal for a pelting
with eggs and tomatoes. Cavendish-Bentinck was quick to
condemn this, but the damage may have been done. It was
known that some of his leading supporters had taken part in
the incident. The N.K.P. office in Nakuru reported that next
day twelve previously uncommitted people asked for Blundell
stickers for their cars. Here was one of the imponderables of
the election: was the Londiani incident vital? Did it affect the
narrowness with which Blundell achieved his 25%? Did it
influence some at least of the 60 people who handed in ballot
papers in the Rift Valley with neither name deleted, thus giving
both candidates the chance to go forward to the general electorate? Blundell's percentage was only 26·7, achieved with a
margin of only 34 papers in a total European poll of 2,031,
being 89% of the electorate.

In the Rift Valley, the central and most important European
reserved seat, Cavendish-Bentinck's tactic of deleting all but
one name had failed, but only just. In two other rural constituencies it was successful: in West and North Kenya. The
Coalition candidate in West Kenya, L. R. M. Welwood, seemed
most conscious of the failing of this form of election, for, as he
wrote in the *East African Standard*, 'it must lead either to em-
bittered Europeans, represented by men they neither trust nor
support, or to frustrated Asians and Africans, who feel that
they have not had the opportunity to vote'. Throughout the
campaign he travelled round addressing joint meetings with
Goord, his opponent. The press noted that most of the questions
were addressed to the latter, who on one occasion refused to
answer any more of the attacks being launched through them

on his leader. The *Daily Nation* described Goord at one meeting as 'something of a Daniel in a lion's den'. It was recognized that the Afrikaner centre of Eldoret would probably be solid against the N.K.P., but the general atmosphere of the constituency made this a veritable uphill fight for their man. It would, indeed, have been surprising if Goord had obtained his 25 %, but he only managed 19.7 %.

One European rural constituency, North Kenya, showed an even greater solidarity of feeling, allowing Campbell, the N.K.P. candidate, only 14.1 %. The atmosphere at Thomson's Falls, one of the main centres of the constituency, was well summed up by a leading Coalition supporter: 'We know each other well here and we have no quarrels; there aren't likely to be many, if any, voters for Mr. Campbell.' Was this just a tightly-knit community or was there here some element also of social intimidation? Certainly the latter was a factor in the North Kenya campaign. Another leading Coalition supporter openly boasted to the writers of this study of the difficulty Campbell was having in obtaining a chairman for his final meeting in Nyeri with Blundell. As a chairman is necessary under Kenya law, to be responsible for the order of a meeting, we were told, with a chuckle, that the N.K.P. might not be able to hold the meeting. When it took place and the speeches were over, hostile questions were thrown first at the chairman, demanding to know who he was, and the suggestion was made that he was really a Government officer. In fact, all present were well aware, in the small society of European Kenya, that the chairman was a local farm manager, but he was not one of the fourteen people who had been bold, or rash, enough to sign Campbell's nomination papers.

The personal attacks on Campbell were such that he decided to answer them in his manifesto, saying he was 'NOT a Communist', a frequent term of abuse for a Liberal in Kenya, and that his P.O. Box number was 'NOT the same as KANU in Nyeri'. This latter smear was interesting since Campbell claimed as his strength that he was on good terms with many moderate educated Africans, that through such friendships he could help the Europeans to gain the confidence of African leaders to form strong moderate policies. He told meetings that in his experience as an educational adviser less than 10 % of

the 1,000 African schoolteachers in the Nyeri district had joined
any political party; they were essentially moderates. Campbell's educational interests, the fact that he had produced the
plan for the introduction of universal primary education for
African children in the Nyeri district that year, did not make a
ready appeal to the overwhelming European farming vote.
Campbell bewailed the fact that, although he travelled 2,500
miles in the first twelve days of the campaign, he could not
get at the voters. They would not come to his meetings. At the
Timau Club one evening there was an audience of nine whereas
the night before Cole had addressed a packed room.

Certainly, Cole's appeal fitted the constituency. One of the
largest land-owners in Kenya, he came of a distinguished Kenya
family, being the son of an early member of the Legislative
Council and the nephew of Lord Delamere, the pioneer of European settlement. The 89.6% support he received was the
highest percent of any candidate in the primaries. In the campaign Cole accepted that there was a serious danger of frustration among Africans if they did not have the opportunity to
exercise their newly-won vote—exactly this effect, it was widely
reported, was produced upon Africans in West Kenya after
the primary shut-out there. However, Cole fulfilled his promise
that if he was the only candidate to go forward from the primary
he would then arrange meetings for his new African constituents. He went further and invited the newly elected unopposed KANU candidate for neighbouring Nyeri, Josef
Mathenge, to meet him at his house. Mathenge accepted but
later made the wry comment which well summed-up the revolutionary situation present in Kenya: 'Mr. Cole's estate is much
larger than the North Tetu division of Nyeri district where I
live'—North Tetu, with 85,000 population, is one of the more
heavily populated Kikuyu areas.

Perhaps the Central Rural constituency focussed best the real
issues in the European mind. Here meetings were not be-
devilled by hostility to the N.K.P. and its leader Blundell since
the Coalition's opposition came from Marrian standing as an
independent. Many in this constituency were heard to say
that it was a pity that both he and Markham could not be
elected, a view reflected in the result where 195 people allowed
both names to go forward. Choice was difficult since on land,

the key issue for the Europeans, Marrian had been with the Coalition to London and, like them, made it plain that he would continue to fight for the British Government to accept its responsibilities in respect of the settlers. Although he disclaimed that it was an election 'gimmick', Markham announced in the middle of the campaign that 'win or lose', the Coalition would go again to London after the election to prepare, if necessary, a court action against the British Government over land titles, and for this purpose a £10,000 fighting fund was to be raised. Marrian said that any questioning of the validity of land titles was a question of the sanctity of all private property, a moving towards the Marxist doctrine of state ownership. In his campaign he played much on the widespread European fears of Communism, which many considered as inevitably associated with African nationalism through the past connections of Jomo Kenyatta. On the other hand, Marrian believed in the possibility of working with the nationalist leaders, deploring the discord in their ranks, whilst Markham maintained that African goodwill to Europeans just did not exist in Kenya. He repeated a forthright declaration that he would not serve under Kenyatta or in a Government of which he was a member, an issue over which there was increasing pressure as the primary campaign was ending.

The three predominantly residential constituencies of Nairobi West, Nairobi South-West and Nairobi Suburban contain mainly civil servants or businessmen. Nairobi West was the one European two-member seat, and was contested by five candidates: two Coalition, C. W. Salter and Mrs. Needham-Clark, two N.K.P., Bompas and Mrs. Hughes, and the independent Howard-Williams who was most outspoken in attacking the complexity of the two-member idea. At least he had one novel policy for this time of drought. This he had already put by motion in the Legislative Council: that the waters of Lakes Victoria and Rudolf should be piped to the arid zones—there were, he said, 'only slight rises of the land'! Howard-Williams's other strength, as he made clear in his election propaganda was his successful Legislative Council motion on behalf of better terms for the police and his pressure on behalf of the civil servants. Nobody seeking votes for these four seats could afford to ignore this last important element, and private meetings, with the press excluded, were arranged so that they could freely put their points to candidates. Nevertheless, Coalition candidates were prone to stress to these urban audiences that Kenya's economy depended on the farmers in the Highlands.

Perhaps it was in these Nairobi constituencies that there was more pressure than elsewhere from thoughtful questioners to know what African support the candidate might expect to receive. N.K.P. candidates like Havelock had to confess their disappointment that there had been no real African response that would build up confidence. The N.K.P. was under attack since none of the Africans and Asians who had been in the New Kenya Group in the Legislative Council was willing to stand under the Party's name. Coalition candidates repeatedly claimed that their party had strong support from other races, as seen from individuals visiting the Coalition's offices because they, too, were 'worried' about the future. Howard-Williams was already looking to the wider electorate with such phrases as 'our African friends'; his chairman did not make the mistake of shutting up a persistent African questioner, as happened at one Nairobi Coalition meeting.

In the countryside it was possible for Europeans to hold their own little election meetings in their Clubs as though this election campaign was no different from those of the past. Not so in Nairobi, where Africans attended European and Asian meetings, often in large numbers. Already in mid-December, Africans in Nairobi West formed an African Voters' Committee and announced they would ask the candidates to meet them; both the lady candidates there had soon to confess that they would be unable to address audiences in Swahili. As the campaign went on African interest in the reserved seats grew and there was some evidence of regret that this had not begun at the time of registration.

When the votes were counted there was some comment that the defeat administered to the N.K.P. candidates in the Nairobi seats might be related to a certain feeling among civil servants. They were taking this opportunity to protest against the Lancaster House conference and the jeopardy in which they felt their careers to have been placed by it. In the outcome Mrs. Hughes was the third N.K.P. candidate to lose her deposit by failing to receive 25% support, whilst Bompas, her running mate, scraped through with 28·01%.

The announcement of the primary results came as a rude shock to the N.K.P. Their eight candidates had managed to obtain only 22% overall support—4,326 permissive votes against 12,128 for the nine Coalition and 3,472 for the four independents. Politicians are optimists by nature but certainly the N.K.P. had been unrealistic in their assessments—even such figures as 40% for Blundell were talked of in otherwise responsible circles in the Rift Valley. Had the percent been set at 33⅓ only Mrs. Shaw and Alexander would have been through to the common roll. The N.K.P. may have had a smoother organization, but it had failed to reach the European voters. The Coalition's whole apparatus was amateurish in the extreme but it did not need efficiency: this was provided by the social structure of the Europeans, particularly in the rural constituencies. The Coalition's lowest figure was 40·5% for Mrs. Needham-Clark, but that was in Nairobi West where Howard-Williams had interposed, putting the Coalition's line and obtaining second place with 54·2%. Cavendish-Bentinck could comment: 'I have succeeded beyond my wildest dreams.' It was clear whom the Europeans had accepted as their leader, but Kenya's constitution did not provide any longer for untrammelled communal representation. Might this not be a Pyrrhic victory?

An indication of the answer was soon provided. Following the Coalition's tactic of concentrating on one electorate at a time, Cavendish-Bentinck despatched, on the day following the primary results, identical letters to the president of KANU and the leader of KADU, asking for a personal meeting. Since the Europeans had made clear whom they trusted he hoped that the African leaders would 'respect the wishes of the European community', for a rejection of the Coalition candidates would be 'a severe set-back' to European co-operation 'in the urgent problems of restoring both economic and political confidence in Kenya', Four days later, Muliro, KADU's deputy leader, gave their answer at a press conference: he could see 'no useful purpose' in meeting Cavendish-Bentinck or other members of the Coalition. He considered Sir Ferdinand's resignation following Lancaster House was directed to breaking the constitution, that he was 'interested in wrecking the economy of the country so that the settlers could be paid off by the British Government' and he described the European leader as 'a die-hard tribalist'. For KANU Gichuru replied in a speech next day to an audience of 10,000 in the Bahati location at Nairobi: they cheered when he announced that in the Rift Valley KANU was instructing Africans to vote for Blundell. But this announcement had been made without consulting KANU's Governing Council. It appeared that a division there might affect the European reserved seats, for Odinga then called upon Africans to support Coalition candidates—an announcement to which Cavendish-Bentinck's first reaction was an embarrassed 'no comment' to the press. Odinga gave as his reason: 'At least with Sir Ferdinand Cavendish-Bentinck we know where we stand. Mr. Blundell gets his support from the Colonial Office . . . Better the enemy you know than the one you do not.' Some interpreted this as an example of Odinga's wrecking tactics.

Pressure was being put on the N.K.P., through letters in the press and in other ways, for them to accept their defeat and withdraw from the election. Havelock replied in the *East African Standard*, saying first, and correctly, that this was not possible—a candidate may not withdraw after nomination. Secondly, he argued that withdrawal would be 'acceding to Coalition pressure to revert to communal elections', a yielding to those who really wanted 'racial representation and political *apartheid*'. Blundell had already announced the party's intention to carry on: 'None of our candidates intends to withdraw. They are fighting on a national policy framed for all voters in Kenya.' On this he carried with him into further battle Bompas who, possibly remembering his earlier words in Legislative Council, was showing some signs of hesitation.

In his constituency of Nairobi West there was the complication of the two-member seat in which voters had but one vote. For the N.K.P. the problem had been solved by the primary result but what was the Coalition to do ? It was faced with the complexity that Howard-Williams's views were the same as theirs and he had beaten Mrs. Needham-Clark. Was there not a danger that on a split vote and with the entry of African support, Bompas would get through? After a fortnight's delay, and an exchange of letters with Cavendish-Bentinck, Mrs. Needham-Clark announced that she was asking her supporters to vote for Salter.

By then KANU had proclaimed support for both Bompas and Howard-Williams. This was a curious and unexpected decision since, if they had followed the Coalition's example and thrown their weight behind Bompas, they might have returned the N.K.P. man. Howard-Williams confessed that KANU's support came as a surprise but he rejoiced in it as 'an unsolicited testimonial' and 'a very considerable compliment'. Was there perhaps some truth in the view that Africans like forthright people? Had they forgiven Howard-Williams his remarks about Africans in the past or had his piped-water dreams roused their imagination? Certainly this and Howard-Williams's work in raising police pay were given as reasons for supporting him by one KADU-minded African Councillor of Nairobi City Council. Howard-Williams showed a continuing flair for publicity— taking his symbol, an ostrich, and turning it into a poster, the bird having three nest-eggs: water, police-pay and the Civil Service; later, on polling-day, he was presenting ostrich-feathers to supporters. A good politician, Howard-Williams was soon happily addressing Africans as 'moi friends!' his voice, said the reporter, taking the audience 'in a warm embrace'. As all other European candidates, he was soon challenged on Kenyatta. Howard-Williams was prepared to leave his release to the Governor who was determined Kenya would not become another Congo, but if there were African unity and stability then Kenyatta would be freed, and, to applause, this might happen within three months: it was 'foreign to the ways of the British to hold a grudge against anyone who had paid the price of his actions'. A guest speaker from KANU followed. He started in the typical fashion of African meetings to the antiphonic repetition from the crowd: 'Uhuru', 'Uhuru na KANU', and then 'Uhuru na Kenyatta', something which, said the reporter, nearly provoked the European chairman to 'a blue fit'.

Here was the problem for Europeans, appealing for the first time to an African electorate. Even the most sincere and friendly candidate found it hard to make real contact. Could it be done with audiences composed of highly politically conscious Kikuyu in Central Rural? There one of Markham's African meetings broke up in disorder when he refused to raise his fingers in KANU's 'V' sign and join in the cry of 'Uhuru na Kenyatta'. In Marrian's case the problem of contact was more essential— for KANU was backing him, arranging meetings and providing a chairman-translator. On one such occasion this gentleman, Dr. Mungai Njoroge, explained to the present writer the need for introducing Marrian at length. Njoroge had six weeks previously been talking about *Uhuru* but now he had to explain why the people there should vote for a European. Indeed on this occasion the Kikuyu women shouted such remarks as 'When I wrap my blanket round me I don't want a bug inside', and 'a dog can't get on with a rat'. In British terms here was the employer seeking votes from the workers, a new experience in Kenya and complicated by the racial question. When it came to questions there was natural pressure over Kenyatta and over land; on neither of these could Marrian succeed in satisfying his audience—the meeting was taking place on that very fringe of the Kikuyu reserve which had long been under claim. Curiously more significant of the lack of understanding was the matter of the British military base being constructed at Kahawa, a few miles down the road. Marrian, like all other European candidates, supported this but African nationalism seeks a neutralist position in the Cold War. Here, as in other cases, Njoroge, after translating Marrian's answers added his own comments, which may be summarized as: 'leave that to us after *Uhuru*'. As Njoroge commented privately: 'Mr. Marrian is too blunt in his answers; he is not a good politician.' Certainly he was not able to rouse the enthusiasm of the crowd with his speech, but this would be difficult through a translator. The atmosphere of an African meeting came rather in response to Njoroge, in the *Uhuru* shouts and the ululations of the Kikuyu women, shrilling their support of particular points. (See plate 2.)

In Nairobi Suburban Alexander, the N.K.P. candidate, made more progress, speaking to Africans in Swahili, with, to support him, Mboya and other KANU personalities. Under the pressure of the constant questions Alexander stated that if the law were changed by an independent African Government so that Kenyatta could become a member of Legislative Council and then Chief Minister, his attitude to Kenyatta would depend on his policies and the extent to which he was accepted by people of all communities. African supporters soon glossed this into an open readiness to serve under Kenyatta. O'Beirne, the Coalition candidate, picked this up and attacked N.K.P. candidates as renouncing their views and convictions to get African support; they were 'captive men', said the Coalition.

O'Beirne and other Coalition speakers found it hard indeed to speak to Africans. Such audiences were heard coming away from O'Beirne's meetings shouting angrily. Another Coalition candidate, Megson, once opened a sentence to a crowd of African workers from a large Nairobi hospital with: 'You are all hospital boys', whereupon he was drowned by shouts of 'We are men, not boys.' His appeal for trust in Cavendish-Bentinck and the Coalition candidates as people the Europeans trusted was greeted with cries of 'We can't', and when he expressed his refusal to serve in a Government under Kenyatta a quarter of the audience walked out.

A small side-light on African reaction was seen in Kericho. There, before the primaries were over, the N.K.P. candidate was being greeted by KANU supporters with cries of 'Uhuru na Mrs. Shaw'. Then there was some hesitation before both the African parties finally decided to support her. The delay was said to be explicable largely in terms of African dislike of voting for a woman; certainly there was no African woman candidate before the stage of the National Seats.

During her campaign Mrs. Shaw drew public attention to a report in a Swahili newspaper that some Africans in the district were being told by their European employers for whom they should vote, and hoped that any such incidents would be reported to the authorities. Such reports were current also in the Rift Valley. Speaking on Blundell's behalf Gichuru told one African audience that he had heard that some farmers were collecting the registration cards of their workers so that they would be unable to vote; if this was so, they should report to the police. Gichuru made the point also that the ballot was secret: anyone warned that he would lose his job for voting for Blundell could and should ignore it.

The Rift Valley campaign provided strange contrasts, while Blundell was vigorously addressing in Swahili large and

enthusiastic crowds, Cavendish-Bentinck, who, after an initial
hesitation, found he had to meet Africans, went mainly to
small gatherings arranged for him by farmer supporters and
spoke only through an interpreter. Blundell had the ability,
after his speeches, of jumping down into the crowd to mingle
and chat with them. After one meeting an African walked up
and, amid cheers, presented Blundell with a 2 ft. 9 in. high
model of a giraffe, his symbol. Did this peaceful animal help
as an emblem? Certainly Cavendish-Bentinck gained no assistance from drawing a hippopotamus with the hide-whip
associations of *kiboko*.   (See plate 1B.)

The nature of African support that the two European leaders
received was interesting. The unimportant Kenya African
Liberal Party, which had been unable to put up candidates
for any open seats when the Coalition refused to find the
money for their deposits, still proclaimed its support for
Cavendish-Bentinck. A Baluhya Political Union meeting at
Gilgil unanimously resolved not to vote for him after their
president, Amalemba, had asked: 'How shall we work with a
man who refused to serve the country because Africans had
attained a majority power in the Legislative Council?' Most
interesting, though, was the effect of the split in KANU.
Whilst Blundell had the Union's official support, Odinga threw
his men into the fray on behalf of Cavendish-Bentinck for whom
he also wrote a letter of appeal which was printed and circulated
by the Coalition despite its conclusion: 'Yours in the struggle—
Kenyatta na Uhuru.' Perhaps one of these strange allies in the
Rift Valley had recalled Churchill's words on the entry of
Russia into the war!

At least one of the Coalition's supporters was deeply perturbed at what was happening. After the election Major Venn
Fey, a Kikuyu-speaker, described in a long letter to the *Kenya
Weekly News* a Coalition meeting where KANU's organizing
secretary for the Rift Valley spoke in Kikuyu with the Coalition's prior authorization. Clearly they had not checked on his
credentials. Fey recorded that the District Commissioner at
Naivasha had previously refused the individual concerned a
licence to speak because of 'his immoderate utterances'; now,
on a Coalition platform, he was taking the opportunity to preach
social disunity. All Europeans, he said, were bitter enemies

and must be driven from Kenya; both Blundell and Cavendish-Bentinck were enemies of the Africans; they were both leopards who had entered the flock of sheep; their only difference was that the former wore a sheep skin and was therefore possibly more dangerous than the latter who stuck to his spots and could thus be more easily destroyed when the time came. The acceptance of such support showed now the weakness of the Coalition in failing to have more than amateurish organization. Newspapers commented in the campaign that few Europeans understood Asian and African politics. The Coalition showed its ignorance in a remarkable degree; it had entered into a place of very deep waters.

The only people who were able to express surprise at the Coalition's overwhelming defeat in the common roll election were Coalition members. Some tried to blame this on intimidation by the African parties. In so doing they only showed their ignorance of African feeling. The Coalition had utterly failed to make any real contact with African opinion. Africans believed—with Amalemba and Muliro as they referred back to the moment of Sir Ferdinand's resignation—that this was a European party which had not, and could not, come to terms with the revolution in Kenya.

As in the primary elections, the voting was heavy and, as then, the highest poll was in the Rift Valley: 89·4%. There, despite Odinga's curious support and that of a few other Africans, Cavendish-Bentinck could only increase the numbers recorded in his favour by 506: to 2,051. Blundell gathered nearly ten times as many votes: 20,009. In the two other rural seats the story of Coalition candidates was the same: Oates in Kericho going from 460 to 643 and Markham in Central Rural from 1,185 to 1,592 where he scored less than one-tenth of the votes. One other Coalition member was elected: Salter, who managed to top the poll in Nairobi West, being followed there by Howard-Williams. On polling day the latter's cars brought in a steady stream of African voters. Bompas explained that he had held no campaign meetings at the common roll stage since he believed that people were 'so bored with them'. Perhaps this was the fulfilment of a pledge in October to the European district association in Kiambu that he would withdraw if he failed to obtain 40% in the primary election. In Nairobi South-

West it had seemed possible that Megson might win unless his
opponent pulled in almost every single African voter. Certainly
Havelock carried out a most energetic personal canvass after
the primary. He succeeded in securing an increase of 1,041
from a possible 1,390. Megson was most noisy in his accusations
of intimidation in this constituency. Apparently he did not
know, or did not desire to know, that it is normal election
practice for candidates' agents to endeavour to record who have
voted so that others may be fetched before the poll closes. This
was N.K.P. practice throughout the primaries and the common
roll election but most Coalition candidates did not think to
make such arrangements.

When all was over Blundell almost went into hiding. He was
receiving abusive letters and dared not visit certain of the leading European clubs. In the main Club of the Rift Valley one
of his known supporters was actually assaulted. This had been
the bitterest election in Kenya's history. Perhaps this was to
be expected. The European settlers knew that it portended the
coming of the end of their way of life. In it they were losing
political power. They believed they could trust neither the
African leaders nor Blundell who, with his party, had tried to
be the bridge between the communities and into the future.
Within a fortnight of the election results the *Sunday Post* of
Nairobi printed a front page banner headline: 'Londiani for
sale' (thirty-seven European farms covering 40,000 acres).
Colonel Gretton Foster, whose remarks had led to the egg-
throwing incident at Londiani a few weeks before, was the
leader in this, declaring 'The farmers involved see no sign of
good will on the part of the Africans and have no confidence
in the future.' A few days later, as if to round off the European
farming story in Kenya, it was announced that Colonel Grogan,
the oldest surviving European leader, present from the beginning and long a strong opponent of Asians, had sold 120,000
acres to Asians for a 'substantial sum' and had sent the money
to Britain. He believed that Kenya was 'no place for his
family'; they, including his three great-grandchildren, would
probably go to Britain in 'dribs and drabs', though he, at the
age of 86, would just stay 'and watch the folly'.

Asian Seats

The campaigns for the Asian non-Muslim seats began in a similar way to that among the Europeans. Naturally the same background appertained: the events of the Congo and the attacks of African leaders in Kenya upon the immigrant communities, made with very specific reference to the Asians. As the months went on, and as approaches by Asians to the African leaders were rebuffed, many in the community considered it necessary for the Asians, too, to seek to build up defences against the future.

In this they were opposed by a party which had developed early in 1960. In its formation the leadership was taken by Chanan Singh, a former Member of Legislative Council defeated in 1956. Returning from a visit to India at the end of December 1959, he held a meeting at Mombasa and obtained 31 signatures to a draft statement. These men were afraid particularly that the Asians would not fully support at Lancaster House the old principle of the Indians in Kenya, the common roll electorate, and in this they were proved right. At first they sought to press their ideas by working as a group inside the Kenya Indian Congress, but in February 1960 decided to come out into the open as an organization. Chanan Singh announced the formation of the Kenya Freedom Party (I.C.F.P.) under his presidency and appealed for members of all races and communities to join them. He was able to develop his ideas in editorials of the *Colonial Times* which thus became the mouthpiece of the new party. However, it had made little impact by the time the Kenya Indian Congress met at the end of the first week of October.

The Congress, the central organization of the Asian Non-Muslim community, resembles in its structure the European Convention of Associations, being composed of delegates from the local Indian associations across the Colony. Formed in 1914, it was originally the voice of all the Asians in Kenya but, with the events of 1947 in the Indian sub-continent, the Muslims broke away. At its formal biennial meetings, normally held around Christmas, the important feature is the speech of its newly chosen President. In 1960, on account of the coming elections, the meeting was advanced to early October and the president was a young and forceful Nairobi barrister, Satish

Gautama. His speech continued the tradition of the president surveying in a 'historical retrospect' the story of the Indians in Kenya since their beginnings. From this historical outlook of the community arose a main theme of Indian speeches during the election: that the Indians had fought the European settlers from the beginning, particularly over the Highlands and for electoral rights, that by these actions they had prevented in 1923 the Colony going the way of Southern Rhodesia and South Africa into *apartheid* and European domination. Whilst there was much truth in this, Gautama also suggested that Harry Thuku, in the beginnings of African nationalism in Kenya in 1921, obtained his inspiration from India and Gandhi through the local Indians. In some of these arguments Gautama was supported before the Congress by Muliro of KADU who reiterated his belief in Kenya for 'Kenyans' but said he had been 'hounded all over the country' for saying this. The question remained how Africans would react to these Asian approaches. Did they not convey something of a patronizing touch? Can a true nationalist allow anything to an outsider? 'Sinn Fein', 'ourselves alone', must be the motto of the nationalist.

Congress resolutions called for the release of Kenyatta and of Makhan Singh, the Sikh Communist Trade Union leader who had been detained even longer, since 1950. On the constitution the Congress declared its support for the African demand for independence and a willingness to renounce 'racial reservations and representations', being satisfied with individual human rights safeguarded by an independent judiciary. To implement their policy on this occasion the Congress decided to sponsor candidates for the elections, the candidates to be chosen by an Elections Committee 'under an independent and impartial chairman'.

On this a split immediately occurred. Eighteen of the thirty-four delegates from the Mombasa Indian Association walked out. They saw that, if the choice of candidates were made centrally, Pandya, the Mombasa sitting member, was likely to receive the Congress endorsement. Their leader, a young lawyer, I. T. Inamdar, promptly announced his own candidature. Inamdar said—and here the parallel with the Convention of Associations the week before was close—that the Congress had always been 'a forum of opinion as distinct from a political party' and that sponsoring of candidates would lead to 'further dismemberment of the Indian community'. Certainly Congress sponsorship in the past had led to such unhappy divisions that for a while the organization had been able to do no more than give 'blanket endorsements' to all Indian candidates. However, Gautama was determined not to leave the matter there. He called a special Congress meeting in Mombasa—which was constitutionally questionable since such a meeting should have been organized by the local Indian Association—and announced that he had not become president for the Congress to go to sleep: Congress had now a clear-cut and well-defined policy, it was incumbent on the community to play a positive role in the country's political life. The K.F.P. subsequently questioned whether the Congress, being a communal organization, ought to sponsor candidates in the new circumstances of a common roll election. Inamdar, who had been associated in the formation of the K.F.P., had to deny rumours that the Mombasa 'rebels' were planning to form a 'branch' of that party; he was to stand as an independent.

At the end of October the K.F.P. issued its policy statement, declaring its objective that Kenya should be a society treating all persons as individuals and 'not as members of a race'; there should be a common roll electorate with universal adult suffrage, in which respects the party proclaimed its disappointment with Lancaster House. On the day before this statement was issued Mboya appeared at a K.F.P. meeting. He discussed the fears of Asian and African civil servants, saying particularly that the appointment of Gavaghan as localization and training officer was 'a wrong move' since he was regarded as the spokesman of the European civil servants. Were there points to draw the Asians and Africans together again, points on which the K.F.P. might well build a support in the Asian community? Mboya called for the minority races to express their confidence in the African leaders, saying they were 'fully appreciative of the interests of everybody'. However, there was now a difference. Previously Asians and Africans had drawn together against European dominance. A fortnight later Gichuru's remarks that Europeans and Asians would 'soon have to kneel' showed where future power lay and destroyed much Asian confidence, especially as Gichuru went on to make a forceful attack on Asian traders and their methods. Old accusations were renewed of unfair practices, that the Asians were preventing the development of African traders. K. P. Shah, the secretary of the K.F.P., announced that, as a supporter of African nationalism, he would write personally to Gichuru on the matter. Meanwhile, Gautama was denouncing the K.F.P. as a collection of 'rebels and upstarts' who were willing to sell out the interests of Asians and Europeans to get into the Legislative Council, whilst their programme was no different from that of the Congress.

Early in December the Congress published an advertisement inviting applications from candidates who wished to stand on behalf of the Congress. They were asked to appear before a committee of forty-one, being the Standing Committee of the Congress and representatives from each of the constituencies. The committee pledged themselves not to work against chosen candidates and a similar pledge was demanded from those who appeared before it, as also that they would be bound by Congress decisions. Apart from Pandya's name, the only widely expected nomination to emerge from the committee was that of C. B. Madan, the non-Muslim Asian minister, for Nairobi Central. As a result there was much talk of 'horse-trading' between certain 'blocks' in the committee, that some people involved had paid the fares of the more distant members to come to vote. J. S. Patel certainly turned out to be a weak candidate: he was a poor speaker and he, a Gujerati Hindu, was set for Nairobi South where the predominant vote was Sikh. Of the two Sikhs who considered applying for a Congress 'ticket', Mota Singh, a member of the Congress Standing Committee, withdrew for the other and when the latter was not chosen, considered himself free to stand as an independent in Nairobi South. For Kisumu the committee chose D. B. Kohli, a Brahmin, and for the two-member seat of Nairobi Central put Jamidar, a sitting member, with Madan.

Travadi, another sitting member, had already made it plain that he, too, would stand for Nairobi Central, though as an independent, and he did not apply for a Congress 'ticket'. He was expected, as a Brahmin known for his religious activities, to appeal to a certain pious vote, especially among the women. Only the day before nomination was it announced that Madan was standing down 'for personal reasons'—rumour, subsequently confirmed, had it that he was to be appointed the first non-European judge in Kenya. The Congress then threw this place open to their rejected candidates. Two, Dr. Sandhu, the Sikh for whom Mota Singh had stood down, and R. B. Bhandari handed in nomination papers, but the latter was rejected on the ground that his seconder, a lawyer member of the K.F.P., had already signed another nomination paper and the law only allowed a voter to exercise one choice. The weakness of the K.F.P. as a party was well shown by the fact that their candidates, K. P. Shah (Nairobi Central), Chanan Singh (Nairobi South) and R. P. Joshi (Kisumu) stood as independents, as did their one Muslim connection, S. K. Anjarwalla in Mombasa.

For the Asian Muslim seats it was widely rumoured that there was an arrangement between three major Muslim communities to divide out the three seats: thus the Muslim minister, I. E. Nathoo, an Ismaili for Kisumu, Zafrud Deen, a sitting member and Sunni, for Nairobi North-East and Anjarwalla of a leading Bohra family for Mombasa. If there was such an arrangement, it broke down in Kisumu where, the day after he had signed Nathoo's nomination paper as his proposer, C. K. Dean, a Sunni, announced his own candidature. The Muslim League and the Ismailia Reform League both formally announced that they were not sponsoring candidates, but Zafrud Deen was president of the former and Nathoo was a leading Ismaili. There was also a feeling in the Muslim communities that younger men might find it easier to work with Africans and this formed something of the basis of the two other candidates in Nairobi North-East: Shaikh Amin and Ahmed Ali.

However much leaders may proclaim that it must and should end, all Asian elections in Kenya in the past—and this was no exception—have been dominated by communalism. The first document noticed on many an Asian candidate's desk, and the first subject of conversation with the agent of any candidate, was the breakdown of the voters' roll by communities. Muslim and non-Muslim candidates alike knew that their first task was to seek and obtain support from the leaders of the various groups: Patels, Shahs, Punjabi Hindus, Sikhs, Goans, etc. on the non-Muslim side, with, on the Muslim, Sunnis, Ismailis, Bohras, Menons, Ithnasharis, etc. It always remained remarkable

how Asian candidates carried the exact figures of voters of
each community in their head so that they could, often most
accurately, foretell the result.[2] The particularly close inter-
locking of communities and constituencies in Mombasa
increased this peculiarity of the situation there so that consideration of those seats has been reserved for the last section of this
chapter. The communal negotiation for votes was described
by one Asian writer in the *Daily Nation* under the heading 'the
same sickening procedure all over again'; he said there was
never a mention of policies and of the grave situation facing
the country, the flight of money and the growing unemployment.

Nevertheless, Asian politicians did seek to discuss these and
other issues in their meetings. In the non-Muslim constituencies
the Congress reputation was at stake through its nomination of
candidates. Gautama, its president, proved to be a forceful
speaker, perhaps better than any of the non-Muslim candidates.
He stumped the constituencies supported by his wife seeking the
women's vote. Gautama's main theme was the Indian struggle
against the Europeans in Kenya as redounding to the benefit
of all. The Congress claimed that its leaders had developed
close relationships with African leaders over the past years, and
through these a community of interests invaluable for the future.
They would support the African leaders and the appointment
of a Chief Minister; they wanted a Committee to be chosen in
the Legislative Council immediately after the election to formu-
late recommendations towards 'a constitution based on
independence'.

At nomination, K. P. Shah made the interesting suggestion
that the Indian community, to show its complete faith in the
common roll, should boycott the primaries. Unfortunately it
was not clear how the idea could have worked within the framework of the constitution. The Congress dismissed it as impracticable and, as the campaign began, Congress candidates were
soon attacking Shah and his K.F.P. friends as 'boot-lickers'
around the African leaders. Travadi gave the impression to
some observers of 'anything the African nationalists can shout,

[2]The as yet unpublished *Social Survey of Mombasa* makes the same comment on the
1956 elections. Those who knew the town well forecast then the results of those
elections with an often remarkable accuracy in the matter of figures.

I can shout louder'. In many matters the non-Muslim candidates were at one. Thus in the key issue of the election all three in Nairobi South agreed at a joint meeting that Kenyatta should be released immediately. The real question was, as so often in Kenya, which candidate commanded most personal confidence. Among Asians communal affiliations were likely to be a deciding factor in answering this.

In Nairobi Central the lowest percentage poll of the primaries was recorded: 54·92%. One commentator estimated in explanation that a fifth of the registered voters had by then left for India because of unemployment or uncertainty about Kenya's future. All the candidates received the necessary 25%, the way being led by the two Congress candidates, followed by K. P. Shah. Nairobi South showed more interest, concentrating on the choice between the two Sikhs: in a 70·66% poll Mota Singh obtained 47·88% followed by Chanan Singh (38·99%). More interest again was aroused at Kisumu (84·05% poll) where the independent Joshi (54·49%) just beat Kohli (51·9%). Trailing behind came the only Asian candidate to lose his deposit through failing to obtain 25%: Bhagat Singh Biant. Whilst he was generally regarded as a weak candidate—he had previously lost Asian elections for Legislative Council in both Mombasa and Nairobi—he did not improve his chances among the non-Muslim electorate by his close identification with African politicians. He was known as friend of Odinga, at whose meetings he had spoken; like an African leader, he carried a fly-whisk everywhere and wore a Kenyatta badge, having obtained one of the rare metal ones made in Czechoslovakia until the Government banned their import.

At the common roll election the Africans were instructed by KANU to vote for the three non-Muslims with K.F.P. leanings. Thus K. P. Shah topped the poll in Nairobi Central, displacing Sandhu, one of the Congress candidates. In Nairobi South Chanan Singh came up to the most exciting finish of the election, one vote less than the victorious Mota Singh. On this the defeated candidate claimed that certain of his votes had been improperly rejected by the Returning Officer and that personation had occurred through the use of the voters' cards of people who had left for India. This in Asian elections—for it was claimed that it occurred elsewhere—appears to be the

modern equivalent of polling dead men in Disraeli's *Coningsby*
(Book 5, Chapter 4), and the answer, now as then, is: 'no doubt
we shall be able to have a good petition.' Certainly it was so
for Chanan Singh for in May the Supreme Court, after examining a number of the ballot papers, found in his favour on both
counts and declared him elected with a majority of three.

Perhaps the most extraordinary common roll result occurred
in Kisumu where the primary non-Muslim result was reversed
in favour of Kohli, despite the fact that Joshi was the candidate
favoured by KANU and was, therefore, expected to increase
the favour already shown by his own community into a walk-
over. However, the Congress took here most hardly its defeat
in the primaries and concentrated on the seat, sending up
leading figures to campaign. They appear to have succeeded
for two main reasons. They convinced a large number of Asians
that Joshi had followed Biant in completely identifying himself
with the Africans so that it was better to switch their votes.
Just before the final poll a letter circulated, allegedly written
by Joshi, saying that he would follow the KANU line in all
things. Besides this, a curious provision at Kisumu told heavily
against him. At the common roll stage the two Kisumu seats,
non-Muslim and Muslim, were thrown together to become
one two-member constituency so voters were free to choose
either the Muslim or the non-Muslim. Apparently the Sikh
vote, limited to Joshi in the non-Muslim primary, switched,
on the instructions of a local leader, to the Muslim Nathoo
on the second stage, and this proved fatal to Joshi.

This Sikh vote was crucial also to Nathoo who won in one
of the most interesting of the reserved seat contests. At the
primary stage Nathoo felt confident enough to stay away
on a visit to Pakistan, arriving only six days before the poll,
and he received 67·52% against Dean's 36·22%. Then the fun
began. Nathoo, campaigning under the slogan, 'The Man who
delivered the goods at Lancaster House', was confident of
African support. This KANU's head office, through the mouth
of Mboya, was prepared to give but the unfortunate Nathoo
was then caught in the split of KANU and its organizational
defects. The local branch decided to make its own choice and its
committee opted for Dean, a factor in this decision being that
the committee had a number of African Muslims who preferred

Dean's Sunni orthodoxy to Nathoo's Ismaili background. Anyway, Odinga endorsed the choice in a public meeting. Then, on the eve of the poll, a letter was put out in Kisumu purporting to come from Kenyatta himself. Addressed to Odinga, who, however, denied receiving it and described it as 'a frame-up', this stated that the dentist who had recently visited Lodwar to pull out all Kenyatta's teeth was Nathoo's brother and that he (Kenyatta) would be 'very grateful' if Odinga and his followers would support Nathoo who was 'on our side'. After the election Kenyatta denied writing any such letters but this may have had some last-minute effect on African voters. In any case, Nathoo was returned with a majority of 154.

In absolute contrast, the Muslim seat of Nairobi North-East hit the headlines at no stage of the election. Although some thought that one of the younger candidates might develop a strong challenge to the established Zafrud Deen, this never really materialized. At the common roll there seemed a possibility that the social worker, Ahmed Ali, might pull up through his contacts with the large non-Muslim side of the electorate and from African voters through his official backing by KANU. However, the leeway proved too great and Zafrud Deen won by 139 votes in a 77·6% poll. One factor in protecting the winner may well have been an agreement to provide Muslim votes in Nairobi South for Mota Singh in exchange for Sikh votes here.

The Protectorate and Mombasa Seats

The acerbities of up-country politics do not normally reach down to inflame political passions at the Coast, something which has been true in the past of all communities. Basking in an indolent tropical atmosphere, Mombasa is 300 miles from up-country storms and, as a provincial capital, often develops its own and different topics of political concern. Whilst in this election no candidate, even at the Coast, could avoid the name of Kenyatta, the reserved seats there had one other problem to bind them together: the Coastal Strip, as the Kenya Protectorate, leased from Zanzibar by the Agreement of 1895, is colloquially known. Its future had been raised at Lancaster House, whilst its dimensions, apart from Mombasa itself, were indicated by the establishment of the Protectorate constituency as an Arab reserved seat. In the year following Lancaster House the coastal Arabs became more and more interested in their position under the Treaty, sending delegations, sometimes accompanied by a European legal adviser, to Zanzibar to interview the Sultan and seek support from the three political parties there. The Arabs and the Europeans in Mombasa took up the idea, first propounded by the Federal Independence Party, of 'coastal autonomy' to make this the slogan of the campaign in their reserved seats; through this they affected the discussion at political meetings of all communities in Mombasa. The attraction was that of an inverted Shangri-la, detached from the evils of Kenya: its racial politics, unemployment, taxation and the uncertainties of *Uhuru*.

Just before Christmas the three prospective European candidates for Mombasa East, Usher, the sitting member, Cleasby, a lawyer, and Captain Hamley, R.N., a former Port Manager. addressed a joint meeting. All were agreed on the objective of coastal autonomy, which Usher regarded 'as perfectly feasible', whilst the blunt Captain Hamley added: 'I'd be daft not to support it'. Before nomination day Usher, who had parted from the N.K.P. after Lancaster House, decided to withdraw also from this campaign; he then remarked that there was no major point of disagreement between the Mombasa European candidates. This made the campaign somewhat difficult. The voters had little choice except, as so often in Kenya politics, between personalities: 'honest Jack', the bluff Hornblower character, or the able lawyer who might put the case clearly in Nairobi. However, nearer polling day Hamley began to have doubts about the wisdom of being too open on the issue: it might have been better to support the Arabs from behind, and also it might lead to trouble with the Africans—it would not be popular in Legislative Council, he said (and here he spoke as a former Nominated Member) to advocate 'tearing a strip off Kenya'. Such changing is never wise in a politician in the last days of a campaign. The voters proved clear in their choice: 88% for Cleasby and only 15% for his unfortunate opponent, the second lowest primary percentage.

Should Cleasby then have, from his strong European base, led a multi-racial campaign for this 'geographical pocket having every attribute of a nation', as he described the Protectorate?

Instead, he left for England a fortnight after the primary poll on some legal business. Doubtless, he went also with the intention of seeing, as the newly elected member, the authorities in England and representing to them the coastal case, to make the point of his election meetings that an autonomous strip would be a better protection for a Mombasa naval base than if the Protectorate were submerged in an independent Kenya.

The main interest of the issue thus focussed necessarily on the Arab constituencies. In Mombasa Central a most interesting campaign developed. Arab elections in the past have been dull affairs: only since 1952 has there been any tradition that they might be contested. There was some dissatisfaction in the community that the sitting member, Sheikh Mahfood Mackawi, had neglected his constituents and was too much of a traditionalist. He was challenged in this by a young and forceful candidate: Abdilahi Nassir. He took advantage of the fact that this was the first time Arab women had had the vote, made much of Mackawi's opposition to this, and appealed to the first 300 Arab women registered voters by having one, the secretary of the Arab Women's Cultural Association, sign his nomination papers.

But the nub of the campaign centred on the relations with up-country Africans. As organizing secretary of the Mombasa Freedom Convention Party, Nassir had participated in the formation of African politics after Lancaster House, attending the Kiambu conferences. He believed that KADU had leanings towards Israel and he joined KANU from which he resigned only in December. His comment was that, like Jinnah in the Indian Congress, he felt he was being double-crossed: he had become convinced of 'the nefarious designs of up-country Africans', and he spoke at meetings of 'Luo/Kikuyu Imperialism'. At Mombasa he had founded a Coast Employment Bureau for Coast people and demanded not 'localization' but 'coastalization' of the Civil Service; for this more educational provision for Coast people—another of his campaign planks— was necessary. His own educational and oratorical ability, greater than that of Mackawi, told as the campaign went on, particularly at the second stage when he had to approach the non-Arab voters. By then, the coastal autonomy issue had sharpened.   Just before the primary poll, Mboya spoke in

Mombasa; to this Nassir replied 'Mr. Mboya is an up-country African. He has nothing to do with our country'; 'we are ready at any time to sacrifice our lives in defending our country's sovereignty—i.e. Mwambao' (the strip). A month later, to fierce Arabic cries of 'Umma Hai' ('the community is alive') he pronounced that the Arabs would 'never accept domination'. Nassir was able to take this strong line since there were only some 350 African up-country voters registered in his constituency. The support Mackawi was receiving from KANU was of little value. His early and open support of the release of Kenyatta did not concern the Mombasa electorate. Nassir saw that it was more important to appeal to the Asian groups who provided over 2,100 of the total electorate of 4,858.

Were the Asians fence-sitting on the issue of the Coastal Strip as Bassadiq, a Protectorate candidate, claimed? This remark was made after a noisy meeting at the beginning of the campaign in the Mombasa non-Muslim seat when Gautama of the Congress spoke on behalf of Pandya. In the packed meeting both were harried on this question. They both tried to take refuge in saying that the Congress had not discussed the matter, and that they would be bound by Congress decisions. Pandya's opponent, Inamdar, was clear in his manifesto that the strip was 'an integral part of Kenya'. For this and other reasons, Inamdar received KANU support, though he insisted that he had given no written pledge to that party. Although in this constituency again the African vote was small, some observers believed that the Asian communities would be so narrowly divided that the African vote might well be decisive. Certainly Pandya was not popular with KANU, being denounced by them for his actions at Lancaster House over the common roll, but he did receive KADU support. At the final stage he defeated Inamdar by 84 in 3,420 votes, in an 88·2% poll of cheering crowds with KANU and KADU vans dashing to and fro with singers and voters.

It might have been thought that the two young lawyers who contested the Muslim reserved seat would have been most careful in what they said about the Coastal Strip. Their electorate of 8,561 contained some 1,600 African voters, though according to one candidate 450 of these were Muslims and would be likely to support the idea of coastal autonomy. On the other side, the trading connections of many Asian Muslims, and links with Zanzibar, might make them favourable to coastal autonomy. Certainly Anjarwalla approached the issue gingerly. He commented that it had been specifically excluded from the Lancaster House deliberations and that, when it was later discussed, he would refer it to the electorate to ascertain their views. He thought that emotions aroused on the issue might delay the country's progress. He was not going to jeopardize his chances with the African vote but his opponent, K. A. Kasmani, was more rash. Speaking three days before the primary poll, he was the first Asian candidate to come out openly for coastal autonomy, believing it 'feasible' and 'practicable' in an East African federation, with, he hoped, Mombasa as its capital—if not, then the Coast could federate with Kenya in 'a greater Kenya'. If this was playing for Asian support, Kasmani failed in this last desperate throw, obtaining only 32 % against Anjarwalla's 70 %.

Kasmani knew he had an uphill fight against a powerful opponent whose father was a leading figure in the important Bohra community. After the primary an interesting meeting was held. Four leaders, two from each of the candidates' communities, Bohra and Menon, met and tried to persuade one of them to stand down and not contest the final poll. In a subsequent statement the leaders declared that elections 'create bad blood and result in dissensions and disunity among the various sections of the community' and that both candidates had 'solemnly and sincerely' agreed to accept their 'Award'. Not unnaturally, in view of the primary result, they asked Kasmani to withdraw but he then refused, telling a Mombasa meeting that one of the judges was a partner of Anjarwalla and that there were illegal financial considerations involved in the 'Award'—anyway, 'the tribunal had not considered each candidate's merit and ability as originally proposed'. In these circumstances election fever increased, KANU supporting Anjarwalla and KADU Kasmani. Only later did the latter discover the views Kasmani held on the Coastal Strip and a few days before the final poll withdraw their support—apparently KADU's local people had not been reading their local newspapers! Nevertheless, the main interest of this election, as in so many of the Asian seats, remained the search for support from

the various Asian communities. The only difference from the
old system was that support had now to be sought first among
the Asian Muslim or non-Muslim groups and then, at the
second stage, among the opposite set of groups, thus doubling
the negotiations. In the proximity of Mombasa's constituencies
it was not unexpected that some trading of votes went on.
In the end, in the two constituencies, Muslim and non-Muslim,
the winners were those who had the strongest traditional support in their own communities.

It remained to see how the Arab candidates would fit into
this system. It was very striking on the final day of the polling
for the Arab reserved seat that, in the tents outside the polling-
station, Nassir had representatives of all the main Asian Muslim
and non-Muslim communities, whereas Mackawi could muster,
apart from one KANU agent, nobody but Arabs. Mackawi had
failed to move out from his own community and make the
necessary contacts with the leaders of the other half of the
electorate, predominantly Asian. It thus came as no surprise
that he should be defeated by Nassir by over 1,000 votes. The
out and out Arab supporter of coastal autonomy and no truck
with up-country Africans had been returned with the strong
support of the Asian communities of Mombasa.

There remained the other Arab reserved seat: the Protectorate. There one of the candidates, Ali Abdulla Shikely, stood
in the name of the Coast People's Party and called on people
to vote for policy not personality, as in the past. In fact, there
was no difference between the policies of the two candidates.
Bassadiq was no less in favour of Coast autonomy than this
curious C.P.P. which had, since its formation after Lancaster
House, made no real progress outside Mombasa or the Arab
community. Bassadiq made much of his appeal to the northern
end of the constituency, in his home town of Mambrui and in
Malindi, ancient rival of Mombasa, playing on the feeling that
at last they had a candidate not produced by Mombasa. Since
the Arab voting strength lay in the north he managed to gain
66·5% at the primary to 34·5% for Shikely. The real interest
lay in the common roll result. Neither of the candidates made
any appeal with coastal autonomy to the African majority.
The week before the final poll first Ngala for KADU and then,
two days later, the local KANU leaders, called on Africans to

boycott the election. As a result only 14% of the electorate polled. Apart from the Arabs who came again, only about another 1,250 voters appeared: some few Europeans, besides Swahilis or Muslim Africans. The Protectorate vote had developed into a striking demonstration of African rural feeling with regard to coastal autonomy. The Arabs, like the Coalition, had failed to contact the African voter and often, particularly with the Giriama, land troubles were at the basis of the antagonism. The effect of the election seemed likely to be an increased tension in Arab-African relations.

CHAPTER V

THE OPEN SEATS

ISSUES

In a real sense there was no national campaign for the open seats. No colony-wide public debate on issues took place, although both national African parties held a large number of meetings and each issued comprehensive manifestoes. Their respective policies, although differing in detail, language and emphasis, were too similar for any substantial debate. What commanded attention was the image each party presented to the electorate, but even this was largely offset by the fact that there were few constituencies where the parties clashed.

KANU produced its policy manifesto first, on 18th November. On the following Sunday KANU held a mass rally at Thika, a township thirty miles from Nairobi, situated between the lands of the Kamba and the Kikuyu. In one of the most spectacular meetings of the election, amidst roars of '*Uhuru*' from a crowd of over 40,000, the party's *Manifesto for Independence and Freedom* was approved by acclamation. As far as KANU was concerned the release of Kenyatta from restriction transcended all other issues. Mboya told the meeting that if Kenyatta was not released no African would join the next Government after the election. In their manifesto they reaffirmed that Kenyatta would be the head of the first KANU government. The 'release Kenyatta' theme was to dominate all other considerations of national significance in the election.

KADU's main election rally took place a month later, at Eldoret, on the day their policy statement was published, 18th December. The contrast in the two meetings was significant. Here there were only some 5,000 supporters, to whom the major party leaders outlined the main features of their policy for establishing an independent but democratic Kenya. But these leaders were fundamentally on the defensive, feeling compelled to answer the attacks made on them by KANU's leadership. They could not ignore the Kenyatta issue, but clearly it had less meaning to them than to a party whose roots were in

KAU. While they sought the release of Kenyatta and of other detainees, they separated this from consideration of his future position. Indeed, at an earlier meeting, KADU's political adviser, Towett, spoke strongly against what appeared to him to be the deification of Kenyatta.

Though the policy statements were mainly devoted to economic and social reconstruction and the establishment of a welfare state under a mixed economy, KANU's was the more dynamic. It rang with a determination to break through the barriers of backwardness and to create a new society. Modern technology would be indispensable in this massive endeavour, but the goal would not be an imitation of the West. It would be a synthesis of the best in Western civilization and African culture. In demanding immediate independence, the manifesto maintained that all must be prepared for sacrifice. Unity was vital; one united movement was essential. KANU was the vanguard and would take steps to bring unity between all splinter groups. Non-Africans were welcomed to identify themselves with the struggle for freedom, but KANU would oppose any effort to impede the rapid achievement of independence. KADU, on the other hand, did not regard itself as an unrestrained instrument for rapid political and social change by exploiting all latent sources of power. Though it uncompromisingly pledged itself to struggle for an independent democratic Kenya nation 'now', it acknowledged as well irrevocable and inherent human rights as the basis of every society, and promised to introduce legislation guaranteeing the normal freedoms enjoyed in all democratic countries. The *Daily Nation* commented that this manifesto reflected 'The decent, honest, Christian views of the party's two main leaders, Mr. Ronald Ngala and Mr. Masinde Muliro'.

Each of the statements sought rapid industrialization, to be accompanied by intense efforts to accelerate African agricultural development. They called for greater opportunities in African employment, higher living standards, and increased educational facilities. KADU advocated eight years compulsory free education in place of the seven suggested by KANU. On the key issue of land, both recognized the need for reform. KANU stressed the vital necessity of a solution to the squatter problem in the Highlands, and a resettlement programme for

Africans, saying, however, that this would not be carried out at the cost of a high standard of agriculture. The land policies were written in general terms; neither party wished to make precise statements before achieving power. Although KADU said nothing about compensation for alienated land, it did promise compensation and recourse to the courts in the event of expropriation of property or nationalization 'in the public weal'. KANU argued that any promises to individuals or groups on land made by Britain were the responsibility of the British Government—their one point of agreement with the Coalition.

Both KANU and KADU called for the abolition of the provincial administration and the replacement of provincial and district commissioners by a democratic system of local government; for the rapid Africanization of the Civil Service; and for a foreign policy aimed not at alignment with the Great Powers, but rather towards the maintenance of friendly relations with all states and the withdrawal of all foreign bases in Kenya.

It is difficult to assess what impact these policy statements had on the electorate. A Gallup Poll type survey of African voters in every constituency during the first two weeks of January revealed that 42% had read newspaper accounts of KANU's statement and 34% KADU's. The Kikuyu, Embu and Meru appeared the best informed, followed by Mombasa Africans, Kamba, Luo, Kalenjin and Baluhya. This survey demonstrated also that only a negligible part of the vote was undecided in terms of party support. The overwhelming majority of the open seats were decisively committed to either KANU or KADU, something already shown in a similar survey of the previous September.

The election scene was dominated essentially by KANU. Little happened nationally that its leaders did not initiate, KADU playing a more reactive role, seeking to gain tactical advantages out of KANU's internal weaknesses. Many of the events in the period before the actual polling were but facets of one problem: the difficulty for KANU of counteracting the fears of the non-African communities regarding their future and of restoring financial confidence in the country, whilst at the same time demonstrating decisively to the African electorate that KANU would implement a policy of major political and social change after the elections. This task was taken up by the leaders, Gichuru and Mboya, during and after their travels in Britain and Europe, during September and October 1960. In contrast to the speeches that Odinga had been making on a tour to the Eastern Bloc in the previous weeks, they spoke of the need to ensure a continuous flow of capital into Kenya, the necessity for rapid economic development and its dependence on investment and non-African skills, and on KANU's intention to do what it could to ensure that conditions were created and maintained which would foster confidence and guarantee security for investors and skilled persons. There would be a need for some expropriation of land after independence, but fair and just compensation would be paid in such cases. On the other hand, non-Africans would have to give up thinking in purely communal terms and co-operate in fostering rapid political and social development. Moreover, KANU wanted no British military base in Kenya and Kenyatta must be released. Mboya, speaking in London on the eve of his return to East Africa, emphasized: 'We do not believe his release will reverse Kenya into violence. We refuse to believe that he is inherently an evil man.'

This programme of moderation and co-operation was challenged almost immediately by the so-called Ginger Group in KANU. Influential in it were Denis Akumu of the Mombasa Dockworkers' Union and Josef Mathenge, the KANU leader in Nyeri. Odinga was clearly associated, being sometimes described as the Group's leader. However, it was less an organized group than a collection of uncompromising nationalists who refused to accept any necessity for moderation. The party must remain true to purely African interests and dedicate itself to the rapid achievement of an African socialism and the ideal of a united Africa. Anything that would inhibit this or tie the hands of a future African Government they bitterly resisted. Their focus of attack was on the suggestion made by Mboya and Gichuru regarding compensation for land appropriated in the Highlands. They staunchly maintained that there should be no such guarantee until KANU was in power.

The Ginger Group had a marked influence on the views expressed in the party's manifesto, delaying its appearance for some weeks. Whilst the group then disappeared back into the party as quickly as it had arisen, the potential and ideas it represented remained. At Naivasha on 13th November, Gichuru deviated from his past moderate approach to tell a KANU meeting: 'We are no longer begging for *Uhuru* from the Europeans and Asians. They will soon have to kneel before us.' As KANU launched its campaign, its task was to win the election despite the fears of European settlers and Asians.

Unfortunately for KANU the campaign started with the failure of a meeting at Ngong in the Masai reserve. Instead of winning the Masai over, it ended in a riot with one KANU Kikuyu supporter speared to death by a Masai *moran*. Here, it seemed, were the elements of ancient tribal strife. Newspaper reports of lorryloads of Kikuyu going to the meeting conveyed the impression of a tribal invasion. The incident strengthened the feeling that KANU was associated with certain tribes and helped to drive the others nearer to KADU.

During November a 'politics of manoeuvre' of an essentially negative character came to dominate the political scene. Positions of leadership within KANU were sought but no outright positive assertion for power was possible as long as Kenyatta was the recognized leader; any contestant for his authority could easily be challenged as a usurper. This constrictive situation fostered a politics of manoeuvring for the best position from which to assert power. In this kind of politics, one does not commit oneself to a decisive course of action, and there is room for errors and mistakes. Since the actual struggle for power has not yet begun, alliances remain fluid and the tactics employed are primarily negative. The objective is to minimize or destroy the leadership of the opponent by accusations of disloyalty to the absent leader. Even the leaders of the opposition party are caught up in these politics in an effort to enhance the position of their party.

Although politics of this character had been present in KANU since its formation, the approach of the General Election made them more intense and overt. This was clearly because another moment of crisis in the long drawn out Kenyatta issue would be reached immediately after the election, for it was implicitly recognized that the Governor would then have to make a new statement on Kenyatta's release. With an expectation by many that the restriction on Kenyatta would be lifted, it is possible to analyse the manoeuvres of the prominent leaders during the election period in the light of their assessment of the likelihood of Kenyatta's imminent return to active politics. No outsider can say what each of these leaders thought was likely to happen, but the manoeuvres themselves give an indication.

KANU's vice-president, Odinga, an old opponent of Mboya, and some prominent Kikuyu leaders, felt and even believed that Mboya and KANU's president Gichuru were vulnerable on Kenyatta. If it could be demonstrated that they were acting equivocally, their stature as national leaders could be diminished. Odinga and his Kikuyu allies sought therefore to make the Kenyatta question the sole issue of the campaign by challenging the sincerity of Mboya and Gichuru. Rumours circulated that they were responsible for the delay in the release of Kenyatta and that they had signed a secret pact with the Secretary of State not to release Kenyatta until much later. These rumours and the whispering campaign of late November, on the eve of Mboya's expected nomination as KANU's candidate for Nairobi East, were alleged to have originated from the Kenya African 'Cairo Office' which was hostile to Mboya and Gichuru. They were denied immediately by Mboya at a dramatic mass meeting in Nairobi when he announced his candidature for Nairobi East. The rumour persisted, nonetheless, and on 11th December the *Sunday Post* published on its front page, with sensational effect, a document already much talked about. This was a declaration, made in 1954, in which the signatories, including Gichuru, condemned Mau Mau and its leaders. Gichuru replied at once, explaining his signature by saying that he had always condemned violence and would continue to do so no matter where violence came from. Having been put on the defensive, both Mboya and Gichuru announced that if documents could be produced proving that they had ever agreed to the continued detention of Kenyatta they would withdraw from public life. At this time no prominent KANU official publicly pressed the attack, although KADU attempted throughout the campaign to exploit this issue.

In a constructive endeavour to bring about the release of Kenyatta, prominent Kikuyu political leaders sought, in late December, to gain the full support of loyalists on the eve of the departure to London of a KANU delegation led by Gichuru. Its object was to press once more for the release of Kenyatta and other detainees, and was timed to coincide with the visit to London of the Governor. The delegation's achievements seemed negligible, and KANU's Governing Council decided, on 20th January, to call for a three-day general strike to begin on 1st February to secure the release of Kenyatta. At this moment, however, KANU was a party rift by factions and on the edge of a major split. The focus of the struggle was centred on Nairobi East, where Mboya's main opposition came not from KADU, but from some Kikuyu leaders in his own party apparently supported by Odinga. The call for the general strike met with little positive support. Not only did KADU reject it, but so did most of the trade unions affiliated to the Kenya Federation of Labour despite Mboya being general secretary. Perhaps the most surprising aspect of this whole incident was Mboya's seeming political ineptness.

Within a week after the announcement of the strike, all pretence of party unity was dropped when Odinga publicly launched an attack on Mboya and Gichuru. He accused Mboya of ruining KANU's plans for the strike by announcing it prematurely, and bitterly criticized Gichuru for failing to take serious steps to secure Kenyatta's release. 'I can only draw the conclusion,' said Odinga, 'that Mr. Gichuru knows for certain that Kenyatta will not be released soon'. He criticized the people of Kiambu for failing to put up a candidate to oppose Gichuru, since, by returning him unopposed, they had sanctioned his signing the 1954 document calling for the continued detention of Mau Mau leaders. What probably sparked this attack was Mboya's statement at a public meeting that until Kenyatta was released, Gichuru, the KANU president, should take the post of Chief Minister and hold it for him. The indications are that Odinga and some other KANU leaders may well have believed that Gichuru and Mboya were making a bid for power. Continuing the attack in a press conference, at which Odinga was supported by four other members of KANU's executive committee, a statement was released in the name of KANU rejecting the suggestion by Mboya that Gichuru or anyone other 'than Jomo Kenyatta should become our first Chief Minister pending Jomo Kenyatta's release'. (See plate 4.)

This open attack by Odinga was denounced by Gichuru as an attempt to create disunity and wreck KANU. He suspended Odinga from his office as vice-president of KANU and called off the general strike. He accused Odinga of officially announcing his support for non-KANU candidates and in giving support to a new political organization which was seeking to challenge Mboya in Nairobi East. Attacks and counter-attacks were made by each faction in which Odinga was characterized as an agent of the interests of the Sino-Soviet bloc and Mboya a stooge of American influence and the child of British imperialism. The conflict reached out to the branches of the party —some supporting each side, and others being split by the struggle radiating from Nairobi. Each faction appealed for support in terms of their loyalty to Jomo Kenyatta. Neither was strong enough decisively to defeat the other, nor could the party afford a formal split with the General Election less than three weeks away. Within a week of Odinga's explosion, the party's Governing Council met. After a heated twelve-hour debate, they declared the suspension of Odinga null and void, delivered a strong rebuke to the national officers who had been the main antagonists, and denied that there was any split in the party. This incredible performance was a recognition by each faction that this was not the moment to commit their forces to a struggle for dominance and power. There were too many unknowns and there remained the immediate problem of winning the election. Mboya was clearly on the defensive, for he had to prove to the Kikuyu voters of Nairobi East his loyalty to Kenyatta, which Odinga and some Kikuyu leaders had sought to bring into doubt in an effort to defeat him.

These 'politics of manoeuvre' not only intensified the Kenyatta issue, but also made KANU heavily dependent in the election on the tribes committed to it. It could not function as an organization committed to its November policy statement, for its leadership remained hopelessly divided; with factions supporting different candidates the party was unable to mount any national campaign. KADU in contrast appeared as a united party drawing advantage from the weaknesses of KANU.

NOMINATION AND CANDIDATES
Nomination day for the open seats was 24th January, 1961.

As this was a common roll election, there was no difference in qualifications for nomination to either the reserved or open seats. Those of education, income and age applicable to African candidates in the 1957 and 1958 elections had been ended. A prospective candidate had to be at least twenty-one years of age, a registered voter, a resident of Kenya for two years immediately before the date of nomination, a British subject or a British protected person, and able to read, write and speak the English language with a degree of proficiency sufficient to enable him to take part in the proceedings of the Legislative Council. Disqualifications included conviction for criminal offences (of or exceeding a twelve month sentence), undischarged bankruptcy, election offences, or holding an office connected with the conduct of the election.

Candidates required a proposer and seconder, and the support of at least seven other persons, all being registered voters of the constituency concerned. The nomination papers, together with a statutory declaration attesting the candidate's consent to nomination and to his English language qualifications, plus a deposit of Shs. 1,000/- (£50), forfeit on failure to secure one-eighth of the votes cast, had to be delivered to the Returning Officer of the constituency between 9 a.m. and 1 p.m. on nomination day.

The £50 deposit and the English language qualification both acted to limit the number of prospective candidates. There were several instances of would-be candidates either unable to raise the sum required or failing to deposit it on time. The Kenya African Liberal Party proved not to have the funds for a single deposit. A few candidates were literally gathering the necessary shillings together during the last few minutes before the 1 p.m. deadline. On the whole the deposit made many think again about standing and brought into better perspective other financial burdens they would have to bear. Nonetheless, a large number of candidates stood who were relatively unaware of the substantial financial support they would need to conduct effective campaigns.

The English language proficiency requirement was a fundamental restriction. In practical terms, it meant that any African candidate had to be able to speak three languages: his own vernacular, Swahili and English. Swahili is particularly important, for it is the African *lingua franca* and the language of African nationalism in Kenya.[1] The vernacular could be used to appeal to fellow tribesmen, but if a wider African audience was to be reached, Swahili was essential. Indeed, a candidate could not follow the election in the open seats without being able to read the national Swahili press. The English requirement eliminated the old Swahili-speaking leaders, and helped to point up the fact that a young, new generation of educated men was coming to power.

Proficiency in English could be established by former membership in the Legislative Council, by possession either of a degree from a University at which the medium of instruction was English or of a diploma from Makerere College in Uganda, or by taking an examination before a language board. About fifty per cent. of the prospective candidates had to adopt the latter procedure. Language boards sat in every Province before nomination day; they consisted of not less than three members, one being a member of the Education Department. No detailed information is available as to their proceedings, but from interviews with candidates it would appear that examiners were generally liberal in assessing proficiency. Not all who passed eventually stood for election. The English requirement eliminated some possible candidates of importance, particularly among the Kalenjin: thus in Elgeyo-Suk an otherwise strong candidate failed. More important, the necessity for this qualification meant that some who might have been more representative of their own people could not even consider standing. The language test highlighted the fact that the member to be chosen had to have something of the quality of a representative in a foreign land.

Ninety candidates successfully filed their nomination papers. A few, particularly those in Northern Province West, had to travel considerable distances. There were several instances where prospective candidates were late; at least three being probably deliberate. Two of these, KANU candidates in predominantly KADU seats, were reluctant to stand and therefore chose this way out. One Returning Officer became worried that there would be no candidate in his constituency and therefore

[1]For interesting comments on Swahili as the language of politics see W. H. Whiteley: 'Political Concepts and Connotations' in *St. Antony's Papers* No. 10 (Ed. K. Kirkwood, 1961) and 'Language and Politics in East Africa' in *Tanganyika Notes and Records*, Nos. 47 and 48, June and September 1957.

telephoned the KANU branch, the locally dominant party, shortly before closing time to ask whether a candidate would be forthcoming. In the last minutes the candidate appeared with his papers and deposit.

There were four distinct groups of candidates: those officially selected by the two national African parties, party-independents of these parties, true independents, and candidates of five locally-based parties. With respect to the first two categories, both KANU and KADU had announced in November that they would contest all thirty-three seats. While this may have been good propaganda to enhance their claims to be territorial-wide parties, neither ever demonstrated any determined effort to fulfil this objective. Neither had the necessary organization or support in all districts. With a few exceptions, party organization was exceedingly sketchy in the rural areas, and the pending election itself practically stopped the spread of party organization. Apart from the urban constituencies, each party tended to concentrate on the constituencies already committed to it. Even in these areas the parties were still engaged in the task of absorbing the former local parties, and in developing branches. Moreover, each national party had severe disabilities: one through its internal conflicts, the other through a paucity of effective leadership.

Though both parties were susceptible to conflicts about nominations, those in KANU were the more intense and posed a major threat to party cohesion. In each party, the branches were to select the candidates by means of local delegate conferences and those chosen would be submitted to the national party councils for approval. KADU's central meeting for this purpose, at Nakuru in mid-January, provided the occasion for one of the few scenes of violence in the election: adherents of the two parties clashed in Nakuru's main street to the accompaniment of broken shop-windows. Of KADU's eighteen official candidates, seven had been members of the last Legislative Council, six others were prominent party leaders, and the remaining five were local leaders. The two selected for the Northern Province seats never stood, and, on the eve of nomination, the original candidate for Nairobi East was replaced by a more dynamic personality in the hope of taking advantage of the KANU clash there.

In contrast to KADU, bitter conflicts characterized KANU's nomination processes. The number of available KANU candidates was far greater than KADU could marshal. They were not, however, distributed evenly across the country. Unfortunately for KANU its concentration of possibles in the three urban constituencies and in its committed rural areas could not be deployed to fight in the KADU dominated regions. Campaigning in the rural areas had to be done in the vernacular. No 'stranger' would be an acceptable candidate. In Northern Province West KANU did, however, put up one outsider, a Kikuyu, though for a specific reason. Whilst he clearly stood no chance, his candidature opened the possibility of a KANU meeting at Lodwar, Kenyatta's place of detention, so causing embarrassment for the administration with the request that KANU speakers should be allowed to go. KANU succeeded in having official candidates in only two KADU areas, though two independents in Kalenjin constituencies were believed to be secret KANU candidates.

KANU's national Governing Council was unable to interfere with any 'local constituency choices', despite frequent complaints that the branch decision was unacceptable to a large number of local leaders. In the vast majority of constituencies contested by the party, many individuals who failed to obtain an official endorsement merely stood as party-independents. At a KANU Governing Council meeting on the eve of nomination, Mboya proposed a motion for the expulsion of all KANU members who opposed official candidates. This was not carried; instead, a resolution was passed that a KANU independent who defeated an official candidate would be eligible to apply for membership in KANU's parliamentary organization. Behind Mboya's motion was an attempt to expel Dr. Waiyaki, the Nairobi branch chairman who had announced his intention of standing as an independent against Mboya. Though the motion failed in the Governing Council, the Nairobi branch expelled Waiyaki a few days later.

The nomination process brought even more to the surface the conflicts in KANU's leadership, making the party even less effective in preparing for the electoral opportunity that lay ahead. During the final weeks of the campaign, any semblance of party discipline gave way to struggles between opposing factions, party leaders supporting different candidates in the hope of out-manoeuvring opponents.

There were twelve independents unconnected with either KANU or KADU and three non-Africans—one Baluchi and two Europeans—of these last one was the Mayor of Nakuru, a chartered accountant and a resident of the town since 1927, the other a former District Commissioner, well known to the Turkana people of Northern Province West. Five candidates were identified with local parties, three being in Tana-Lamu and two in North Nyanza.

The following tables contain information on age, religious background and experience of the open seat candidates, excluding the two Europeans. As Table 1 shows, this was an election of young men. At least sixty-seven were under forty and fifteen of these under thirty. The youngest candidate was twenty-two and the oldest fifty-five. There was no appreciable difference between the two national parties in age structure. Most of the national party leaders were between thirty and forty, although KANU's president and vice-president were about forty-six and fifty respectively and came from the older KAU generation of leadership. At least four other KANU candidates over forty were previously associated with KAU, including its former acting president, Odede.

TABLE I

Age of Candidates

Age Group	KANU		KADU		Independents	Other Parties	Total
	Official	Independent	Official	Independent			
Under 30	5	6	1	–	2	1	15
30–34	11	7	3	2	6	2	31
35–39	8	4	7	–	1	1	21
Over 40	5	6	5	–	1	–	17
Unknown	1	–	2	–	–	1	4
All Candidates	30	23	18	2	10	5	88

The tribal diversity of Kenya is well illustrated since twenty-four distinct tribal groups were represented among the candidates. However, fifty-five came from only four tribal groupings —Baluhya, Kamba, Luo, and the Kikuyu, Embu and Meru. The Baluhya were found in all four categories of candidates, while the candidates of the other major tribes were all affiliated to KANU. Most constituencies were dominated by a single tribe; only a few candidates stood in rural areas where they were not identified with the majority group. Of the urban constituencies, the candidates in Nairobi East and Nakuru Town were Kikuyu, Baluhya and Luo; Mombasa East had one candidate whose distant origin was Nyasa, and two from the coastal tribes.

The religious affiliations of the candidates are indicated in Table 2. Well over half considered themselves Protestants, although stated denominations of both Protestants and Catholics were often only nominal. Religion is not a major factor in Kenya African politics, nor an issue between the parties. Leadership in the national parties reflects affiliation with both Protestant and Catholic churches. The Muslim candidates were in the coastal constituencies, with the exception of the Somali from Northern Province East. Only in one constituency (Kisii) did religious connections seem likely to play a decisive part, though there was talk in at least three others of an instructed Catholic vote—and one successful candidate did

TABLE 2

Religious Affiliation of Candidates

Religious Groups	KANU		KADU		Independents	Other Parties	Total
	Official	Independent	Official	Independent			
Protestants	21	11	11	1	5	2	51
Catholics	4	5	3	1	1	–	14
Muslims	1	–	–	–	2	2	5
Unknown	4	7	4	–	2	1	18
All Candidates	30	23	18	2	10	5	88

acknowledge to one of the present writers that Catholic priests had been active on his behalf.

The most striking feature of the educational background of the candidates, as shown in Table 3, is that nearly half had some training at institutions of higher education. At least twenty had completed college degree programmes and ten had been engaged in post-graduate studies. Again there was no appreciable difference between the two national parties in the candidates' standard of education. Only a few had not proceeded beyond primary education, and most had received at least two years of secondary education. About a third had part of their education outside East Africa, attending colleges or universities in South Africa, the United States, India and Britain. Of the fifty candidates who had no more than a secondary education, only thirteen were successful in the election; educational background was by no means a decisive factor but it was clearly given consideration by the electorate. The ability to represent effectively the district in the Legislative Council was well understood.

A factor which Table 3 does not indicate is the association and friendship formed between many candidates and other leaders while at school. The Alliance High School at Kikuyu and the Holy Ghost College, Mangu, run respectively by Protestant and Catholic missions, were the two most important secondary schools where most candidates and other members of the Western educated élite first came into contact with one another. It is difficult to develop meaningful political generalizations about the continuing significance of these school associations, but clearly they were of some relevance. For example, the KADU candidates for the Coast rural seats of Kilifi and Kwale, Ngala and Matano, were school mates. In other cases former class associates were opponents. Perhaps the most important aspect of these early school associations was the existence of a widespread web of educated people who possessed considerable knowledge about many of the candidates and were thus able to act as communicators of information to others.

The data in Table 4 requires some qualification. Well over a third of the candidates—and a majority of those over forty—have pursued more than one occupation. Here dominant occupations only have been listed, with the exception of three

TABLE 3
Education of Candidates

Educational Level	KANU				KADU				Independents		Other Parties		All Candidates	
	Candidates		Successful		Candidates		Successful		Candi-dates	Suc-cessful	Candi-dates	Suc-cessful	Candi-dates	Suc-cessful
	Official	Ind.	Official	Ind.	Official	Ind.	Official	Ind.						
Primary or Secondary	13	15	5	—	11	—	5	—	7	1	4	2	50	13
Makerere College (E.A.), not necessarily degree standard	5	1	4	—	1	—	—	—	1	—	1	—	9	4
Overseas Non-Degree Higher Education	3	2	2	—	3	1	3	—	—	—	—	—	9	5
Outside East Africa : College Degree Education	5	3	4	1	2	—	2	—	—	—	—	—	10	7
Post-Graduate Degree Education	4	2	3	—	1	1	—	1	2	—	—	—	10	4
All Candidates ...	30	23	18	1	18	2	10	1	10	1	5	2	88	33

TABLE 4 Candidates' Occupations

Types of Occupation	KANU				KADU				Independent		Other Parties		Legislative Members Elected and Nominated		All Candidates	
	Candidates		Successful		Candidates		Successful		Candidates	Successful	Candidates	Successful	Previous Members	Re-elected	Candidates	Successful
	Off.	Ind.	Off.	Ind.	Off.	Ind.	Off.	Ind.								
Teachers	11	10	8	1	8	–	5	–	4	–	1	–	9	7	34	14
Labour Leaders	3	–	1	–	–	–	–	–	–	–	–	–	1	1	3	1
Political Organizers	3	1	2	–	–	–	–	–	–	–	–	–	–	–	4	2
Politicians (various past occupations)	1	1	1	–	1	–	–	–	–	–	–	–	–	–	3	1
Private Managers and Clerks	1	3	–	–	3	–	2	–	–	–	1	1	1	1	8	3
Lawyers	2	–	1	–	–	1	–	1	1	–	–	–	–	–	4	2
Medical Practitioners	–	–	–	–	–	–	–	–	1	1	–	–	–	–	1	–
Journalists	–	–	–	–	1	–	–	–	1	1	1	–	2	1	3	1
Civil Servants	2	1	1	–	3	1	2	–	1	–	–	–	2	1	8	3
Businessmen and Farmers	7	7	4	–	2	–	1	–	2	–	2	1	3	1	20	6

candidates who had no basic occupation other than as political organizers, and three political leaders who have pursued various occupations. Two of the latter had once been teachers, and the third a journalist. A factor affecting the careers of a few candidates was their detention during the Emergency.

The significant part played by teachers in African politics is highlighted by this data. Not only had over a third of the candidates been teachers in recent yeais, but their political role is also very evident in African District Councils. Teachers are leaders of opinion, and hold high status in African society. They are organized in the Kenya National Union of Teachers, in which several candidates held office. Only three candidates may be called labour leaders, but recruitment from the labour movement has been an important aspect of Kenya politics. Mboya is the most outstanding example, but many minor political leaders have come up through the trade unions. To date Kenya has produced only a few African lawyers; two of the unsuccessful candidates had recently started legal practices. In the civil service category are three former central government officers (an education officer, a policeman and a journalist), a chief who resigned his position in order to stand, and four who had been local government employees.

Table 5 indicates political experience as interpreted by membership in the Legislative Council, local government councils, or central or district government committees. With the exception of Odede, a nominated unofficial member of the Legislative Council before being detained in 1953, and Moi, appointed in 1956, the remaining seventeen had only been in the Council since the African elections of 1957 and 1958. Eleven of the fourteen sitting African Elected Members were re-elected, as well as one Specially Elected Member who stood in North Nyanza. Two of the former nominated African members who contested seats were defeated. About a third of the successful candidates had had no experience on government councils or committees. Table 5 also indicates that KANU could more easily find candidates with political experience; KADU was more dependent on a limited number of established leaders, and was largely restricted to the less politically developed areas.

In considering political experience, it should be noticed that

TABLE 5

Political Experience of Candidates

Categories of Experience	KANU				KADU				Independents		Other Parties		All Candidates	
	Candidates		Successful		Candidates		Successful		Candidates	Successful	Candidates	Successful	Candidates	Successful
	Official	Ind.	Official	Ind.	Official	Ind.	Official	Ind.						
Legislative Council:														
1952–53 … …	–	1	–	–	–	–	–	–	–	–	–	–	1	–
1956–60 … …	6	3	6	–	–	7	–	5	1	–	1	1	18	12
African District or Urban Boards or Councils …	14	8	7	–	8	–	4	–	1	–	2	1	33	12
Central or Local Government Committees …	14	9	9	–	9	–	6	–	3	–	1	1	36	16

well over half of the candidates were national leaders, branch party officials, or leaders of local parties. Eight were former detainees or restrictees during part of the Emergency and of these five were successful.

THE CONSTITUENCIES

KANU candidates contested twenty-five open seats, KADU eighteen. There were thirty official KANU candidates, but another twenty-three party members stood as party-independents. KADU avoided having more than one official candidate for each contested seat, and only two independents could be classified as KADU-independents. Despite the number of seats each party contested, they opposed each other in only ten. In four (Machakos, Central Nyanza, Kilifi and Kipsigis) the opposition was fundamentally token. Twelve independents stood in seven seats while five local parties had candidates in three seats.

Unopposed Seats

In six seats only one candidate successfully completed the nomination procedure and was therefore elected. One was the only independent who remained totally free of all party connection: a Somali, Ali Ahmed Lord, in Northern Province East. He attained fame in a curious way. A prospective candidate from Northern Province West, disqualified by a past criminal record, came to Nairobi after nomination day and announced in turn at the headquarters of KANU and KADU that he was Lord, the newly elected member. Neither party's officers had ever seen Lord, so, believing the impostor's story, each party courted him. Before the hoax was finally discovered, he had attended a KANU Governing Council meeting, was booked to speak at a KADU meeting and, it is believed, made a financial profit from his activities. Thus an unknown newly elected member from a remote area rapidly achieved prominence through the machinations of an impostor. The fraud was regarded with considerable humour by the two political parties, which reflects well on their tolerance, though, as KADU's general secretary confessed, it showed up their administrative inefficiency.

KANU's unopposed candidates were its president, Gichuru,

for Kiambu, where there was talk of his keeping the seat warm for Kenyatta, and Josef Mathenge from Nyeri. These two Kikuyu districts stood apart from the other KANU committed areas: their branches managed to ensure that only one candidate should stand. In Fort Hall, a Kikuyu two-member constituency, there were only two official candidates, though a KANU-independent did decide to contest the election. In contrast to most other rural areas, the effectiveness of party organization among the Kikuyu was remarkable, though it was backed by oath-taking ceremonies on behalf of candidates.[2] It hardly needs to be recorded that this organization reflects forty years of political activity. Within six months of KANU's branch being formed in Nyeri district, it had more than 35,000 card-holding members, and a party structure reaching down to the village level. A local mass meeting with no national leaders present could attract 15,000 people, the majority of whom would be women. Nevertheless, such political unanimity as existed in Nyeri could only be achieved with some degree of pressure, comparable perhaps to the 'social intimidation' in the neighbouring European reserved seat of North Kenya. In Nyeri town one leading butcher found it expedient to change his political allegiance from KADU to KANU, and, it was believed, one prospective candidate was strongly advised that his candidature would be unwise.

Three KADU candidates were elected unopposed: from Elgon-Nyanza, Narok and Kajiado. Elgon-Nyanza, a predominantly Baluhya area, was the home district of KADU's deputy leader, Muliro, who had originally been elected to the Legislative Council in 1957 from Nyanza North which at that time combined both North and Elgon Nyanza districts in one constituency. Muliro subsequently strove to develop local parties in both districts, but his main strength lay in Elgon Nyanza. KANU hoped to oppose him but their candidate failed to produce his deposit on time.[3] As a result Muliro was left free to campaign for other KADU candidates to the disadvantage of KANU in at least two constituencies.

Narok and Kajiado are Masai districts, and were politically

[2]Clyde Sanger in *The Guardian*, 8th May 1961.
[3]The prospective candidate, Christopher Makhoha, petitioned, claiming the Returning Officer had improperly refused his deposit but the Supreme Court dismissed the petition in May, describing the candidate's story as 'improbable'.

bound together in the Masai United Front, one of the tribal constituents of KADU. John Keen, KADU's general secretary, was returned unopposed for Kajiado with the backing of the members of Kajiado's traditionally minded District Council. It was thought that at Narok J. K. Tipis, a sitting member of the Legislative Council and KADU's official candidate, might be opposed, though he again had Masai traditional support. At the request of KADU's All-Union Executive Committee, John Konchellah, President of the Masai United Front, stood down. Yet the Front's general secretary, David Lemomo, was adamant in his determination to stand as an independent— because of KADU's 'racial exclusiveness'. He argued that political parties should be open to all races and that land ownership in the Highlands should not be regarded as in dispute. A combination of factors prevented his candidature at the last moment, and Tipis was returned unopposed.

Contested Seats

Campaigning in the contested seats was carried on under the handicap of Government restrictions on public meetings. Any political gathering of fifty persons or more required a licence from the local District Commissioner. This specified the place of meeting, the names of the permitted speakers and the times between which the meeting might be conducted, the hours allotted being usually during daylight and ending well before dark. Such African features of public gatherings as dance and song necessitated special permission, whilst any songs to be sung, or motions to be put, had to be submitted for prior censorship. Since licences were issued at administrative discretion curious discrepancies ensued, through differing views of the security situation. In Nyanza Province a rigid restriction was imposed on the number of meetings per week per district. It appeared almost as if the Mau Mau Emergency must have taken place there and not in the Central Province where a much freer attitude prevailed! There, as in most of the Colony, it was recognized that an election was taking place, that restrictions should be eased. With the exception of Nyanza, candidates could obtain licences for as many meetings as they requested, subject only to the proviso that a licence would not usually be granted for the same time and neighbourhood as another meeting. Some District Commissioners assembled the candidates at nomination and planned with them a schedule of public meetings, keeping rival candidates apart in different areas of the constituency. In two Nyanza constituencies, North and Kisii, candidates circumvented the full harshness of the restrictions by agreeing among themselves to hold, with the District Commissioner's consent, joint meetings. Many candidates in Nyanza resorted also to unlicensed so-called 'private meetings', legal if less than fifty persons were present; some were prepared to confess that on occasion, faced with a crowd of eager supporters, they had risked the penalties of violating the law. Certainly a prosecution in the middle of the campaign might well have strengthened a candidate in the popular mind, but none took place for any such offence.

The typical rural meeting consisted of a hundred or so people seated under the trees, but among the more politically conscious Kikuyu crowds would be larger. In Fort Hall, the one Kikuyu contested seat, attendances sometimes reached 15,000 and more, and the meeting was as much a social occasion as a political event. The freer attitude of the authorities allowed traditional dances and these formed an integral part of the meeting. In marked contrast to other tribes large numbers of Kikuyu women attended, their ululations shrilling assent to speakers' points.

Such typical African sounds underlined issues which touched African heart-strings. These were not far to seek: ever present questions like those of land and of race relations, questions which gave an edge to the demand for independence and the release of Kenyatta, spoken of as the father of Kenya's nationalism. Besides such national issues, there was everywhere a demand for increased educational facilities and oversea scholarships. Candidates had to discuss the need for more agricultural and trading loans, less restriction in the marketing of crops, the need for more hospitals and health centres, increased responsibility for the local District Councils, the recasting of laws to eradicate racial discrimination, and land claims. Education was clearly the most important issue, followed by land and agricultural development. There was little difference between candidates on these matters. What often told was whether the educated, necessarily English-speaking, candidate could

convince the voters that he was still in touch with traditional
values and could still, despite frequent absence from the tribe,
represent their problems and aspirations.

Most candidates sought to hold meetings across the constituency, but in so doing they had often to travel beyond their
own particular local support. In assessing prospects and results
it was important to note both the areas of the constituency with
high or low registrations of voters and the candidates' local
affiliations through residence, family, clan and marriage. Such
connections, it appeared, might well prove important in seats
with large numbers of candidates and particularly in those
two-member seats which had been specially designed to give a
chance to minorities. Certainly these last seats encouraged a
crop of locally based candidates.

As the constituencies were so large few attempted to campaign without a car, and some official candidates had the use
of a party van. Campaign expenses proved far greater than
most contestants had anticipated. Exact figures are unknown
but the average rural candidate spent between £300 and £400,
and some well over this figure. This went not only on transport,
handbills and posters, but on entertainment and services. Only
a few had adequate funds; the majority appeared to meet most
of their expenses themselves, little coming from party sources.

KANU dominated Rural Seats

In this group *Fort Hall* was exceptional. It was the one place
where there was little doubt that the party's official candidates,
two in a two-member constituency, would be returned, for the
third candidate, a KANU-independent, had little support. The
interest lay in the size of Dr. Gikonyo Kiano's majority.
Minister of Commerce and Industry since April 1960, he had
represented Fort Hall and Kiambu since 1958. Now he needed,
by obtaining a large majority, to make plain his dominant
position in the district, and hence his importance in Kikuyuland, as a basis for influence at the national level. He talked of
KANU and KADU dropping the 'N' and the 'D' to come
together after the election as KAU again, and looked to some
such unifying leadership role for himself. On his return from the
United States in 1956 with a Ph.D. in Political Science, he had
rapidly established himself as a major political personality both

in his home district of Fort Hall and in Nairobi. His prestige was enhanced not only by his own educational attainments, but also by his help in sending many students to America for study. He had actively worked to heal the rift between loyalists and ex-detainees in his constituency and had developed, by the time of the election, a well organized branch of KANU. With a shrewd appreciation of political realities in Fort Hall, he established relations with former leaders of KAU and brought many within the structure of the new KANU branch. His journal, *Kirinyaga* (Mount Kenya), circulated throughout Kikuyuland, advocating unity and the end of the divisions in Kikuyu society.

As a running mate for the two-member constituency, Kiano sponsored Kariuki Njiri, the son of a well-known retired senior chief. Like Kiano, he had both received his higher education in America and married an American Negro wife. As the campaign developed, it became apparent that in sponsoring Njiri, Kiano might have jeopardized his own chances of a commanding majority: Njiri had much support in the south of the district. Moreover, Kiano made the mistake of joining in the attack on Mboya, first in the district and then more publicly in Nairobi. In the outcome Kiano only beat Njiri by 2,276 votes in a poll of 95,197. This largely unexpected result did not enhance his position in KANU or in national politics.

The two-member constituencies of Kitui and Machakos in the Southern Province are populated by the Kamba. Although this tribe had made its support for KANU clear, there were some doubts whether their allegiance would hold firm, particularly after KANU's big Thika meeting. There, on the borders of their own country, many Kamba felt slighted at the lack of prominence accorded to them and their representatives.

This doubtful feeling may have been a factor in Muimi's actions. The sitting member and Minister for Health and Social Welfare, he hesitated for some while between KANU and KADU before finally deciding to stand as an independent in *Kitui*. In this vast and remote area perpetually on the edge of famine, politics were slow in developing. Outside influences have come more from Mombasa, with which the district has labour-migratory connections, than from Nairobi. Registration had been low, political activity has tended to be confined to teachers, and at the time of the election the KANU branch had no more than 400 card-holding members. As elsewhere the demand for a rapid improvement in educational facilities was a dominant issue; besides this all candidates stressed the need to find ways of overcoming the district's great shortage of water.

Muimi, a teacher before becoming a minister, was opposed by two practising teachers: Frederick Mati and Eliud Mwendwa, the official KANU candidates. Mati was one of the few Kitui Kamba with a university degree; he had directed the only independent school in Kamba country before the Emergency, during which he was for a time restricted. Mwendwa had been a member of the local District Council for nine years and had membership in KANU's national councils. These two conducted an intensive campaign together. Since they made no effort to divide the district, it seemed possible that one might obtain the overwhelming majority of votes and the other lose to Muimi. He, however, was soon on the defensive, suffering from the reputation of neglecting the district in the past and of being unwilling to commit himself on many issues. One curious feature was the visit during the campaign of Kiano who spoke at meetings with Muimi. This intervention made little difference. Mati and Mwendwa won easily, largely on the cry that a change was needed, and that Kenya should be made aware of the Kamba and of Kitui.

In the other Kamba constituency, *Machakos*, there were eight candidates for the two seats. This large number was encouraged in part by the lack of authority and organizational weakness in KANU's local branch which was in a constant state of turmoil over struggles for leadership. The serious doubts about the status and effectiveness of the party encouraged people with prospects of support from their home areas or from locally influential people to stand.

Unlike Kitui, Machakos lies directly within the political influence of Nairobi, 'the nerve centre of Kenya African politics'. Through the township of Machakos, which is now less than an hour's journey from Nairobi on a tarmac road, politics radiate into the district. Nairobi's proximity was underlined by three of the candidates being residents of the capital, one a City alderman, whilst others also had close ties. Despite this and despite the Kamba being the third largest tribe in the country, they had never in the past played any significant role in national politics. Now they were demanding, in examining candidates, that the Kamba should achieve their rightful place, but this required effective leadership.

Of the eight candidates, it soon became evident that the real choice lay between Henry Mulli, George Nthenge and William Malu. Mulli, a graduate of Fort Hare in South Africa, was the only practising teacher, though during most of the quarrelsome pre-nomination period he was at Oxford, reading for the Diploma in Education. This he interrupted somewhat reluctantly after Christmas to return and contest the election—indeed, he at first hoped that he might conduct his campaign from Oxford. His advantage, besides his educational qualifications, was that he was well known to Kamba leaders. He had been a neighbour and friend of Paul Ngei (the Kamba convicted with Kenyatta for organizing and managing Mau Mau), and had been detained himself through failing to assist the Government in the Kenyatta trial. Like other Kamba candidates, he campaigned for the release of Kenyatta and Ngei, the latter's name being raised in the tribe to the same significant quality as that of Kenyatta nationally.

Nthenge, the other candidate returned with Mulli, had tried to stand in 1957 but was then disqualified on technical grounds. A well-known and successful businessman in Nairobi, he had played a large part in the development of the Kamba woodcarving industry so well known to tourists in East Africa.[4] Apart from this contribution to the Kamba economy, he had been active in their politics, both in Nairobi and Machakos, had aided Kamba students to go abroad for study, and had helped to provide legal counsel for the Kamba in a recent important case arising from a clash with the Masai over cattle thefts. Not only was Nthenge vice-chairman of the KANU Machakos branch, but he had founded the New Akamba Union to foster Kamba unity and, incidentally, his own political career. He conducted one of the most extensive campaigns, emphasizing the need for the Kamba to play their full part in a new African Government.

[4]For its history see W. Elkan: 'The East African Trade in Woodcarvings'. *Africa* XXVIII No. 4, October 1958.

Malu, the leading unsuccessful candidate, appeared at first as a likely winner. He had long been active in politics: an official of the Mombasa branch of KAU (1950-2), first chairman of KANU's branch in Machakos and the party's national treasurer. However, his power locally appeared to be waning, as seen by his recent failure to maintain the position of vice-chairman of the District Council, and his inability to control discontent within KANU found expression in his electoral defeat, since he was the party's first choice. Less than 15% of the total vote went to the other five candidates; among them was the sitting member, David Kiamba, returned unopposed in a by-election in 1959, and the one KADU candidate who obtained less than one per cent. of the vote.

In *Meru*, also, five of the eight candidates lost their deposits. Again KANU's weakness encouraged this proliferation; here the branch had only been established in November. The sitting member, Bernard Mate, elected in 1957, recovered his position to top the poll from a nadir in public esteem when, in 1959, he had failed to gain election to the Meru District Council. An engaging personality, a graduate of the University of Wales, he understood the problems of his district and could express his views forcibly. While not a militant KANU nationalist, he argued effectively that the Meru would be left behind in the new national developments unless they were represented by a man with experience and education. The other winning candidate was Jackson Angaine, the former chairman of the Meru KAU branch (1948-52), a past secretary of the African District Council, and the present chairman of the KANU branch. The only other candidate who commanded any substantial support was Justus Kiecha, a teacher and local KANU official, who came from Nyambeni division in eastern Meru which had about forty per cent. of the votes—and there his supporters were reported as carrying corn cobs, his symbol.

Many of the Meru candidates were local teachers. Several of them had been successful in the 1959 District Council elections, and, realizing they had some support, were encouraged to stand in what appeared to be a very open race. One factor which seemed of less significance than in the 1957 election was the influence of the *Njure Ncheke*, the traditional body of Meru elders. With an electorate embracing a substantial sector of the adult population and an expanding body of educated men no longer prepared to leave leadership to their illiterate and conservative elders, this traditional body has been gradually losing its power. Its influence exists and is important, but a modern election conducted on a near-universal franchise allowed new forces to make themselves felt.

Embu, to the south of Meru, is ethnically the most heterogenous district in Central Province, having three distinct peoples: Kikuyu, Embu and Mbere. Though possessing similar social and political organizations, the three groups live in separate territorial divisions. The local KANU branch recognized this ethnic complex by deciding that there should be two official candidates for the one seat: one from the northern divisions of Embu and Mbere, the other from Ndia and Gichugu. While Ndia is a Kikuyu division adjacent to Nyeri district, Gichugu, situated between Ndia and Embu, reflects a merging of the two cultures, Jeremiah Nyagah, who was elected for Nyeri and Embu in 1958, had family ties in both Embu and Mbere. He was one KANU candidate, the other being Robert Ndegwa Maringa from Ndia. A third to stand was Nahashon Njuno, as a KANU-independent.

As in many rural areas, the election stimulated political interest and concern for the future. Shortly after the end of the Emergency in January 1960, the Embu African Democratic Party had been formed. In September it was replaced by a KANU branch, though this was not formally registered under the Government regulations until January 1961, owing to the insistence of the Government that Njuno should not be the general secretary or an office bearer. Many of the local party leaders were ex-detainees, as was the case elsewhere in Central Province. The party rapidly received widespread support in the district as the organization through which independence could be quickly achieved. Yet this KANU branch also was riven with faction so that, as we have noted, it had to leave the final choice of the district's representative to the electors.

An extremely active campaign ensued, the three candidates holding between them over 80 licensed meetings after nomination day. Nyagah, a former teacher and a practising Anglican, was not a strong party man. In advocating Kenyatta's immediate release 'so that he can join in the most exciting task of history-building in Kenya' he sought, like many ex-loyalist Christians, to heal the divisions of the past. Maringa, a Makerere College trained teacher, suffered through recent absence from the district, teaching in Meru. He stressed the need for a change, drawing attention to Embu's unfavourable educational progress as compared to that of Nyeri district and to Nyagah's failure to send any significant number of Embu students to America. Njuno, the most ardent nationalist but the least educated candidate, competed with Maringa for votes in Ndia and Gichugu. Nyagah, with an overwhelming vote in Embu and Mbere (some estimates put it at 95 % or more), was able to maintain his position. His prestige, derived originally from being the first educated Embu, had been enhanced by his becoming Deputy Speaker in 1960, the first African in Kenya to hold this post. In the campaign his national stature was indicated by help from both Mboya and Kiano.

In Nyanza Province KANU dominated the constituencies of Kisii, Central and South Nyanza, the last two being mainly Luo in population. South Nyanza is overwhelmingly so, apart from the small Bantu enclave of the Kuria near the Tanganyika border.

In *South Nyanza*, although several people indicated their intention to stand, only two candidates finally emerged: Lawrence Oguda and Samuel Ayoda. Oguda, elected for Nyanza South in 1957, had lost the seat in 1959 when convicted of sedition. At the by-election, Ayoda, who had been a teacher since his return from America in 1956, was elected unopposed. A close friend of Mboya, who comes from this constituency, Ayoda, continued throughout 1960 to build his political support, not only as the sitting member but also as a member of the African District Council and chairman both of the South Nyanza branch of the Kenya National Union of Teachers and of the KANU district branch. In May 1960, Ayoda founded the South Nyanza Parents' Association, which he regarded as more important to his election campaign than the local KANU organization. Education was the key to progress and through this association, of which Mboya was patron, he rapidly expanded the number of his supporters.

Oguda was a more controversial candidate, it being widely reported that he had neglected the constituency when he was its member. Differences then with two leading chiefs in his home division had cost him further support. However, it seemed possible that he might regain his strength through having been a 'prison graduate', for so he was hailed by Odinga on the completion of his sentence in 1960. This support introduced into the constituency something of the national dispute between the KANU leaders: whilst Oguda had Odinga's blessing, Ayoda, besides being the official KANU candidate, had Mboya's. Ayoda's steady campaigning and his efforts to end the historic antagonism between the two traditional Luo regions, Karachuonyo, the northern, and Milambo, the southern, were rewarded. He obtained two-thirds of the vote and must have gained a considerable number in Milambo, the poorer area from which Oguda came, as well as from his own home region of Karachuonyo.

The highlands constituency of *Kisii* had a larger electorate, though a smaller population, than South Nyanza. Of the five candidates, James Nyamweya, a lawyer and vice-chairman of KANU's district branch, seemed a particularly good choice as the official KANU candidate. Before the branch was formed in July 1960, he had been chairman of the local Kisii political association, had taken part in the formation of KANU at the Kiambu conference and, as a close colleague of Ayoda, was vice-president of the South Nyanza Parents' Association. His law practice was centred in Kisumu, though he had opened a branch office in Kisii township in March 1960. He campaigned with confidence and assurance but did not stress that he was the official candidate. Of the four KANU-independents, Lawrence Sagini appeared to have the best prospects. He had received his higher education in America, had taught in local schools for nearly nine years, and shortly before the election had been appointed an assistant education officer in the district. As an ardent Catholic, he could hope for sectarian support, since religious considerations played an important part locally. His politics appeared closer to KADU than to KANU; while a friend of Muliro, he was not officially affiliated to KADU, something which might have been dangerous to his prospects in KANU-minded Kisii. Perhaps one of Sagini's most important assets was his ability to identify himself with the difficulties and problems of the people. He toured the constituency with a wooden model of his symbol, a giraffe, mounted on the roof of his car.

One of the other three party-independents, Zephaniah Anyieni, a salesman, had decided to stand because he believed that Nyamweya was too moderate, but he in turn was soon accused of talking too much like a Nairobi politician. He was disappointed by the failure of audiences to raise questions concerning national policy and, as a true African nationalist, he showed a keen interest in the fate of Lumumba, the Congo leader. Thomas Mongare Masaki, a teacher and the KANU branch propaganda secretary, surprisingly came third, despite the fact that he had to campaign without possessing a car. The fifth candidate, John Kebaso, received less than a thousand votes. By far the oldest, he sought to capitalize on the African respect for age. He had been a founder member of KAU. However, the fact of having been a nominated member of the Legislative Council did not increase his popularity. The campaign was conducted without bitterness, all the candidates appearing to be on friendly terms. Thus they found it easy to overcome the Nyanza restrictions on public meetings by sharing theirs, one candidate sometimes cheerfully introducing an opponent.

It was widely held that Sagini was returned because of Catholic support. Catholics and Seventh Day Adventists form the two largest denominations in the constituency, and both churches play an important role in the lives of the people. If the religious issue was decisive, Nyamweya was somewhat at a disadvantage since he had to share the S.D.A. vote with two other candidates. Sagini did not publicly raise the religious issue but rather emphasized the need for social justice. He concentrated on the northern section of the district, where he had strong family ties and where the majority of the vote was concentrated. Undoubtedly it was this substantial northern support, including important Catholic areas, that elected him. Nyamweya's support was more uniform but in his home location of Nyaribari, in the north of the constituency, he was believed to have lost votes because of the opposition of a senior chief to his family.

Central Nyanza, a predominantly Luo district, became established as a prominent centre of African nationalism during the political standstill in the Kikuyu areas enforced by the Emergency. Here leadership came from Oginga Odinga, who had founded the Luo Thrift and Trading Corporation in 1946, an organization which helped Africans to establish businesses. In 1953 he became president of the Luo Union and played a leading part in its reorganization and expansion. This rapidly became the largest tribal organization in East Africa with branches not only in all the main urban centres, but in all the rural Luo locations of Nyanza Province. Although the Luo Union was not a political association, these efforts in building Luo unity and social awareness provided substantial support for Odinga's sweeping victory in the 1957 election for Nyanza Central. In November 1956, he revived the *Nyanza Times*, a nationalist weekly printed in Luo and English. Giving up the presidency of the Luo Union in 1957, Odinga concentrated on establishing his position as a major nationalist leader in the country and in amassing political support in Central Nyanza. Until KANU's Central Nyanza branch was formed in August 1960, the African District Association (Central Nyanza) was Odinga's main vehicle for political action.

In October, the KANU Central Nyanza branch, headed by the former chairman of the African District Association, a loyal follower of Odinga, began an intensive effort to establish a nucleus of organizations in all locations and sub-locations of the district. '*Uhuru* Chiefs' or location political leaders were appointed and, above them, divisional organizers. In December, elections to the Location Councils were held throughout the district. KANU's local leaders only belatedly saw their importance as a means of power. Their hurried campaign was only partially successful, hardly more than a third of their candidates being elected. Personality and past records of individuals appeared more important assets than the status of local party leaders. Nonetheless, KANU was established as the major political force in the district, although the pending General Election produced a rift in branch leadership over the choice of candidates for the two Central Nyanza seats.

Apart from Odinga, six other KANU members sought to be official party candidates. Of these six, the most important were Odede, the former president of KAU, and Argwings-Kodhek, an old associate of Odinga. At a delegates' conference in Kisumu on 29th December the Central Nyanza KANU branch decided to allow all seven candidates to contest the election for the party. They argued that since all prospective candidates were active KANU members, and since the party had no effective opposition in the constituency, it would not be in the interests of the branch to decide between factions. Refusing to accept this, Odinga mobilized his forces and, at another delegates' conference two weeks later, he and Argwings-Kodhek were selected as the two official KANU candidates. While Odede thus lost the struggle for party backing and his supporters were dismissed from their positions as branch officials, he nonetheless contested the election as a party-independent. With the exception of Joseph Mariwa Gek, a school teacher, the other prospective KANU candidates stood down.

Two other candidates, from the Baluhya locations in the west of the constituency near Lake Victoria, stood as well: James Osoga, a teacher, campaigned as a KANU-independent though he had not sought KANU nomination, and Henry Odaba, a farmer, as KADU's official candidate. These two, together with Mariwa Gek, were no more than 'locational' candidates with restricted support. As, in contrast, Odinga's pre-eminence gave him widespread strength, interest concentrated on the battle between Argwings-Kodhek and Odede for second place. Although Odede was believed to have the support of Mboya, he had to campaign on his own, whilst Argwings-Kodhek received the active support of Odinga, having, like him, the backing also of the KANU branch. These two candidates appeared to have unlimited financial resources, which were widely believed to have been derived from Odinga's Communist contacts. In the Legislative Council in December 1960, on a motion concerning the Government's withdrawal of his passport after his Iron Curtain visits, he said he had £10,000 but explained: 'I received it from some friends. I received it from Great Britain towards education for some students, and I am using it for that purpose, and if I can help the students go to Russia or to America or anywhere else, then I shall use it'.[5]

In the middle of February, two weeks before polling, a structured sample survey of this constituency was undertaken

[5]Leg. Co. *Debates*, 9 December 1960, p. 442.

by the writers with the help of an African research assistant. A total of 261 voters was interviewed. For this purpose the constituency was divided into twelve areas on the basis of locational boundaries, ten locations being combined to form five survey areas, while each of the other seven locations formed a separate area. Thus about twenty voters were interviewed in each of the twelve areas. Care was taken to include representatives of different age and occupation groups, equal in proportion in each area. Of those interviewed, 128 were farmers of whom 52 were women, 59 were in the category of literate voters, and 74 were local leaders (traditional, church, administrative or political). The main purpose was to ascertain what the voters knew of the election, how they obtained their information and what factors would influence their choice. As a check, each voter interviewed was asked to name his favoured candidate. Table 6 gives the results of the survey, as compared with the final results of the election in percentages:

TABLE 6

Status of Candidates: Survey and Election Results

Candidates	Survey Results in Percentages	Election Result in Percentages	Difference in Percentages
Argwings-Kodhek, C. M. G.	14	26	12
Mariwa Gek, J. C.	1	2	1
Odaba, H. D.	1	5	4
Odede, F. W.	5	2	3
Odinga, O.	39	58	19
Osoga, J. C. N.	10	7	3
Refuse to state or uncertain	30	—	—
Total ...	100	100	—

Apart from Argwings-Kodhek and Odinga, the sample survey had no more than a 4% differential from the election results. Undoubtedly the overwhelming majority of those who refused to answer or were uncertain voted for Argwings-Kodhek and Odinga. Osoga's and Odaba's support was only in the Baluhya locations, while Mariwa Gek's was confined to three locations south and east of Kisumu. Neither Odede, Odinga nor Argwings-Kodhek, as Luo candidates, had appreciable support in the Baluhya locations. Odede received his greatest support in his home location, Uyomo, with scattered votes elsewhere. The survey confirmed the widely held view that Argwings-Kodhek's major support was in the central and northern part of the constituency, for he had family ties in Gem and Alego locations in the centre of this area. Odinga completely dominated his home location of Sakwa and had much support in all the Luo locations with the exceptions of Gem and Uyomo. Since the locational boundaries coincided fairly accurately with the former tribal boundaries among the Luo and Baluhya, the survey clearly demonstrated the importance of parochial voting.

Fourteen per cent. of those interviewed had no knowledge of the number of candidates; 34% believed there were no more than five; 50% thought there were six and 2% said there were seven. The voter was then asked to name the candidates, indicating party affiliations; Table 7 shows the percentage response.

TABLE 7

Knowledge of Candidates and Party Affiliation

Candidates	Able to give his name (in percentages)	Able to name Party affiliation (in percentages)
Argwings-Kodhek, C. M. G.	75	57
Mariwa Gek, J. C.	44	15
Odaba, H. D.	50	31
Odede, F. W.	66	18
Odinga, O.	83	68
Osoga, J. C. N.	45	19

The most widely known were the two successful candidates, and the poll clearly showed Odinga to be the dominant political personality. Whilst most of Argwings-Kodhek's past political activity had been in Nairobi, he had done considerable local spade-work for his candidature during 1960. Odede was only released from detention and restriction in 1960. His slowness to begin his campaigning helps to explain why only 66% knew of his candidature. Knowledge of candidates' party affiliations was poor. Possibly that may have been caused by the confusion over the selection of the official KANU candidates and the fact that Central Nyanza was an overwhelmingly KANU constituency. Unlike candidates in many other rural districts, the KANU official candidates proclaimed on their posters their official status as party contestants.

Seven choices were presented to those interviewed in asking how they had learned what candidates were standing: 30% said that they had been told by other people; 27% indicated information from a newspaper and 19% from the radio; 15% by attending political meetings; 2% had met a candidate personally; while 1% said they had seen the names in an official Government notice. Only 4% indicated that they had learned in other ways, and 2% gave no response. While this data clearly demonstrates the importance of oral communication, the increasing significance of the press is also evident. The most widely read daily paper was *Taifa Leo*, a Swahili paper which paid particular attention to African politics.

Table 8 shows factors influencing voters in their selection of candidates. Each person was asked to state his first, second and third choices of certain possible influences. The candidate's

TABLE 8

Factors influencing Choice of Candidates in Percentages

Factors	1st Choice	2nd Choice	3rd Choice
The candidate's policy	34	37	11
His past services to the people	23	27	19
His sub-tribe or Location affiliation	5	2	3
Being an official party candidate	2	2	5
His educational qualifications	5	7	8
His religious background	1	1	1
His courage to fight Government	2	3	4
He is an independent candidate	1	2	3
Other	19	10	31
No response	8	9	15

policy and past services to the people emerged as most decisive. Among the main considerations voters stated under 'other' were that the candidate should be a courageous fighter for the rights of the people, that he should work hard for the district, and that he should be a man both popular among his people and of high integrity and ability. Being an official party candidate was clearly of little significance.

Ninety per cent of those interviewed stated that there were problems they expected the candidate to help with if elected: 18% regarded increased educational opportunities as paramount; 13% looked to land problems as the main area for improvement; 5% wanted relief from taxation; and 3% considered the problems of unemployment as most vital. Under 'other', three groups of problems were outstanding: most frequently mentioned was the desire for help in all phases of development; secondly, a specific need for business opportunities and loans; and thirdly that the candidates should work for Independence.

Perhaps the most unexpected aspect of this election was Odede's failure to capture more than a scant 2% of the vote. His detention and restriction had been a major political issue in the past few years. In 1957 Odinga had campaigned as Odede's champion, describing him as a martyr of colonialism for whom he would stand down at the first opportunity. Nevertheless, Odede received no great ovation when he was finally freed in 1960 and Odinga made no public overtures to support his re-entry into politics. As a personality, Odede lacked Odinga's flamboyance and failed to project himself as a fully committed nationalist. In Luo eyes his views in support of land consolidation were suspect, and his moderation in all policy matters even encouraged the rumour that he was pro-government. The general view that being a 'prison graduate' was a major asset may hold true only as long as another group of men has not taken over power during the interval.

KADU dominated Rural Seats

In these six contested seats KANU opposition, where provided, was merely token. Official KANU candidates opposed Ronald Ngala, KADU's leader, in Kilifi at the coast, and Towett, KADU's political adviser, in Kipsigis. In Baringo and Elgeyo-Suk independents were accused of being secret KANU candidates.

Ngala had represented the Coast since 1957, remaining

closely in touch with the area, more particularly with his own
Giriama people of *Kilifi* district. Seeking desperately for a
candidate there, KANU persuaded, after nomination day, Seif
Suleman, an independent, to accept their name and support.
Although Suleman tried hard to find issues that would take
votes from Ngala, there was little doubt of the outcome. Ngala's
hold over the Giriama was demonstrated by his receiving 98%
of the poll—KANU's first chosen candidate was clearly wise
to miss the last ferry at Kilifi before nominations closed on
24th February! Towett's victory in *Kipsigis* was even more
spectacular. With 91·8% of the electorate voting, Towett
obtained 56,445 votes, the two opposing KANU candidates
collecting between them less than 200—even here KANU split
what few votes it had! Certainly the two KANU candidates
were regarded by the Kipsigis as something of a joke. On one
occasion the press reported that one of these candidates had at
a meeting an audience of precisely one: Towett, who had come
as a good democrat to hear what an opponent had to say.
Ngala's and Towett's enormous majorities showed their un-
doubted right to speak on behalf of their people, whilst providing the most striking examples of the 'one party tribe'
system.

Since the coastal strip of *Kwale* district where the vast
majority of the Digo live was included in the Arab Protectorate
seat, the Kwale seat was dominated by the Duruma. This was
a distinct advantage for KADU, for, while the Digo are KANU-
minded, the numerically smaller Duruma followed KADU.
Robert Matano, a Makerere trained education officer, was
nominated by the KADU district electoral conference. Another
Duruma, Peter Mwero, who failed to get KADU's endorsement, stood as a party-independent. Mwero had no politically
organized following, but hoped to be able to win through intensive campaigning, clan affiliations and the influence of his
father, vice-president of the District Council and chief of
Mwavumbo location; there were even rumours that the candidate was trying to obtain the support of local witch doctors.
Matano, on the other hand, had the backing of Ngala who
had a large following in the district. One of Matano's main
problems was to get the scattered electorate to vote, and during
the campaign he spent a considerable amount of time teaching

the Duruma how to mark their ballot papers properly. In the lowest open seat poll (55·3%) Matano won easily.

Of the four Kalenjin constituencies, *Baringo*, stretching northward from the settled areas of the Rift Valley into the vast arid regions of northern Kenya, is the most isolated. Not until 1944 was the first intermediate school established in the district, whilst only a few years ago mail still came by runner to Kabarnet, the district headquarters. New and improved roads now link parts of the area with the Highlands, and the Tugen, who form about 90% of the population, were eager not to be left behind in the development of a new Kenya. As in Kipsigis, Baringo possessed an established political leader: Daniel arap Moi, a former teacher elected in 1957 to the Legislative Council for the Rift Valley. He had played an important part in the developments leading to the formation of the Kalenjin Political Alliance and was now chairman of KADU's All-Union Conference.

Tugen interest in politics rapidly increased after Lancaster House with issues of land settlement schemes, education and increased political responsibility uppermost. Moi conducted an intensive campaign though his sole opponent was a relatively unknown teacher, E. K. Bomet, from the extreme southern part of the district. Bomet, who stood as an independent, was branded as a KANU man. In his defence he maintained that there was no difference in the policy statements of the two parties. In an attempt to save at least his deposit, he hoped to win the support of other teachers and educated people. But the Tugen had found their leader in Moi, who appealed not only to emerging educated groups, but also to the traditional elders who still possessed great influence. Bomet was unable to retain his deposit in this unbalanced contest.

To the west of the Kamasia hills of the Baringo district lies the narrow and tapering district of Elgeyo-Marakwet. It was joined with West Suk to the north-west to form the *Elgeyo-Suk* constituency. KADU's official candidate was an Elgeyo, William arap Murgor, chief of the Irong division, who had resigned to contest the seat. The other candidate, John arap Chemweno, son of the Marakwet Senior Chief, claimed to be an independent although he was accused of being a 'secret'

KANU candidate. The electorate of 16,471 was made up of 7,644 voters in Elgeyo, 5,549 voters in Marakwet, including some Elgeyo, and 3,278 in West Suk. With both candidates having a substantial following amongst their own people, the Suk appeared to hold the balance. KADU's leaders, such as Moi and Muliro, had diligently courted this vote. While no KADU branch had yet been established in Elgeyo-Marakwet, one had been formed in West Suk. Murgor's proposer and seconder were Suk KADU office bearers and he made every effort to gain the support of the influential Suk elders. Chemweno, on the other hand, found the overwhelming majority of his sponsors in his own area. Despite the apparent importance of the Suk, Murgor's victory was won with heavy Elgeyo backing, both in their own area and in Marakwet, the majority of the Suk vote going to Chemweno.

The most interesting election in the KADU dominated areas was undoubtedly the contest for *Nandi*.[6] The Nandi district may be described as the keystone of the Kalenjin region; to the secondary school at Kapsabet, the district's centre, have come many future Kalenjin leaders. While the Nandi had never been in the mainstream of African politics, their leaders recognized after Lancaster House the need for a political organization to protect Nandi interests, particularly their extensive claims in the Highlands. As late as 1919-1920 parts of their reserve in the Kipkarren Valley and Kaimosi were excised for European farms. Furthermore, they feared the encroachment of other and more populous land hungry tribes. Thus they joined with other Kalenjin-speaking peoples to form the Kalenjin Political Alliance and took part in the decision to create KADU in opposition to the thrust for power by KANU.

Shadrach Kimalel, a Makerere educated Nandi teacher at the Government secondary school in Kapsabet, was selected by the local KADU committee. Though Kimalel had played only a minor part in the new political organization, he possessed the background and educational qualities that his sponsors regarded as vital to represent the Nandi effectively. At the end of November, a Nairobi lawyer, M. J. Seroney,

[6]The authors are much indebted to Mr. A. T. Matson of Kapsabet for the paper he contributed on which this account of the Nandi election is based. The paper is being deposited in the library of the Institute of Commonwealth Studies, Oxford.

announced his intention of standing as an independent. Seroney's candidature was received with some suspicion in the district, for, while he was a Nandi, most of his adult life had been spent elsewhere, either studying overseas or following his profession in Nairobi. Suspicions were also engendered by his previous lack of apparent interest in Nandi affairs, his alleged membership of KANU and reported association with Mboya, and the withdrawal of the proposed KANU candidate from the election in his favour. It was also thought that, whether his candidature was inspired by anti-KADU elements in Nairobi, or by personal motives, his interest in the district would soon cease after the election and the Nandi would lack adequate representation.

Surprisingly, Seroney received almost immediate support when he returned to contest the seat. With considerable skill he concentrated on lessening or removing the suspicions that surrounded his candidature. He maintained that he was not a member of KANU, but had joined KADU and was fighting on the KADU policy statement. Moreover, whether elected or not, he would move his law office to nearby Eldoret in order to be of service to the Nandi in the future. In addition, Seroney was able to take advantage of the fact that the Nandi were by no means unanimously committed to having only one candidate stand and that there was considerable opposition to the long established authority of the older Protestant ruling groups. The prospective candidate Kaptingei, who was to oppose Kimalel, stood down for Seroney and became his proposer, while the leading Catholic elder, a man enjoying respect throughout the district, became his seconder. This gave Seroney not only Catholic support but also backing in KADU, since the seconder was chairman of a KADU branch in the district. Support rapidly came from many of the District Council members. Very soon Seroney had electoral committees functioning in nearly all locations and was in command of the district's embryonic political organization.

Seroney's nomination papers indicated support from people of all ages, of both religions and sexes, spread geographically throughout the district; Kimalel's from his family, members of his *pororiet* (a Nandi political unit) and the Protestants. However, he had one Kikuyu and one Nandi Muslim as sponsors, as well as Isaac Koskei, the leader of the Kalenjin Political Alliance. Seroney's nominators were generally more popular figures, for Kimalel's chief supporters and agents included men who had made themselves unpopular over the years by their brave but uncompromising denunciation of Nandi weaknesses.

During the campaign both candidates used the KADU party van as if the question of official recognition had been covertly dropped. They shared public platforms, but there were few large formal meetings. Both candidates concentrated more on talks to small groups, at markets, women's clubs and other meeting places. As in most rural constituencies, there was inevitably a lack of organization at the main meetings with the usual long delays. A type of 'meeting' of possible importance was that in which leading Catholics exhorted the faithful after Mass on Sunday to vote for the Catholic candidate, Seroney. He obviously spent more money on the campaign than Kimalel, and in the last fortnight of the campaign his posters and photographs appeared throughout the constituency.

As both candidates were standing on the KADU policy statement, it was inevitable that speeches followed much the same lines, with the local issues dominant. Seroney appeared to be the more convincing speaker. Kimalel tended to confine himself to a statement and explanation of the KADU policy declaration, whereas Seroney roamed over a wider field and advanced more of his own opinions. Since questions largely concerned local matters, this necessarily put Kimalel at a disadvantage as his opponent had never taken part in making some of the more unpopular decisions. There were two obvious personal differences which may have had some influence. Kimalel was a teetotaller, whereas Seroney was always willing to have a cheering glass with the voters. Secondly, Seroney campaigned in clothes which were almost out at the elbows, whilst Kimalel was always neatly dressed. The latter gave the impression of Nonconformist rectitude and respectability, the former of a man who was obviously pleased to be able to become an ordinary Nandi again.

As in all constituencies, symbols played an important part. The ballot would seem to have favoured Seroney as his was the motor car. Much play was made of the distinction between the car and the elephant (Kimalel's symbol) in speed and use-fulness, it being said that the elephant crushes people beneath his feet, while the motor car picks up the pregnant woman and takes her to hospital.

Seroney won by an overwhelming majority. In seeking, as many voters essentially did, the ablest representative for the tribe, Seroney's abilities told: he was a lawyer, had travelled widely, spoke with determination and conviction, and answered questions more easily. From a historical point of view, Kimalel represented the non-drinking, progressive, Protestant oligarchy, whose long rule had become irksome to many Catholics, younger Protestants and pagans. The fact that he had been a nominated member of the District Council for the past two years probably did not help his chances, particularly since he had tried loyally and reasonably to justify what seemed to many to be unnecessary and harsh byelaws. Seroney was in the strong position of not having been involved in local matters, and was therefore able to express the opinion that it seemed to him that certain matters ought to be examined again. Throughout the campaign the initiative rested with Seroney who represented the new order, while Kimalel had the unfortunate task of defending many of the acts of the ruling generation.

Other Rural Seats

Four rural constituencies remained which could not be clearly classified as strongholds of either KANU or KADU. In Tana-Lamu and Northern Province West there was no direct clash between the two national parties. Both constituencies contained widely differing groups, and tribal parochialism was decisive.

In *Tana-Lamu* there were the Pokomo, a Bantu riverine people who formed the overwhelming majority of the population of Tana River district, and the Islamic communities of Lamu district, the most significant of which were the Bajuns, an Arabized Somali people. Two of the four candidates were Pokomo. One of these, Martin Jilo, a former police officer, stood for KADU which had attempted to organize particularly among the Pokomo. Their registration was considerably lower than that of the Muslim electorate of Lamu district so that Jilo's chances were slight, even had they not been diminished by a teacher candidate, Juda Komora of the Tana River

Pokomo Union. Was there any possibility that Jilo would get in
through a split coastal vote? There, too, two candidates were
nominated, both standing for Muslim interests and coastal
autonomy. However, the Baluchi, Khermohamed Ali, who
represented the ineffective Coast People's Party, lost his deposit,
as did Komora, so that Ali Jeneby, a Bajun standing in the
name of the Shungwaya Freedom Party, was elected with a
safe majority.

In *Northern Province West* the vote of the pastoral Turkana
dominated; they accounted for some 10,600 of the 14,517
electorate. Four candidates were nominated: L. E. Whitehouse,
a former District Commissioner, was asked to stand by the
Turkana because they could not at first find a member of their
own tribe; Peter Areman, a Turkana, who had been teaching
at a Catholic Mission school in West Suk, and a last-minute
candidate; Godfrey Kariuki, a Kikuyu and general secretary
of KANU's Thomson's Falls branch; and John Lenayiarra, a
Samburu school teacher. During the campaign Whitehouse
realized that large numbers of Turkana tribesmen were moving
out of the district into Uganda and the Sudan because of the
severe drought, and so would not be present to poll. In order
not to split the Turkana vote, he 'withdrew' in favour of
Areman, who won easily. Lenayiarra could do little more than
save his deposit with the Samburu votes. There was, however,
some comment—not least from the Samburu, a KADU-
minded tribe—when Areman joined KANU. This only became
widely known after the election, though the Kenya Broadcasting
Service had announced this at Areman's request three days
before polling started.

Although an independent stood for *Taita*, the election there
was in reality fought between the KANU and KADU candidates. The area had been in Ngala's Coast constituency since
1957 and he had been a teacher in the district. Nevertheless,
the KADU leader proved unable to counteract the support
KANU rapidly established among the Taita. KANU's candidate, Dawson Mwanyumba, was an old established Taita
political leader, controlling the KANU branch, and an ardent
nationalist. He responded to the over-population and land
hunger of the Taita hills with the demand that land should be
taken from the neighbouring Tsavo Royal National Park:

Africans are more interested in land for humans than for game. KADU's candidate, Apolo Kilelu, had to take up the same cry. A teacher educated at Makerere and St. Andrew's University, he had, however, been absent from the district for many years, and was never able to capture the initiative.

The two-member constituency of *North Nyanza* had the distinction of the largest number of candidates: nine, representing both national parties, the Baluhya Political Union and a local party besides independents. The conservative Kenya African Liberal Party had announced a prospective candidate, but he, like several other hopefuls, did not stand. None of the parties could claim widespread support. KANU drew most of its backing from the heavily populated southern part of the district, while KADU's tended to come mainly from the north and centre. Party organization was superficial, and party affiliations of the candidates were not significant factors— indeed, one KADU candidate took the party's name off the second edition of his posters. Local parties had existed before the national parties were formed, but these had never attracted any substantial following. Though an educationally advanced district with a strong basic structure of local government, it is also one of the most fragmented areas in the country, both politically and culturally. No less than thirteen tribes, of whom the most prominent are the Wanga and the Maragoli, live in the district, each conscious of its own traditions and culture. There has for some years been a movement to bring those who are Bantu together as Baluhya, a name which came into existence only in the 1920s. Situated to the north of the Luo and west of the Nandi, the district contains small but important enclaves of these peoples. One Luo, supported by some people in his own location and what he grandly called the Kenya National Congress, stood, but lost his deposit. The other eight candidates were all Baluhya, but parochialism was here a governing factor.

Ideally, each national party would like to have had but two candidates, each representing different sections of the district. This, however, implied a degree of party organization and discipline which did not exist. Dominating the scene were the aspirations of a number of candidates who calculated their chances independently of party. Such a situation was of little consequence in constituencies committed to either KANU or KADU, but in North Nyanza the national parties were confronted by a formidable tribal party.

KANU's candidates were related to the predominant tribes in the west and the south of the constituency: respectively, a Wanga, John Washika, and a Maragoli, Jafetha Oyangi. The former was an ex-detainee and the latter a national leader of KANU's Youth Wing who returned from Nairobi for the contest with a band of tough supporters. Whilst Washika came third with strong support from his own tribe, Oyangi was beaten for fourth place by his fellow Maragoli, A. S. Lukalo, a secondary school teacher educated in Britain, standing as a KANU-independent. No less of a nationalist than the official KANU candidates, he was helped by his greater education, an asset he emphasized by his poster portraying him in his B.A. hood and gown. At least one of the two seats should have gone, by population, to Maragoli but there was yet a third candidate from there, Jephtha Avugwe Luseno, a former nominated member of the Legislative Council and a KADU candidate. Indeed, there was a suspicion that Muliro, keenly interested from his home in Elgon Nyanza in North Nyanza politics, had favoured Luseno's candidature to split still further the Maragoli vote. Muliro was supporting Edward Khasakhala, who gained second place; another teacher, he had been general secretary of the North Nyanza District Congress, the antecedent of KADU in the district. KADU's weakness consisted in not having a representative from the northern and western areas, although they did seek to put up from this area Christopher Siganga, a Community Development officer. He was, however· absent from the district at nomination and his papers were not completed in time.

Perhaps the most striking feature was Musa Amalemba's successful candidature. Amalemba, who had spent most of his adult life in Nairobi working as a journalist, had been a member of the Nairobi City Council and was elected in 1958, with European and Asian backing, a Specially Elected Member of the Legislative Council. As we have seen, he was bitterly condemned for this by many of the African Elected Members. Their campaign against him had made him a well-known figure. Nevertheless, he became and remained Minister for

Housing until the election. His name was linked with the New Kenya Group and he firmly believed in a multi-racial approach to Kenya's problems, feeling also that Africans should work with the existing constitution and then attempt to correct its faults.

After a private meeting with several Baluhya leaders in North Nyanza early in July 1960, Amalemba launched the Baluhya Political Union with himself as President. The Union rapidly became a political force not only in North Nyanza, but perhaps even more among the Baluhya in the towns of Kenya. The divisions of the Baluhya tribes have hindered this educationally advanced group from playing an effective role in politics. Now many of them believed that they were being treated with contempt by Luo and Kikuyu leaders, saying particularly that they had not received a fair share of the scholarships to America which these politicians controlled. Whilst urbanized Baluhya may have felt this more keenly, there was a widespread feeling in the district as well that they must have political unity to have a rightful place in the new Government.

Drawing upon the organized support of the B.P.U., Amalemba plunged into the campaign determined to prove to all that he could be elected by his own people. Though he appealed to Baluhya sentiment and the need for unity, Amalemba rejected expediency in stating his political beliefs. He continued to advocate a moderate approach. He stressed that the Governor had never closed the door on Kenyatta's eventual release, and it was up to Kenyatta to make known his views as to the kind of life he intended to follow. Land titles of all races should be respected, whilst, for both economic and security reasons, Britain's military base in Kenya should remain. His posters boldly proclaimed: 'the basis of the right type of *Uhuru* is God, Unity, Responsibility, Peace and Justice'.

Amalemba and Khasakhala were returned with comfortable majorities, Amalemba leading by over 6,000 votes. Both benefited from the split in the voting, and each possessed on his own behalf considerable support in certain parts; no candidate could claim widespread support. Khasakhala was helped considerably by Muliro's backing, particularly in the northern part of the district. Amalemba was believed to have

had the support of a large Catholic vote. Both could command
the majority of votes in their own home locations.

The Town Seats

The three seats of Nakuru Town, Mombasa West and
Nairobi East had a special significance, for towns are normally
the forcing ground of nationalism. In the mixing of towns tribal
feeling may wane through detribalization, or, under the shock
of the new situation, may even be intensified. The urban election
results might serve as a measuring rod of African nationalism
in Kenya, of its vitality and power, and thus of the nationalist
party, KANU, and its control of tribal rivalries. At the same
time there was much talk that neither of the main tribes in
KANU, Kikuyu and Luo, should be allowed to gain all these
seats where, through labour-migration, they were well represented. Since Mboya, as the sitting member for Nairobi, would
contest Nairobi East, it was felt centrally in the party that there
should not be another Luo town representative. For this reason,
Mboya persuaded his fellow trade unionist Akumu not to
stand in Mombasa, and the KANU candidate became Thomas
Chokwe, a Giriama. Central direction could not, however,
control the situation in *Nakuru*.

There the local branch was as badly riven by faction as any.
Three KANU candidates submitted nomination papers, each
claiming to be the official choice. Arthur Ochwada, the party's
assistant general secretary, basically caused the split by seeking
to control the branch to obtain local backing for his candidature. Unlike the two other KANU candidates, he had no
residential connection with the town. They, Zephanin Adholla,
a Luo, and E. P. Getata, a Kikuyu, had both been detainees
during the Emergency, though Getata was now linked with
Moral Re-Armament. All claimed to be supporters of Kenyatta,
putting on their posters his picture, one having the frontispiece
photo of Kenyatta from his book *Facing Mount Kenya*. There was
talk that of the three candidates each was connected with one
of the national leaders—Ochwada with Odinga, Adholla with
Mboya and Getata with Gichuru—so that their quarrels were
reproduced in miniature. Gichuru, as president of KANU,
visited Nakuru in a vain attempt to end the branch's quarrels.
Getata appeared to have more than a head start since well

over a third of the registered voters were Kikuyu, and certainly he courted them through the Kikuyu Welfare Association; however, his chances were lessened by the departure before polling day of a large number of Kikuyu because of the growing unemployment in the town. In the result he proved to be the strongest KANU candidate, obtaining only 27 votes less than the winner.

This was Wafula Wabuge, KADU's candidate. He could expect the support of his fellow Baluhya, who were said to regard Ochwada as a tribal traitor; indeed, the Baluhya Political Union was reported as working behind the scenes for Wabuge. At the polling station Muliro, KADU's deputy leader, stood outside, seeking particularly to win the Asian vote. They had a registration of 1,911 which might well be crucial in the 8,250 electorate. It was largely through looking to this group that Geoffrey Bellhouse, Nakuru's Mayor, dared to stand though a European. He could, of course, expect the bulk of the 731 European votes and hoped to gain a sufficient number of moderate Africans to profit from KANU's disunity. At least he succeeded in defeating Ochwada who suffered the humiliation of being the only one of the five candidates to lose his deposit. Most striking of all, the rurally orientated KADU defeated the urban nationalism of KANU through the latter's organizational weakness and personal rivalries.

The contrast in *Mombasa West* was complete, for there was one of the few well-disciplined KANU branches. They put up only one candidate, though others besides Chokwe had aspired to the nomination. The three candidates were all coastal men, the others being Francis Khamisi, the African sitting member, for KADU, and Abdurahman Omar, a teacher, with the support of the African Muslim Society. The latter's intervention was of little consequence; this was essentially a party struggle between KANU and KADU. Khamisi was KADU's Coast regional secretary and had been one of the founders of KAU, although he withdrew from it and returned to Mombasa in 1948. In 1955 he started the Mombasa African Democratic Union and was its president until the Union was dissolved in 1960. After the founding of KANU Khamisi became the first acting chairman of the Mombasa KANU branch, but shortly afterwards joined Ngala to help establish KADU in the Coast Province.

Both parties conducted an intensive campaign for this vital urban seat, holding a number of large public meetings at which the national leaders spoke before nomination day. Thereafter, few could spare the time to travel to Mombasa. At a major KADU rally on 5th February only one out of seven of KADU's national leaders billed to speak was present. There were few fundamental issues dividing the candidates. Both were uncompromisingly opposed to coastal autonomy and both raised a number of social and economic issues which touched coastal Africans. Khamisi's past activity on behalf of Mombasa market women was probably the reason for the large number of women who wore his clock symbol on their traditional black coastal over-dress. However, immigrant male labour dominated. As KANU was united, Chokwe had behind him up-country dock labour as well as local tribes like his own Giriama. KADU was driven more and more on the defensive. Looking at the symbols voters wore as they entered the polling stations, it was not difficult to forecast a win for Chokwe and the end of KADU's hopes of controlling the coastal seats.

The most dramatic open seat contest took place in *Nairobi East*. The one predominantly African seat in the capital was of clear importance in the leadership struggle and the sitting member had been, since 1957, the controversial Tom Mboya. With the end of the Emergency the Kikuyu had returned to the African residential areas in the east of the city which formed the bulk of the new constituency. Over 60% of the registered electors were from the Kikuyu and the allied Embu and Meru, with the Kikuyu in the commanding position. The next largest ethnic group were the Luo with slightly more than 10% of the vote, followed by the Kamba and the Baluhya. Whilst five candidates contested the seat, the struggle appeared to lie between Mboya and Dr. Munyua Waiyaki, a Kikuyu. Would the crucial Kikuyu vote be swayed by tribal feeling?

Mboya was selected in November by KANU's Nairobi branch as their official candidate. In his opening meeting before 20,000 people, he had to deny rumours that he and Gichuru had made a secret pact with the Secretary of State to delay the release of Kenyatta. The meeting was a great triumph for Mboya and a defeat for those leaders who were trying to undermine his position in Nairobi and among the Kikuyu.

Nevertheless, the questioning of Mboya's and Gichuru's loyalty to Kenyatta continued. Shortly before nomination day, the anti-Mboya forces announced their firm intention to put up a candidate, although there had long been rumours that this would happen. He proved to be Dr. Waiyaki, KANU's Nairobi branch chairman. Although subsequently expelled from the party he was, nonetheless, openly supported by Odinga, KANU's vice-president, and a formidable array of KANU Kikuyu political leaders. Throwing aside all party considerations, these men backed Waiyaki's independent candidature in the hope of defeating Mboya as the major obstacle to positions of dominance in the party and country.

The campaign that followed was an amateurish endeavour to undermine Mboya's integrity in the eyes particularly of the Kikuyu electorate. It was suggested that Mboya was seeking to keep Kenyatta in continued restriction to become himself Kenya's first Chief Minister, whilst Waiyaki and his supporters portrayed themselves as the only trustworthy champions of Kenyatta's interest. In the hope of establishing the honesty of his position, Waiyaki signed on nomination day an affidavit that, if elected, he would resign his seat in favour of Kenyatta upon the latter's release from restriction and that Kenyatta should be the first Chief Minister. An unsigned document, 'The Secrets of Mr. Mboya', which sought to bring him into disrepute by grossly distorting some of his past actions and by questioning his motives, was distributed during the first week of the campaign. Waiyaki denied responsibility for this, but adopted the same reasoning and illustrations in his speeches. Throughout ran the appeal to Kikuyu loyalty, with Kikuyu leaders, such as Dr. Mungai Njoroge, chairman of KANU's Central Province Consultative Committee, speaking for Waiyaki. He also had as spokesmen two former labour leaders dismissed from the Kenya Federation of Labour. Mboya was portrayed by them, and by others, as a stooge of American interests and a threat to an independent African labour movement.

Mboya concentrated his entire effort on meeting Waiyaki's challenge. In his determination to gain the initiative, no allegation went unanswered. Dominating all else was the issue of Mboya's loyalty to the leadership of Kenyatta. At an early

meeting in Bahati, a Kikuyu stronghold in Nairobi East, Mboya
and Gichuru signed a pledge of fidelity to Kenyatta, of refusal
to participate in a new Government without his unconditional
release, and of insistence that he be the first Chief Minister,
calling also on all KANU members to pledge themselves to
vacate any seat selected for him upon his release. (See plate 5.)
The campaign against Mboya and Gichuru was driving them
into extreme positions from which it would be difficult to
negotiate after the election. In seeking closer identity with
Kenyatta and the Kikuyu electorate, Mboya brought in as
speakers Kenyatta's Kikuyu lawyer, former KAU leaders and
other leading Kikuyu. Their themes were the unity of KANU
and Mboya as KANU's representative in Nairobi East;
tribalism as the worst enemy of African unity, and Waiyaki
and his supporters as its representatives.

The efforts of the other three candidates attracted little
attention. Akoko Mboya, a Luo lawyer, and Clement Were,
who had been rejected by KADU as its candidate, had difficulty
in attracting audiences. KADU's candidate, Martin Shikuku,
the party's youth wing leader, was somewhat more successful.
Both Ngala and Muliro campaigned for him, that KADU
might at least gather a respectable number of votes. Though
Shikuku attempted a spirited campaign, with vehement attacks
on Europeans, and particularly on Cavendish-Bentinck, it was
clear that he and his party were on the side lines. Mboya and
Waiyaki all but ignored them, equally with the other candidates.

It was difficult for the observer to believe that Mboya could
be defeated. A Gallup Poll type survey in late January gave
Mboya 67·4% against Waiyaki's 7%; Shikuku received 25·6%,
while the other two candidates had no support. Nonetheless,
Mboya intensified his campaign. Every public meeting was
carefully planned to accentuate the drama and significance of
the occasion. Traditional dances by Kikuyu, Kamba and Luo
became a part of nearly all meetings. Posters appeared pro-
claiming Mboya's past services and his loyalty to Kenyatta and
KANU. He was hailed with the cry '*Ndege*', the Swahili for
'aeroplane', his symbol. This was aptly turned into a reference
to Mboya's airlift organization for sending students to America,
just as, in 1957, the punning significance of the 'Cock' emblem

had been exploited to fix Mboya in the minds of many Kikuyu as a 'hero'. Thus he has often been spoken of since, especially for his efforts in seeking an end to the Emergency restrictions on the Kikuyu.

Waiyaki's last public meeting, in Bahati three days before the poll, attracted some 10,000 people. It was a curious meeting, for while Josef Mathenge, who had been returned unopposed for Nyeri, and Kenyatta's daughter, Margaret, spoke, both declared that their presence on the platform did not mean that they were supporting Waiyaki. Nonetheless, their remarks cast doubts on Mboya's statements, particularly regarding loyalty to Kenyatta. When Waiyaki rose to make his final plea, Mungai Njoroge interrupted. Arguing that Kenyatta was the only true leader, he suggested that all candidates contesting Nairobi should stand down. The day before polling began, the other four candidates went to the District Commissioner's office with this intention, but Mboya ignored this as the act of defeated and desperate men.

The climax of Mboya's campaign was a mass KANU rally, attended by about 22,000 people on the eve of the poll. It was undoubtedly the most spectacular meeting of the election. Traditional dances were performed and a long array of speakers condemned all forms of tribalism. Halfway through the meeting a low-flying plane towing Mboya's banner flew overhead, interrupting the speaker as the crowd, making KANU's 'V' sign, shouted '*Ndege, Ndege*'. Mboya reaffirmed his own and Gichuru's pledge on the leadership of Kenyatta, regretting that, instead of discussing the real issues of the election, time had been wasted in refuting the allegations of Waiyaki and his supporters. He placed his own feelings on these attacks within the context of Kipling's 'If', a poem he quoted at some length.*

Polling took place on 26th and 27th February. On the first day, a Sunday, 75 % of the electorate voted. The overwhelming majority in the long queues bore Mboya badges. Despite this outward expression of support, the dominant rumour of the campaign persisted: that while the Kikuyu might shout Mboya's name and wear his symbol, they would in secret vote tribally. This belief among non-Kikuyu marked well the prevalent suspicion of that able tribe. Otherwise, Mboya's victory

*Plate No. 5 depicts a scene at this meeting.

seemed certain; what was utterly unexpected was the measure of his success. He captured 90 % of the votes, all the other candidates thus losing their deposits.

This victory was in many ways a personal achievement, indicative of Mboya's organizational skill. Not only did he command Kikuyu votes, but his appeal embraced also the other tribes in Nairobi. While in 1957 he had stood as a workers' candidate, in this election he campaigned and was returned as a truly national leader. In accounting for the massive Kikuyu vote in support of Mboya, a Luo, it may be suggested that the Kikuyu have gone further than most tribes in developing a national outlook. Both their long involvement in politics and the destructive social and psychological consequences of the Emergency helped to foster, at least in an urban situation, the values of ability and achievement over purely tribal qualifications. Mboya demonstrated the requisites needed for modern leadership, whereas Waiyaki's primary claim was a regressive appeal to tribal solidarity. The result was a resounding defeat for the tribalists who had been urging the Kikuyu to vote for Waiyaki, and it led many non-Kikuyu Africans to reconsider their suspicions of that tribe. Mboya's victory in this urban seat thus suggested the possibility of a new and significant opportunity to build a common national loyalty among Africans.

The popular feeling for Mboya was well shown in the scenes in the African area of Nairobi on the night of the announcement of the result. The courtyard of Solidarity House, the headquarters of Mboya's Kenya Federation of Labour, was filled with a great rejoicing crowd, cheering and shouting '*Ndege*'. Africa and Europe appeared to meet: the traditionally garbed Kikuyu dancers contrasted strangely with the quiet, western-dressed Trade Union officials in the well-furnished offices of the fine building erected with Trade Union money from Britain and America. Cheering crowds thronged the streets, but were watched by squads of police and of the paramilitary General Service Unit. Armed with rifles and batons, they were determined to contain Nairobi East. Barring the approach roads to the centre of Nairobi, they prevented the spread of the rejoicing, and used tear gas twice during the night to disperse the crowds. This confrontation seemed to sum

up well the problem of the immediate future: would victorious
nationalism sweep all before it or would the organization of the
civil service administration and its forces check the onward
rush?

Part Three
AFTERMATH

CHAPTER VI

POST-ELECTION MANOEUVRES

After scenes of great but orderly excitement, polling ended on
27th February in Kenya's first General Election on a common
roll basis. During nine days 884,787 voters, or nearly 84%
of the electorate, had voted in the forty-four contested seats.
In the open seats KANU easily emerged as the dominant
party with nineteen of its official and party-independent candidates returned. Its victory was even more pronounced for
67·4% of all the votes cast could be credited to it. KADU
polled only 16·4% of the votes, but nonetheless gained eleven
seats in the new Legislative Council. Three new African members remained unaffiliated to either of the two national parties.
In the reserved seats six victorious European candidates—all
except the three Coalition representatives and the one Mombasa
independent—had received KANU support. Likewise in the
non-Muslim Asian seats KANU had backed the two victorious
Kenya Freedom Party candidates (including, that is, Chanan
Singh who won on an election petition), and in the Muslim the
independents Nathoo and Anjarwalla. KADU also had supported the New Kenya Party candidates and in Pandya had
one specific Asian whom they had fully backed, whilst
KANU had opposed him in common with the other Kenya
Indian Congress candidates. There remained the two Arabs,
apparently hostile to all up-country Africans, and the Muslim
Zafrud Deen in some position of independence between the two
African parties. In the reserved seats Africans had supported
overwhelmingly those European and Asian candidates who
appeared willing to co-operate with them in a common effort
to achieve national sovereignty and racial integration.

KANU leaders, and indeed those of KADU as well, fully
expected the Governor to meet their overall demonstration of
responsibility during the elections, the peace and order in
which the elections had generally been conducted, with a compromise over the continued restriction of Jomo Kenyatta.
African leaders were in a confident and conciliatory mood, and

there were discussions of a joint approach in forming a government party in the Legislative Council. But this atmosphere was short lived. In a broadcast on the evening of 1st March, the Governor, Sir Patrick Renison, announced that Kenyatta's release would not be effected until a government had been formed and found workable. In the same speech, he offered a mild compromise by stating that Kenyatta would be moved after a few weeks from Lodwar to Maralal, a healthier place and somewhat easier of access from Nairobi. After a government was formed, its African ministers, religious leaders and, at a later date, journalists, would be allowed to visit him to ascertain his views and intentions. Kenyatta's refusal to make any statement or reveal his thinking had influenced the decision not to release him. Security rather than political considerations were to control the moment of his release. Thus he was not to be freed in any dramatic gesture, as had happened with his old colleague, Nkrumah, after the Gold Coast (now Ghana) election of 1951.

As the Governor was speaking, Gichuru and Mboya of KANU and Ngala and Muliro of KADU were at Government House. How would they react, particularly KANU's leaders who were pledged not to enter a government until Kenyatta was released? There were, of course, significant differences from the situation in the Gold Coast in 1951. No African party had emerged in Kenya as the sole challenger to colonial rule. Although the centre of electoral power rested clearly with KANU, it was not a united party easily capable of translating its victory into governmental authority. The election results confirmed KANU's strength in the country, but did not resolve the issue of where real power lay within it. The Kenyatta issue continued to control KANU politics. While leaders and factions could still manoeuvre for positions from which to assert power, had any attempted fully to assume it, they would have been accused of arrogating to themselves the mantle reserved for Kenyatta. With opponents ready and able to employ the very effective weapon of disloyalty to the charismatic leader in exile, no faction could command a majority position in the party. 'We divide and you rule' said an Indian nationalist leader at the Round Table Conference on India in 1930.[1] It seemed that

[1] Quoted in R. Coupland, *The Indian Problem*, 1833-1935 (1942), p. 36.

the election results had left the Governor and his advisers room for manoeuvre.

The immediate request of the four leaders was that officials of their respective parties should be allowed to see Kenyatta. Two days after his broadcast, the Governor modified his original statement by agreeing that the four invited to Government House for the broadcast might go. KADU's parliamentary group approved, but there was suspicion amongst the KANU leaders concerning Mboya and Gichuru. Mboya had just won an overwhelming victory in the Nairobi East multi-tribal constituency. It seemed to some that Gichuru and Mboya were preparing to make a bid for power and would attempt to persuade Kenyatta that they should co-operate in forming a government. If this succeeded Gichuru and Mboya might achieve positions of authoritative leadership. After a six-hour meeting on 4th March, KANU's newly formed parliamentary group flatly rejected the Governor's offer that their president and general secretary should visit Kenyatta. Significantly, the resolution of refusal was proposed by Argwings-Kodhek, a close associate of Odinga who had spearheaded opposition to any compromise on the Kenyatta issue. KANU's Central Province Consultative Council (a Kikuyu body) also passed a resolution that KANU would never co-operate in the formation of government unless and until Kenyatta was freed.

Yet KANU sought to avoid a complete deadlock, for Gichuru appealed to the Secretary of State to visit Kenya and review the situation. But could Macleod act? Some believed he was then in a weak position on account of a growing feeling in the Conservative Party in Britain that too many concessions had recently been made to African nationalism. Moreover, Sir Roy Welensky, in resisting the proposed Northern Rhodesian constitution, had strengthened this Conservative attitude. Thus many in Nairobi thought that Macleod was in no position to instruct the Governor to release Kenyatta. Instead, the Secretary of State insisted that this was a security matter which must remain the Governor's responsibility. At the same time African leaders considered that the Governor was being ill advised by senior administrative officers who refused to recognize the possibility that Kenyatta could be a constructive force in the future. If the influence of these officers could be overcome, perhaps concessions could be obtained which would bring about a new situation permitting the African leaders to co-operate in forming a government.

Besides individual loyalty KANU Elected Members may have held on the Kenyatta issue, two further factors largely explain how KANU was, despite factions in its leadership and organization, able to maintain its cohesion during the immediate post-election period. In the first place, KANU knew itself to be the most powerful party in the country and, strong in its expectations, had every anticipation of forming the first government under the Lancaster House constitution. As events unfolded during March, KANU leaders appeared to believe that a compromise over Kenyatta could be made, thereby enabling them to co-operate in forming a government. Secondly, individual Elected Members were inhibited from breaking away from the party for fear of the displeasure of their KANU oriented constituents. Local party leaders and defeated KANU candidates might well campaign against them. The politics of manoeuvring could continue, at least in the immediate post-election period, without threatening the dissolution of the party. Thus, KANU presented a misleading appearance. It was not necessarily a party which would split if confronted with a situation threatening its integrity and the survival of its leadership.

The National Members

During this period of indeterminate manoeuvring and deteriorating prospects for forming a stable government, the election reached completion with the choosing of the National Members. The twelve National Members were elected by the Legislative Council sitting as an electoral college. First the Speaker held an informal meeting of the Council to explain the complexities of the procedure. National Members were to be elected in three sections: African, European and Asian-Arab. There were to be four Africans, four Europeans, two Asian non-Muslims, one Asian Muslim and one Arab (the last four comprising the Asian-Arab section). Each member of Legislative Council was entitled to one vote in each of the three sections. The balloting was to be secret. A minimum of seven votes was required for election. If after the first ballot any seats remained unfilled, balloting would continue until the four members from each section had been elected. This system had been designed to protect minorities: a group of seven or more members might be effective on the first ballot. Had the thirty-three African members been united, they could nevertheless have dominated the balloting. They had the electoral power to ensure the election of at least three-quarters of the candidates in each of the three sections.

An initial effort was made by the KANU and KADU elected members to co-operate. After the Speaker's informal meeting, a list of twelve candidates sponsored jointly by KANU and KADU was published. The list had been composed at a meeting under the chairmanship of Odinga, all present undertaking that they would support no other candidates. There was some bitterness on the part of the non-African groups that the African members were seeking to dominate the election. They had some justification for this attitude since Odinga said of the KANU-KADU meeting: 'We did not go very far to consider the support of the people within their own communities. As they were national seats they had to be considered on that basis.' As prospective candidates required support from two members of each of the three racial sections, a united racial group could veto nomination. Carried to extremes, this potential veto power could have prevented the electoral system working. In one case the Europeans did exercise a veto: not one of them was willing to sign the nomination papers of the KANU-KADU Arab prospective candidate, Sheikh Mahfood Mackawi. Inter-racial negotiations were necessary to produce true national members. In the event, the African Elected Members failed to maintain a united front. Three independent African members, Amalemba, Lord and Jeneby, were free to sign any nomination papers. Moreover, two KANU and two KADU members had been absent from the joint African parliamentary members' meeting. They made it clear by signing other papers that they did not consider themselves bound by the decisions of their colleagues. That firm discipline was lacking was evidenced by the fact that even some who had attended the meeting signed other than the approved nomination papers. Finally fifty-two candidates were nominated. Illustrative of the general lack of restraint, the independent African member, Lord, signed twenty-five nomination papers, and the independent European, Howard-

Williams, twenty-four.

The Legislative Council lobby became a scene of confusion as prospective candidates of all races and from all parts of the country sought signatures. One KANU-KADU European nominee, Derek Erskine, had some difficulty in obtaining support from any of the European members. He had previously been a member of Legislative Council but resigned in 1951 over the fingerprint issue, thereby winning considerable African popularity and losing the political support of his own community. The European Elected Members would have liked to prevent Erskine's return to the Legislative Council. At the last minute, however, two N.K.P. leaders signed his papers in return for promised African support for their favoured candidate, Rhoderick Macleod. In another move calculated to enhance Macleod's chances, N.K.P. members supported at least one 'bogus' European candidate, to try to split the African vote. Some already defeated in the general election tried but failed to obtain nomination as National Members.

Of the fifty-two nominees, four categories will illustrate the kind of people competing. Ten had failed in the general election: seven Africans, two Europeans (both Coalition) and one Asian Muslim. Two others could perhaps be included in this group: Macallan, who had stood down for Cavendish-Bentinck in the Rift Valley and S. G. Amin, a senior Indian leader who had not received a Congress 'ticket'. Of all these, only two were elected: Odede, who had stood in Central Nyanza as a KANU independent, and Kilelu, KADU's candidate in Taita. Apart from Odede, candidates included six other former Legislative Council members: two Nominated, two Specially Elected, and two Constituency Elected Members. From this group two were successful: Erskine and Bruce McKenzie, the then Minister of Agriculture. A third category comprised political party officials: Macleod, executive officer of the N.K.P.; Mulindi, chairman of the Baluhya Political Union; Konchellah, president of the Masai United Front; the secretaries of two KANU branches (Mombasa and Machakos); and the assistant information secretary of KADU. Of these only Macleod and Konchellah were elected. Then there were the women. Mrs. Gecau of Kiambu, a health visitor and social worker, received much popular backing but little support from voting members of the Council.

Outside, people remarked that there was only one woman Elected Member—Mrs. Shaw from Kericho—and suggested that there should also be at least one elected African woman. Margaret Kenyatta, the daughter of Jomo Kenyatta, was much canvassed but she neither received the African parties' nomination nor did she campaign on her own behalf. The KANU-KADU nomination list included the name of Mrs. Susan Wood, a leading proponent of multi-racialism who had been defeated in the European elections in 1956; and she lost here by a narrow margin in the final ballot.

The actual voting was not only by secret ballot but was conducted behind locked doors. However, this electoral College unlike the Sacred College of Cardinals, was not placed under an oath of secrecy and it was therefore soon possible to ascertain that the election had been completed in two ballots. This was surprising since the Asian-Arab section was divided into three separate groups—Asian non-Muslim, Asian Muslim, and Arab —and this in itself might have necessitated three ballots. Moreover, the divisions among the Elected Members, and particularly in KANU, suggested that the voting might be protracted. That it terminated so quickly must be attributed largely to the presence of two disciplined groups: the eleven KADU members and the four of the N.K.P. By their conjunction and a strict adherence to instructions, they were able to give two candidates in each section the requisite minimum of seven votes. This was the basis for the success on the first ballot for the four African seats of the two original KADU nominees, Apolo Kilelu and Peter Okondo, with nine and eight votes respectively. They were beaten only by Odede who was returned largely with the help of Asian votes. Apart from some support for Odede, the undisciplined KANU votes were split ineffectively among five other candidates. On the second ballot, the KADU-N.K.P. block voted solidly for Konchellah, who appears to have been supported also by the remaining European members.

In the European section also three candidates were elected on the first ballot. The N.K.P. negotiations with the African parties ensured the return of Macleod, although he was second to McKenzie. The disciplined KADU members split their votes as instructed between these two candidates. Erskine came third, being elected very largely by KANU votes. On the second ballot John Porter, an educationalist, who had obtained only one vote on the first ballot, received the support of the KADU-N.K.P. block and was elected. Mrs. Wood and S. V. Cooke, both on the KANU-KADU list, were defeated for they could only share the split KANU vote.

In the Asian-Arab section the main KADU vote was given to Jan Mohamed, a Muslim businessman from Machakos who was there associated in a bus company with the failed KADU candidate. The KADU-N.K.P. block also supported Sheikh Alamoody, who had resigned from the Council of State to stand for the Arab National seat. Thus these two were elected, whilst KANU support ensured the return of F. R. de Souza, a Nairobi lawyer and member of the K.F.P., to one of the two Asian non-Muslim seats. In the second ballot S. S. Patel, a Nakuru lawyer and a supporter of KADU, won the second Asian non-Muslim seat with the largest number of votes accorded to any of the National Members. The ineffectiveness of the Asian-Arab group throughout the balloting was shown very clearly in the voting for the Asian-Arab section. The Asian-Arab group which K. P. Shah would not join, held discussions, but because of the split between the Muslims and non-Muslims, their nine votes were ineffective on the first ballot. Although they put their support behind S. G. Amin on the second ballot, they were then overwhelmed by the African vote for S. S. Patel.

In the election KADU's discipline had been triumphant, as both Gichuru and Mboya confessed to the press. The initial agreement between the two parties that there should be general support for two members from each African party had broken down in the nomination process. KADU felt released from any commitment, and therefore strove for as many African seats as possible. Although a minority party, it obtained three new members to KANU's one. It prevented the election of Bomet, Moi's defeated rival in Baringo, whom it suspected had been nominated by KANU in an attempt to break up Kalenjin unity. Instead of having to vote for Bomet, KADU was now free to vote for the surprise candidate, Konchellah. KADU's effectiveness could also be seen in that three Asians and three Europeans were returned very largely with its support. By means of this election KADU substantially strengthened itself for the political struggle ahead.

The Formation of the Government

In the interval between the Governor's decision concerning the continued restriction of Kenyatta and the election of the National Members on 16th March the clash between the African parties and the Government had shown no hope of being resolved. Ngala and Muliro, KADU's leader and deputy leader, together with J. K. Tipis, had visited Kenyatta on the 8th, despite KANU's refusal then to take part in the visit. Nothing fundamental seemed to result from the interview, although Kenyatta began to re-emerge as a personality after having been for so long a voiceless symbol of African nationalism. The KADU leaders reported no specific instructions except that Kenyatta wanted African leaders to have a united front on all national issues and he regretted that KANU had not taken part in the visit. The delegation had not sought Kenyatta's advice on forming a government, because they expected this to be undertaken by KANU. They indicated that Kenyatta regarded the Lancaster House constitution as a basis for a further move towards independence. Moreover, Kenyatta was not bitter against the people of other races and would be delighted to meet the press and discuss his views.

Throughout March KADU leaders refrained from offering to join the government. The moment had not yet arrived which would permit them seriously to consider such a move. The party's interests were national, but its electoral basis was narrow. It had only a token foothold in the urban centres, and its rural support was limited to a few committed areas. Its strength resided in its leaders' acceptance of collective responsibility and their unity in opposing KANU. While KADU was not committed to the unconditional release of Kenyatta as a prerequisite of their participation in government, it had to show that it was as concerned as KANU for his immediate release from restriction lest it forfeit any chance of commanding substantial African support in forming a government. Thus Ngala and Towett resigned from their positions in the Caretaker Government as a protest against the Governor's continued refusal to modify his position on this issue. Though KADU's position on the Kenyatta question differed from that of KANU, it was nonetheless crucial for the future of the party.

Immediately after the National Members had been chosen, a

joint KANU-KADU parliamentary delegation was announced in response to Kenyatta's request to see leaders of both parties. This apparent revoking of KANU's earlier decision not to visit Kenyatta revealed in part a search for leadership able to speak with authority in order to bolster the party's position and to overcome any internal threats to its integrity. Political initiative was slipping away and had to be regained. Others saw in the visit the hope of avoiding a major constitutional crisis. Several Asian leaders appealed to Kenyatta in an open letter, urging him to tell the African leaders to participate in forming a government. They considered it 'a serious error' on the part of the Governor to maintain Kenyatta's restriction, but, as the decision had been taken, the speediest way to gain his release was to ensure that the conditions which were thought to justify his continued restriction no longer prevailed.

The KANU-KADU delegation visited Kenyatta at Lodwar on 23rd March (plate 7a and b), thus initiating a new phase in the crisis. The delegates said they had not raised the question of whether they should co-operate in the formation of a government. They were concerned rather with the problem of unity and their parties were pledged to work together in full consultation on two major issues: the immediate release of Kenyatta and the achievement of full independence in 1961. Gichuru stated that Kenyatta fully approved of KANU's decision not to take part in government without his unconditional release. Despite this joint declaration, KADU's position remained more equivocal. Their leaders who had seen Kenyatta earlier had left for the All-African People's Conference then being held in Cairo. In their absence Moi reiterated the party's position that the question of Kenyatta's release was a separate issue from that of forming a government. Before leaving for Cairo Ngala had emphasized that his party had no intention of merging with KANU, although they appreciated the principle of co-operating with other political parties on national issues. Perhaps as a portent of the future, he added that while it was not possible to form a party government, it might be feasible to consider the formation of a national government.

Before KANU's delegation set off for Cairo, to rally support from other African leaders and independent states for Kenyatta's release, Mboya bitterly blamed the Governor for the post-election 'instability, economic disintegration and crisis'. The Lancaster House constitution had served its purpose and a new constitution must be produced immediately. 'Let us embark on the next stage of our struggle to create a constitution that puts Government truly into our hands.' The apparent impasse between KANU and the Government had become a deadlock. During the Colonial Secretary's brief stop in Kenya after the Tanganyika constitutional meeting at the end of March, Gichuru again emphasized that KANU was not prepared to take part in any government until Kenyatta was freed. Nonetheless, Macleod still believed that there was a 'reasonable chance' of breaking the deadlock, because both major African parties desired to see the country advance.

Shortly before the Legislative Council was due to convene on 4th April, its opening was postponed indefinitely. On 6th April, the deadlock received further formal recognition from the Speaker. In a curious action for one in his position, he appealed to the Elected Members at a special meeting to accept an artificial majority in the Legislative Council by means of Government nominees, a reserved power which remained to the Governor under the Lancaster House constitution. The only alternative would be government by decree. With KANU seemingly not prepared to acquiesce in the Governor's use of his nominatory power, government by decree appeared more and more the only possible course. On the other hand, if the Governor was prepared to give a firm assurance that Kenyatta would be released after a government was formed, undoubtedly KADU and perhaps even KANU might regard this as sufficient basis for co-operation.

After Kenyatta's move to his new place of restriction at Maralal, he was permitted to give his first press conference since his arrest in 1952. Held on 11th April, it lasted for three hours. He was questioned by some sixty journalists on subjects ranging from female circumcision to the current constitutional deadlock. He declared that he had always been an advocate of non-violence and was dedicated to achieving freedom for his people by constitutional means. Europeans and Asians need not fear an independent African government as long as they were willing to become citizens without special privileges. He denied ever having had any Communist affiliations and maintained that there was no place for Communism in African society. The question of land titles should be gone into by an independent African government, but Kenyatta felt personally that European farmers working their land efficiently and thereby contributing to the economy had no need for fear. He rejected the Corfield Report on the Origins and Growth of Mau Mau as 'a pack of lies', a one-sided document aimed at crushing Kenyatta. Regarding his own future political role, he stated that it was up to the African people to decide. On the constitutional crisis, he believed that the Governor and the political parties should come together to find a solution. The Lancaster House constitution had already served its purpose, a roundtable conference should be called immediately to discuss the next step towards independence. Remarking on the width of the gulf between Kenyatta's aims and those of the Government, *The Times* correspondent wrote: 'This is the real basis of the Government's reluctance to release him, for all the talk about this being "a security risk", the fear being that his release would lead to sustained pressure for more and more concessions until total independence had been attained.'[2] Gichuru stated that KANU was delighted with Kenyatta's views on the need for rapid political change.

Although the Governor did not reply directly to 'Mr.' Kenyatta's statements (from the time of Kenyatta's move to Maralal, Government had acknowledged his changing status by referring to him as 'Mr. Kenyatta' rather than 'Jomo Kenyatta'), he nonetheless regarded it important to state clearly his policy on political advancement. His views were expressed in a statement on 14th April, and included the following:

'The Lancaster House constitution was devised to provide an agreed first step towards independence. Subsequent steps are responsible government, internal self-government, and final full self-government.

It is possible to pass through these stages quickly, but the Governor believes that to pass on to a second stage before the first stage is working would endanger the whole method of the planned approach which led other territories in the Commonwealth to stable independence.

The abandonment of such a planned approach could lead to a

[2] *The Times*, 13 April 1961.

landslide in which the human rights of individuals, minority tribes and communities, together with the administrative and economic structure of Kenya, would be in danger of being overwhelmed.'

Thus the Governor rejected the suggestions of Kenyatta and KANU leaders that the Lancaster House constitution had 'served its purpose' and should be superseded immediately by another.

Although KANU had given up all hope of persuading the Governor to grant them any concessions, KADU appeared determined to find some way out of the deadlock. Ngala went on to London after the All-African People's Conference. If Ngala were to succeed, he had to gain some concession on Kenyatta. He submitted to the Colonial Secretary a new memorandum setting out a case for immediate release. In an attempt to reverse the Governor's decision, he discussed the issue at separate meetings with Conservative and Labour Members of Parliament. After several days of protracted discussions with Macleod, Ngala had to admit that his aim of securing a promise of immediate release would not be forthcoming. Macleod, however, urged Ngala to see the Governor upon his return to Kenya, for he had sent to the Governor a formula which would cause a revision of attitude on the Kenyatta issue.

Immediately following Ngala's return from London, discussions were held between KADU leaders and the Governor which culminated in an announcement on 18th April that KADU would participate in the formation of a government. Kenyatta would not be immediately released from restriction, but the Government would now build a house for him and his family in his home district of Kiambu in readiness for his release 'in due course'. Other points were that there would be an elected Leader of Government Business and that KADU would be given effective control of the Colony's affairs. Anticipating KANU's opposition, Ngala said, 'We are not going into Government: we *are* the Government. We are not just co-operating with a colonial administration.' Moreover, KADU would be the dominant party in Government, although it would require support from other members of the Legislative Council.

KADU needed to fulfil at least four conditions to succeed in forming and maintaining a stable government. First, in order to enhance the new Government's prestige and stave off KANU's opposition, KADU's ministers would have to be able to effect Kenyatta's release within a very short period of time. Secondly, they would require financial assistance from Britain on a scale sufficient to make a visible impact on the critical problems of the unemployed and landless amongst the African electorate. Thirdly, they must be able to show that co-operation had helped to accelerate the pace of political development. Rapid constitutional progress towards independence would be essential if they were to refute KANU's attacks that they were willing agents of colonial rule. Finally, KADU would need to strengthen its numerical support and attract as associates men of ability. It would require support from the Asian and European members, the African independents, as well as from a few KANU Elected Members.

Britain and the colonial administration could assist in meeting the first three challenges: the Kenyatta issue, financial aid and constitutional progress. KADU's basic weakness as a rural minority party remained. Yet KANU's divisions appeared to increase KADU's prospects. Before the elections there had been talk, especially among KADU members, of a possible realignment of parties and individuals after the election. KADU leaders believed that they might be able to detach some of the Elected Members from KANU. It was known that some were dissatisfied with their party's apparently uncompromising refusal to join in the formation of a government without Kenyatta's prior release. Others, like the Kamba members, felt that they were not accorded enough prestige in the party. The leadership conflicts fostered the impression that defectors might be forthcoming.

KADU's decision to co-operate in forming a government had created a crisis for KANU. No longer could loyalty be maintained through an expectation that the party would rapidly achieve its objective and become the first government under the Lancaster House constitution. A new situation had arisen in which dissatisfied KANU members might be tempted to join KADU in governing the country. KADU offered at least one ministerial post, together with the possibility of being able to effect rapidly the release of Kenyatta and to take real steps towards the early achievement of independence. Should the four Kamba members join KADU in government, then KANU would clearly be open to the attack that it was predominantly a Kikuyu-Luo party. If KANU was to continue as the dominant African party and be in a position effectively to challenge a KADU government, the party could no longer afford disunity in its leadership and lack of discipline in its ranks.

The formation of the new Government was formally announced on 27th April. While the four colonial civil servants retained their ministerial positions as set forth in the Lancaster House constitution, Ronald Ngala became Leader of Government Business. The creation of this position was meant to convey a sense of political advance; indeed, Nkrumah first held this title as a stepping stone to that of Chief Minister. Ngala showed some courage in also accepting the portfolio of Education, an area in which rapid advance had been demanded by Africans throughout the elections. Associated with Ngala as ministers were his KADU colleagues, Muliro and Towett, but the fourth African post was assigned temporarily to a civil servant in the hope that a KANU elected member might yet be detached to join the Government. The single Asian ministry went to Jamidar, whose acceptance was supported by the other two Kenya Indian Congress elected members on the Government benches. Thus previous alignments in the Kenya National Party in 1959 were re-established in part, Jamidar and the Indian Congress co-operating with those African leaders who had helped form that multi-racial party. In addition, the new Government was supported by the leaders of the N.K.P., men who had taken the lead in forming in 1959 the multi-racial New Kenya Group. Havelock retained the portfolio of Local Government and, after some hesitation, Blundell once again accepted the ministry of Agriculture. This co-operation by the N.K.P. with KADU had been forged during the election for the National Members, despite the dependence of the N.K.P. on KANU support for its candidates at the time of the common roll elections. The Government thus appeared as a combination of many of those who had sought in 1959 a multi-racial approach in the Legislative Council. Although this apparent relationship seemed to be strengthened by the third European minister being Peter Marrian, the successful European independent with a Capricorn background, and by Musa Amalemba

14

subsequently accepting a position as a Parliamentary Secretary, it was not the multi-racialism of the Lennox-Boyd constitution. African party politics had replaced multi-racial politics as the dominant factor in the Kenya of 1961. A new Government led by Africans but with representatives from other races now shared authority with the colonial administration. Lacking a working majority in the Legislative Council, however, it could only be maintained by the Governor's appointing eleven nominees to the Government benches. Sir Patrick Renison was thus compelled to employ the reserve power of nomination which he had told the Lancaster House conference he desired to abandon.

When the new Legislative Council met on 11th May, the majority of the Elected Members sat on the opposition benches. The main force of the opposition rested with KANU, which was supported by two European National Members, Erskine and McKenzie. McKenzie had refused to retain the portfolio of Agriculture and had broken with his former N.K.P. colleagues. He saw the dangers of this minority government, and the likely embitterment of feeling between races and tribes. He actively supported KANU and its policies both in the Council and at public meetings. Soon he was denouncing in the Council the 'gerrymandering' of the constituencies—although the reply was quickly made that he had been in the Government when the Working Party reported. Asian support for KANU consisted of the three Kenya Freedom Party members and the four Muslim Asians. Nathoo had already co-operated with KANU by accompanying Gichuru on a delegation to London. Thus KANU, like the Government, could claim that it had multi-racial support for its position. Also on the opposition benches were the Coalition members, the independent Howard-Williams, and the two Arab Elected Members. Their interests were not the same as KANU's, but neither were they identified with the Government. Like KANU, they represented the majority of their communities.

Although the Lancaster House conference had left critical issues unresolved, particularly Kenya's future land policy, it had established the fact that eventually the African majority would dominate. The direction of political change was no longer in doubt, but the rate of change towards independence

was left to future negotiation. African leaders returning from
Lancaster House were determined to achieve independence
in the shortest possible period of time. For the first time since
the banning of KAU in 1953, these leaders could campaign
on a colony-wide basis and build national parties to achieve
their objectives. African mass politics had finally received in a
real sense the stamp of legitimacy. In this new political environment, the fragile and limited politics of the Blundell multi-
racial group which was to have been the linchpin of the new
constitution simply disintegrated. By the time of the election it
was no more than a European faction commanding only the
barest support in that community. The multi-racialism of the
Lyttelton and Lennox-Boyd constitutions had given way to the
nationalism of the African majority.

Kenya's new democracy spoke in the election, but since the
majority of Africans had linked their cry for freedom with
'Uhuru na Kenyatta', the colonial government was unwilling
to accept the result of the election in terms of the votes cast.
Kenyatta remained to the Governor and his civil service
advisers, as well as to the majority of the Europeans, 'a leader
to darkness and death'. With power still in the hands of the
colonial government, the Governor rejected the wish of the
overwhelming mass of the voters. Kenyatta was not released
and an impasse was soon reached with KANU, in terms of
votes overwhelmingly the majority party.

Commanding only minority support from the newly enfranchised electorate, the new Government appeared inherently
unstable, an instability made more pronounced by the determination of an incensed opposition to bring the Government
into disrepute. Mobilizing its forces, KANU and its supporters
aimed at dispelling the idea that Kenya could move system-
atically to independence under KADU's leadership. KADU,
on the other hand, appeared determined to succeed in its new
role and it had some formidable weapons. On the day the new
Legislative Council met, it was announced that the men who
had been tried with Kenyatta would be allowed to return to
their home areas. The budget was presented five days later, and
the civil service Finance Minister was able to state that British
financial aid to Kenya for the current year would be at least
£18½ million in grants and loans. When Bernard Mate, Meru's

senior member, crossed the floor of the Council and accepted the portfolio of Health and Welfare, KADU began to show increased confidence. On 13th June, the Leader of Government Business, Ngala, announced the hope of achieving internal self-government for Kenya by the end of the year. He hoped, and expected, that the Government would arrange the appointment of a Chief Minister by October, and an increase in the number of elected ministers—the intention being that the Chief Minister would hold talks with the Colonial Office for the next constitutional change to take place in 1961. Without referring explicitly to the statement which Hugh Fraser, the Under-Secretary of State, was reported to have made during his visit to Kenya in May that independence was 'several years and several constitutional conferences ahead', Ngala maintained that there was no need for several conferences before achieving independence. The Lancaster House constitution was sufficiently flexible to allow this, although talks and discussions with the British Government would be prerequisites. Blundell, who during the election campaign had sought to reassure the European electorate that independence was in the distant future, was now denouncing in the Legislative Council 'itinerant people' who came to Kenya and dictated details of the Colony's constitutional advance.

KANU's answer to the announcement of constitutional advance was a demand for independence in 1961 and the immediate release of Jomo Kenyatta. While rejecting the 'planned' programme towards independence of KADU and the colonial administration, it was at the same time inhibited in launching a massive attack against the Government outside the Legislative Council. Not only did its branches continue to remain poorly organized, but the new unity within the senior leadership was by no means completely consolidated. Perhaps of even greater importance was the danger involved in developing massive resistance in the country. Ugly memories of the Emergency were still fresh in the minds of the people, and KANU leaders had no desire to precipitate a new one. Arrests of men alleged to be 'planning violence' against Ngala and other members of the Government and their families were reported, and there existed a small hardcore of extremists who might seek to gain control of any resistance movement.

Although KADU may have achieved a major tactical advantage over KANU in forming the first government under the Lancaster House constitution, it remained a government of minorities. As KANU leaders sat frustratedly in opposition searching for constitutional means with which to bring down the Government, grave uncertainty about the future persisted in all communities.

Overshadowing the parliamentary struggle in Legislative Council was the unmistakable authority of Jomo Kenyatta. To the vast majority of the African population Kenyatta was not only the paramount leader, but also the symbol and embodiment of their nationalism. In the search for unity and coherence of purpose, his authoritative leadership continued to grow in stature and remained unchallenged. No longer could the colonial administration deny his commanding role in Kenya's nationalism. Indeed, Kenyatta may provide the cohesion necessary for concerted action in the future. If Kenya is to have a peaceful and constructive transition to independence, the real powers of the past and of the future must come to terms with the realities of the election results.

APPENDIX I

Common Roll Election Summary

53 Seats (44 contested)

Party	Votes	Percentage	Seats
Kenya African National Union (Official and Party-independent)	590,661	67·4	19
Kenya African Democratic Union (Official and Party-independent)	143,079	16·4	11
Baluhya Political Union	28,817	3·3	1
New Kenya Party	28,284	3·2	4
Kenya Indian Congress	10,488	1·2	3
Kenya Coalition	8,891	1·1	3
Kenya Freedom Party	5,263	0·6	2
Kenya National Congress	4,561	0·5	0
Shungwaya Freedom Party	3,748	0·4	1
Coast People's Party	1,693	0·2	0
Tana River Pokomo Union	699	0·1	0
Independents—African	13,917		1
Arab	5,712		2
Asian Muslim	11,880	5·6	3
Asian Non-Muslim	4,648		0
European	12,768		3
Totals	875,109	100	53

RESERVED SEATS

EUROPEAN

Constituency and Candidate's Name	Primary Result	Common Roll Result	Electorate Primary	Electorate Common Roll	Valid ballot papers Primary	Valid ballot papers Common Roll	Percentage poll Primary	Percentage poll Common Roll (including spoilt papers)
125. CENTRAL RURAL (1)								
MARRIAN, P. (Ind.)	804 44·81%	10,073	2,211	14,148	1,794	11,665	81·14%	85%
Markham, Sir Charles (K.C.)	1,185 66·05%	1,592						
23. KERICHO (1)								
SHAW, A. R., Mrs. (N.K.P.)	234 36·96%	2,572	780	4,042	633	3,215	82%	80·6%
Oates, C. O. (K.C.)	460 72·67%	643						
38. MOMBASA EAST (1)								
CLEASBY, R. P. (Ind.)	644 85·64%	Returned	958	1,298	752	—	78·53%	—
Hamley, C. W. (Ind.)	115 15·29%	—						
3. NAIROBI SOUTH-WEST (1)								
HAVELOCK, W. B. (N.K.P.)	602 30·3%	1,643	2,588	3,978	1,984	3,221	76·67%	82·8%
Megson, F. L. (K.C.)	1,498 75·5%	1,578						

¹The figure before the constituency name conforms to the maps, that after indicates the number of seats in the constituency.

EUROPEAN—contd.

Constituency and Candidate's Name	Primary Result		Common Roll Result	Electorate		Valid ballot papers		Percentage poll	
				Primary	Common Roll	Primary	Common Roll	Primary	Common Roll (including spoilt papers)
7. NAIROBI SUBURBAN (1)				2,355	5,100	1,813	4,170	76·99%	82·8%
ALEXANDER, R. S. (N.K.P.)	649	35·8%	2,799						
O'Beirne, D. P. R. (K.C.)	1,249	68·8%	1,371						
4. NAIROBI WEST (2)				4,462	5,636	3,484	4,289	76·7%	77·9%
SALTER, C. W. (K.C.)	2,207	63·34%	1,647						
HOWARD-WILLIAMS, E. L. (Ind.)	1,889	54·21%	1,372						
Bompas, F. W. G. (N.K.P.)	977	28·04%	1,261						
Needham-Clark, M., Mrs. (K.C.)	1,413	40·55%	9						
Hughes, E. D., Mrs. (N.K.P.)	812	23·3%	—						
29. NORTH KENYA (1)				1,256	11,971	934	—	74·4%	—
COLE, D. L. (K.C.)	837	89·6%	Returned						
Campbell, L. (N.K.P.)	132	14·1%	—						

26. RIFT VALLEY (1)									
BLUNDELL, M. (N.K.P.)	542	26.7%	20,009	2,286	25,528	2,031	22,060	89%	89.4%
Cavendish-Bentinck, Sir Ferdinand (K.C.)	1,545	76%	2,051						
28. WEST KENYA (1)									
WELWOOD, L. R. M. (K.C.)	1,734	82.5%	Returned	2,436	10,296	2,102	—	86.29%	—
Goord, A. B. (N.K.P.)	414	19.7%	—						

ASIAN NON-MUSLIM

19. KISUMU TOWN (1)									
KOHLI, D. B. (K.I.C.)	804	51.9%	1,246	1,857	5,672	1,549	2,317	84.05%	75.1%[2]
Joshi, R. P. (Ind.)	844	54.49%	1,071						
Biant, B. S. (Ind.)	346	22.34%	—						
40. MOMBASA LIWATONI (1)									
PANDYA, A. J. (K.I.C.)	1,540	57.87%	1,752	3,161	3,946	2,661	3,420	84.15%	88.4%
Inamdar, I. T. (Ind.)	1,166	43.81%	1,668						
5. NAIROBI CENTRAL (2)									
SHAH, K. P. (K.F.P.)	3,532	45.72%	4,229	14,066	17,191	7,725	11,917	54.92%	70.9%
JAMIDAR, A. (K.I.C.)	3,888	50.33%	3,431						
Sandhu, G. S. (K.I.C.)	3,828	49.55%	3,379						
Travadi, K. D. (Ind.)	2,979	38.56%	878						

[2] This figure relates also to the Muslim reserved seat in this two-member constituency.

Constituency and Candidate's Name	Primary Result		Common Roll Result	Electorate		Valid ballot papers		Percentage poll	
				Primary	Common Roll	Primary	Common Roll	Primary	Common Roll (including spoilt papers)

ASIAN NON-MUSLIM—contd.

Constituency and Candidate's Name	Primary Result		Common Roll Result	Electorate Primary	Common Roll	Valid ballot Primary	Common Roll	% Primary	Common Roll
2. NAIROBI SOUTH (1)									
Singh, Chanan (K.F.P.)	770	38·95%	1,034						
Singh, Mota (Ind.)	939	47·5%	1,031						
Patel, J. S. (K.I.C.)	734	37·13%	680						
				2,798	3,486	1,977	2,745	70·66%	80%

ASIAN MUSLIM

19. KISUMU TOWN (1)									
Nathoo, I. E. (Ind.)	397	67·52%	1,008						
Dean, C. K. (Ind.)	213	36·22%	854						
				649	5,672	588	1,862	90·6%	75·1%

39. MOMBASA TUDOR AND OLD TOWN (1)

Candidate									
ANJARWALLA, S. K. (Ind.)	2,219	70·73%	3,838	4,266	8,561	3,137	5,496	73·5%	66·2%
Kasmani, K. A. (Ind.)	1,006	32·07%	1,658						

6. NAIROBI NORTH-EAST (1)

Candidate									
DEEN, K. ZAFRUD (Ind.)	1,155	54·2%	1,684						
Ali, Ahmed (Ind.)	613	28·8%	1,545						
Amin, Shaikh M. (Ind.)	766	36%	1,293	3,082	5,958	2,128	4,522	68·82%	77·6%

ARAB

41. MOMBASA CENTRAL (1)

Candidate									
NASSIR, A. (Ind.)	705	35·95%	2,373						
Mackawi, S. M. (Ind.)	786	40·08%	1,242						
Balala, S. M. (Ind.)	523	26·67%	9	2,454	4,858	1,961	3,624	79·91%	76%

33. PROTECTORATE (1)

Candidate									
BASSADIQ, O. S. (Ind.)	1,460	66·58%	2,088						
Shikely, A. A. (C.P.P.)	758	34·56%	1,401	3,018	24,503	2,193	3,489	74%	14%

Appendix

OPEN SEATS

Constituency and Candidate's Name	Result	Population (1948 Census)	Electorate	Valid ballot papers	Percentage poll (including spoilt papers)
TOWNS					
42. MOMBASA WEST (1)					
Chokwe, T. M. (KANU)	8,576	1948 figures of the towns are in no way relevant to these three constituencies	17,701	13,565	78·3%
Khamisi, F. J. (KADU)	3,230				
Omar, A. (Ind.)	1,759				
1. NAIROBI EAST (1)					
Mboya, T. J. (KANU)	31,407				
Waiyaki, M. (Ind.)	2,668				
Shikuku, M. (KADU)	1,557		39,458	35,787	91·6%
Were, C. H. (Ind.)	79				
Mboya, G. P. A. (Ind.)	76				
27. NAKURU TOWN (1)					
Wabuge, W. (KADU)	2,124				
Getata, E. P. (KANU)	2,097				
Adholla, Z. (KANU)	1,521		8,250	7,182	87·8%
Bellhouse, G. L. (Ind.)	1,129				
Ochwada, A. A. (KANU)	311				

CENTRAL PROVINCE

10. EMBU (1)					
Nyagah, J. (KANU)	43,943				
Njuno, N. N. N. (KANU Ind.)	19,135				
Maringa, R. N. (KANU)	16,240	202,611	88,738	79,318	89.7%
24. FORT HALL (2)					
Kiano, J. G. (KANU)	47,995				
Njiri, K. (KANU)	45,719				
Mbarathi, D. (KANU Ind.)	1,483	304,457	103,750	95,197	94%
8. KIAMBU (1)					
Gichuru, J. S. (KANU)	Unopposed	258,085	74,507	—	—
11. MERU (2)					
Mate, B. (KANU)	31,986				
Angaine, J. (KANU)	30,021				
Kiecha, J. (KANU Ind.)	20,231				
Kamunde, S. A. (KANU)	6,025				
Ethaiba, H. (KANU Ind.)	3,427				
Mbogori, E. K. (KANU Ind.)	1,846				
Mbogori, N. (KANU Ind.)	1,288				
Mburea, E. (KANU Ind.)	299	313,702	107,584	95,123	88.4%
9. NYERI (1)					
Mathenge, J. (KANU)	Unopposed	184,363	82,704	—	—

COAST PROVINCE

Constituency and Candidate's Name	Result	Population (1948 Census)	Electorate	Valid ballot papers	Percentage poll (including spoilt papers)
35. KILIFI (1)		Population figures omitted on account of the excision of the Protectorate constituency from these 2 districts			
NGALA, R. G. (KADU)	16,305		20,389	16,613	81·1%
Suleman, S. S. (KANU)	308				
36. KWALE (1)					
MATANO, R. S. (KADU)	917		2,583	1,416	55·3%
Mwero, P. J. (KADU Ind.)	499				
37. TAITA (1)					
MWANYUMBA, D. (KANU)	8,681	62,051	12,144	10,377	85·4%
Kilelu, A. P. (KADU)	1,632				
Zawadi, S. P. (Ind.)	64				
34. TANA AND LAMU (1)					
JENEBY, A. M. (S.F.P.)	3,748	40,286	8,640	6,963	80·6%
Jilo, M. T. (KADU)	2,224				
Komora, J. (T.R.P.U.)	699				
Ali, K. (C.P.P.)	292				

NORTHERN PROVINCE

	Un-opposed	Population			
44. NORTHERN PROVINCE EAST (1)					
Lord, A. A. (Ind.)	Un-opposed		1,622	—	—
43. NORTHERN PROVINCE WEST (1)		Population figures are not possible for these two constituencies owing to the way the boundaries were drawn			
Areman, P. A. (KANU)	7,112				
Lenayiarra, J. K. (Ind.)	1,208				
Kariuki, G. G. (KANU Ind.)	194				
Whitehouse, L. E. (Ind.)	194		14,517	8,708	60·3%

NYANZA PROVINCE

	Un-opposed	Population			
18. CENTRAL NYANZA (2)					
Odinga, A. O. (KANU)	46,638				
Argwings-Kodhek, C. M. G. (KANU)	21,136				
Osoga, J. C. N. (KANU Ind.)	5,938				
Odaba, H. D. (KADU)	3,751				
Odede, F. W. (KANU Ind.)	1,770				
Mariwa Gek, J. C. (KANU Ind.)	1,440		458,849	98,804	80,673	83·3%
17. ELGON-NYANZA (1)					
Muliro, M. (KADU)	Un-opposed	See North Nyanza	63,096	—	—

NYANZA PROVINCE—contd.

Constituency and Candidate's Name	Result	Population (1948 Census)	Electorate	Valid ballot papers	Percentage poll (including spoilt papers)
22. KIPSIGIS (1)			61,753	56,603	91·8%
TOWETT, T. (KADU)	56,445	152,391			
KORIR, K. (KANU)	102				
BARMALEL, T. (KANU)	56				
21. KISII (1)		South Nyanza and Kisii	35,232	30,906	88·9%
SAGINI, L. G. (KANU Ind.)	9,436	546,590			
NYAMWEYA, J. (KANU)	8,318				
MASAKI, T. M. (KANU Ind.)	6,642				
ANYIENI, Z. M. (KANU Ind.)	5,563				
KEBASO, J. K. (KANU Ind.)	947				
16. NORTH NYANZA (2)		In 1948 North Nyanza and Elgon-Nyanza were one district with a population of 635,580	142,458	118,647	84·6%
AMALEMBA, M. (B.P.U.)	28,817				
KHASAKHALA, E. (KADU)	22,625				
WASHIKA, J. (KANU)	16,098				
LUKALO, A. S. Z. (KANU Ind.)	14,700				
OYANGI, J. M. (KANU)	12,601				
AKATSA, W. B. (KANU Ind.)	12,114				
OMORO, I. N. Y. (K.N.C.)	4,561				
LUSENO, J. A. (KADU)	3,800				
KHASIANI, J. (KANU Ind.)	3,331				

20. SOUTH NYANZA (1) AYODA, S. A. (KANU) Oguda, L. (KANU Ind.)	13,993 6,729	See under Kisii	27,136	20,722	76·9%

RIFT VALLEY PROVINCE

30. BARINGO (1) Moi, D. A. (KADU) Bomet, E. K. (Ind.)	5,225 503	72,147	6,730	5,728	86·1%
32. ELGEYO-SUK (1) Murgor, W. C. (KADU) Chemweno, J. K. S. (Ind.)	7,532 6,116	107,328	16,471	13,648	83%
31. NANDI (1) Seroney, M. J. (KADU Ind.) Kimalel, S. K. (KADU)	13,286 1,547	80,796	18,351	14,833	81·3%

15

SOUTHERN PROVINCE

Constituency and Candidate's Name	Result	Population (1948 Census)	Electorate	Valid ballot papers	Percentage poll (including spoilt papers)
14. KAJIADO (1)					
Keen, J. (KADU)	Unopposed	29,482	2,732	—	—
13. KITUI (2)		211,254	14,000	9,958	71·1%
Mati, F. M. (KANU)	5,219				
Mwendwa, E. N. (KANU)	3,295				
Muimi, J. N. (Ind.)	1,444				
12. MACHAKOS (2)		351,405	80,570	65,130	81·5%
Mulli, H. N. (KANU)	21,076				
Nthenge, G. W. (KANU Ind.)	18,836				
Malu, W. M. K. (KANU)	15,383				
Ndile, J. K. (KANU Ind.)	7,002				
Mutiso, P. K. (KANU Ind.)	1,674				
Kasyoka, J. M. (KANU Ind.)	409				
Mangeli, B. (KADU)	380				
Kiamba, D. I. (KANU Ind.)	370				
15. NAROK (1)					
Tipis, J. K. (KADU)	Unopposed	37,648	5,025	—	—

SUMMARY

Electorate: Unopposed seats	353,251	Valid votes	875,109
Contested seats	1,057,866	Spoilt papers	9,678
Total	1,411,117	Total	884,787

Percentage poll: 83·63%

The returns, taken from the *East African Standard*, 3rd March 1961, have been compared with the Kenya Information Service press handouts, and the figures have then been further checked. The party designations derive from field work and therefore do not always conform to those of the *E.A.S.*

APPENDIX II

The Press and Broadcasting

When the overwhelming mass of an electorate is illiterate and the fundamental means of communication are still oral, it is difficult to judge the impact of the press in an election. The political meeting is probably more important. Nonetheless, newspapers and journals are read by literates, and by them to non-literates, and the ideas and information are then often rapidly transmitted by word of mouth. Certainly in this election leaders and literate voters were very conscious of the role of the press.

Kenya's oldest established paper is the *East African Standard* (daily, 24,300, weekly edition 42,600).[1] It has a long history of ownership connection with the leading European political figures, and has been mainly written for the European community, settler, official and commercial. In the past few years, however, it has begun to devote an increasing attention to African politics. The same firm publishes also a weekly, *Baraza* (48,000), in Swahili for African readers. The established position of these two papers has been challenged by the appearance since Lancaster House of some new and lively ones, owned by a company in which the Aga Khan, the leader of the Ismaili community, has a large interest: East African Newspapers. They publish the *Daily Nation* (15,000), the *Sunday Nation* (32,000), and *Taifa Leo* ('the nation today', 33,000), the last having in *Taifa* (55,500) a weekly edition. The latter two are published in Swahili, the first of these being the only daily paper in that language. Considerable efforts have been made to develop the circulation of these two papers in the African rural areas, and they were undoubtedly the most significant papers for the open seats, giving a more extensive coverage of African news than any other paper. The *Daily Nation* also carried more information on African and Asian politics than did the *Standard*. The *Nation* and its stable companions were more sympathetic to African aspirations, being particularly well informed on developments inside KANU.

Throughout the election the *Standard*, although claiming to seek an impartial position, leant more towards the policies of Michael Blundell and the N.K.P. Coalition supporters were heard to say that the press was against them, but then in Kenya the *Standard* has often been spoken of among Europeans in the past as 'the press'. As the election campaign went on, the Coalition had less and less reason for complaint. The important *Kenya Weekly News* (9,000) of Nakuru, which also claimed to be seeking an impartial position, leant in the Coalition direction, whilst the Nairobi *Sunday Post* (14,600) came out clearly for them. The letter columns of these two journals, together with those of the *Standard*, reflect well the range of opinion of the resident Europeans. These weeklies also carried some news and comment on African politics.

On the Asian side the oldest existing paper is the *Kenya Daily Mail* (daily,

[1]Bracketed figures denote approximate circulations as at 1 December 1960.

2,000, weekly ed. 3,000). This was founded by J. B. Pandya, father of A. J. Pandya, and is owned by Pandya Printing Works Limited. Like most other Asian owned papers, it is published in English and Gujerati, the predominant language among the Asians. Other important Asian papers are the *Daily Chronicle* (4,000) and the *Colonial Times* (5,000), the latter a weekly which in the election voiced the views of Chanan Singh and his Kenya Freedom Party. The *Colonial Times* has some features designed for African readers. One Asian owned paper, *Jicho* (20,000), is printed in English and Swahili and has an African editor.

Kenya's independent vernacular press remains small, comprising only a few papers, with limited circulations. Perhaps the most significant in the Kikuyu areas is *Kirinyaga* ('Mount Kenya', 10,000); owned by Dr. Kiano, it advocated unity and the end of divisions in Kikuyu society. Two Luo papers of some importance are *Ramogi* (7,000) and the *Nyanza Times* (no figures available). The former, published in Nairobi, carries a considerable amount of news of Nyanza Province; the latter, fundamentally a militant paper, gave unquestioned support to Odinga and Argwings-Kodhek in their Central Nyanza campaign. In November 1960, KANU started a party weekly: *Sauti ya KANU* ('voice of KANU', 35,000); printed in Swahili, it has a wide distribution. KANU also publishes periodically, in Kikuyu, *Wiyathi* ('Freedom'), which supported Mboya in Nairobi East. KADU initiated a party paper in December: *Nyota ya Haki* ('Star of Justice', no figures available).

The *East African Standard* published daily, after nomination day, short policy statements from most candidates of all racial groups, together with their pictures. *Taifa Leo* also published brief biographical sketches. The government regional papers[2] gave candidates in the open seats the opportunity of making brief statements, a facility offered also by the government weekly *Habari* (15,500), a Swahili paper with a colony-wide circulation.

The Kenya Broadcasting Service gave election information not only through its regular news bulletins, but also in special election programmes. It was consistently reported that the radio was able to reach more persons than were the newspapers. A recent survey for the Kenya Broadcasting Service revealed that there were at least 52,000 African households with radio sets and it was estimated that the African audience potential was over 275,000. Programmes are provided in English and certain Asian languages, besides Arabic, Swahili, Kikuyu and other African vernaculars.

Allotment of election broadcasts was made on principles laid down by the Council of Ministers. Each recognized national party was permitted

[2]

Paper	Language	Approximate Circulation	Published
Sauti ya Pwani	Swahili	5,500	Twice monthly
Matemo	Kikuyu	10,000	Fortnightly
Mutai	Kamba	7,500	Twice monthly
Kalenjin	Nandi	5,000	Monthly
Nyanza Citizen (North)	English/Swahili	3,500	Twice monthly
Nyanza Citizen (South)	English/Swahili	3,500	Twice monthly
Ilomen le Maasai	Masai	1,500	Monthly

one fifteen-minute broadcast on the three National Services simultaneously (English, Asian and African), two of fifteen minutes on one or other of these National Services, and three of ten minutes on a regional programme (Western, Central and Coast), these last being in any language the party might choose. Independents unconnected with any national party were each permitted one four-and-a-half minute broadcast on a regional programme. All broadcasts had to be pre-recorded by K.B.S. to ensure that no party or independent had an advantage in knowing what was being said by another.

Eight national parties were recognized for these broadcasts: the Coalition, the N.K.P., the Kenya Indian Congress, the Kenya Muslim League, the K.F.P., KANU, KADU and the Kenya African Liberal Party. The last was removed from the list when it failed to nominate any candidates, whilst special arrangements were agreed for the Muslim League and the K.F.P. when it was found that their members were standing as 'independents'. These arrangements fitted in the general rule that the addresses should be on behalf of a party and that the speakers were not to canvass for themselves as individuals. A number of people spoke for their parties though they were not candidates: thus, Gautama and C. B. Madan for the Congress, and Dr. S. G. Hassan for the Muslim League, whilst the Coalition and the N.K.P. each had Africans to speak in Swahili on their behalf.

The Asian broadcasts tended to become little historical sermons. Nearly all the performers could have benefited from production assistance. Undoubtedly the most effective speaker was Gichuru for KANU, though his repeated stress on Kenyatta did nothing to allay European fears. KANU lost one national programme opportunity because of a speaker's failure to make the recording before the closing date. For an independent to qualify to speak he had to sign a statement that he was not affiliated to any national party, and this eliminated the party-independents, but did allow Dr. Waiyaki, expelled from KANU, to put his anti-Mboya line in Nairobi East. Few independents broadcast: either because of the shortage of time between nomination day, when they were officially informed of these facilities, and the closing date for the pre-recording, or because they believed it would have little effect on the electorate. Thus from the western region station the only independent to broadcast was Joshi, in Hindustani, but he lived in Kisumu. Certainly the need to travel to a K.B.S. studio ruled out for many independents any thought of broadcasting.

SELECT BIBLIOGRAPHY

1. *Official Documents*

Report of the Kenya Constitutional Conference, held in January and February 1960, Cmnd. 960.

Report of the Working Party appointed to Consider Elections under the Lancaster House Agreement, Kenya Sessional Paper No. 7 of 1959/60.

The Kenya (Electoral Provisions) Order in Council, 1960.

The Legislative Council (Constituency Members) Regulations, 1960.

The Legislative Council Ordinance, 1960.

The Legislative Council Election Rules, 1960.

Legislative Council Debates, particularly:
    on the Working Party report, 14-21 June 1960.
    on the Legislative Council Bill, 14-16 December 1960.

2. *Comparative Material*

G. F. Engholm: 'African Elections in Kenya, March 1957' in *Five Elections in Africa* (1960), edited by W. J. M. Mackenzie and K. E. Robinson.

T. E. Smith: *Elections in Developing Countries* (1960).

Susan Wood: *Kenya, the Tensions of Progress* (1960).

INDEX

Havelock supported by Gichuru and Muliro at a private meeting for African civil servants at the opening of his common roll campaign

b. Cavendish-Bentinck campaigning in the Rift Valley for the African vote. See p. 108

2. Mungai Njoroge introduces Peter Marrian to an African audience. See p. 106

3. Kenya Freedom Party makes the KANU sign.　a.　*above:* Chanan Singh in Nairobi South.　b.　*below:* K. P. Shah's prominent car symbol in Nairobi Central

4. Odinga's Press Conference at KANU's Headquarters in January in which he attacked Mboya, whose portrait is on the wall.
Left to right: Argwings-Kodhek, Ochwada, Odinga, Njoroge, Kibaki. See p. 132

5. Mboya's eve of poll meeting. Standing in the car Gichuru in striped shirt and Mboya in beaded cap. Note Mboya's aeroplane symbol and the Kenyatta picture with Mboya in the heart of Kenyatta. See p. 179
Inset: Mboya and Gichuru signing a pledge of loyalty to Kenyatta during the campaign. See p. 178

6. Polling station scenes.

a. *above*, Turkana women carrying their registration cards in the traditional cleft sticks. b. *below*, Kikuyu women queueing in Fort Hall

7. At Lodwar on 23rd March 1961.

left: Mboya, Gichuru, Matano with
Kenyatta

b. *right:* Odinga with Kenyatta.
See p. 194

. KANU leaders outside Legislative Council building at opening meeting on 11th May.
Left to right: Chokwe, Mboya, Gichuru, Mwanyimba, Odinga, Mathenge

8. The Governor opening the Legislative Council on 11th May. Government Front Bench, *left to right*: Minister for Works, Jamidar; Minister for Labour and Housing, Towett; Minister of Defence, Swann; Minister for Commerce and Industry, Muliro; Minister for Education and Leader of Government Business, Ronald Ngala; Minister for Legal Affairs, Griffith-Jones; Minister for Finance, K. W. S. Mackenzie; Chief Secretary, Coutts; Minister for Tourism, Mervion; Minister for Local Government, Havelock; and Minister for Agriculture, Blundell